Appetite for Excess
A Chef's Story

Chef Todd Hall

ClearSky Publishing
San Clemente

Copyright 2017 by Todd Hall

All rights reserved. No part of this book may be reproduced in any form or by any electronic or mechanical means including photocopying, recording and information storage and retrieval systems—except in the case of brief quotations imbedded in critical articles or reviews—without the permission in writing from its publisher, ClearSky Publishing.

Published by:
ClearSky Publishing
645 Camino De Los Mares
Suite 108-276
San Clemente CA 92673
www.ClearSkyPublishing.com

Cover Design: Reyhana Ismail: reyhanaismail.design@gmail.com
Book Design: Scribe Freelance | www.scribefreelance.com

ISBN: 978-0-9965453-6-5
First Edition

Printed in the United States of America

Contents

I Survived 5
Foreword 7
Chapter 1 11
Chapter 2 25
Chapter 3 35
Chapter 4 40
Chapter 5 49
Chapter 6 52
Chapter 7 57
Chapter 8 66
Chapter 9 71
Chapter 10 76
Chapter 11 90
Chapter 12 100
Chapter 13 108
Chapter 14 118
Chapter 15 122
Chapter 16 125
Chapter 17 129
Chapter 18 133
Chapter 19 147
Chapter 20 152
Chapter 21 158
Chapter 22 163
Chapter 23 171

Chapter 24...177
Chapter 25...181
Chapter 26...185
Chapter 27...189
Chapter 28...193
Chapter 29...197
Chapter 30...206
Chapter 31...209
Chapter 32...212
Chapter 33...216
Chapter 34...223
Chapter 35...229
Chapter 36...239
Chapter 37...243
Chapter 38...246
Chapter 39...254
Chapter 40...263
Chapter 41...271
Chapter 42...279
Chapter 43...284
Chapter 44...292
Chapter 45...297
Epilogue 300

I Survived

I WAS ASKED TO TELL you what this book is about—that's a complicated assignment. I have led a very complex and beautiful life; to describe it in a couple of paragraphs is challenging.

I am extraordinarily fortunate to have been born with the gift of cooking—I love to cook food, and people love for me to cook for them. I also love to do drugs. If it were not for my children, cooking, and this book, I would probably still be doing drugs. A fog lifted when I kicked dope for the last time, and my memories became loud and clear. I needed to try to make sense of the last thirty years; cognitively, emotionally, spiritually, and chronologically.

I wrote the book as a self-prescribed recovery tool. I decided to confront my past, head on—as much of it as I could remember, as opposed to running away and getting high. I started at the beginning and tried to remember everything I could about my life. While writing, I felt the pain that I had always tried to escape; it was cathartic—it felt right—so I kept doing it. I also felt joy, peace, and a sense of accomplishment as I relived the wonderful parts of my life.

I wrote this book ten years ago and it sat in my computer until 2016. After losing my son Parker to a heroin overdose, I knew it was time to share my story with the world and do my part to build awareness of this insidious disease, called addiction. At the end of this book and at the end of each day, I have thanked God for the same thing…

That I survived.

Foreword

MAKE NO MISTAKE, I have no more business writing a book than you do preparing a ten-course degustation menu for the Prince of Wales. If I were preparing the meal it would be less of a burden than dealing with a lifetime of feelings all stirred up and felt again as I try to explain what happened on paper.

Be that as it may, I am compelled. No, I am haunted with a sense of urgency to compile my life in some sort of chronological order if only to make sense of what the hell happened in the last thirty years.

So what am I to do here? How does one start something like this? Am I supposed to be articulate, entertaining, and funny? Is it now my job to titillate your senses with an expansive vocabulary and clever dialog? Just like I titillate your senses with robust sauces, intense flavor profiles, and stunning presentations? I do have a talent for writing, but it is pretty much limited to beautiful menus and nasty emails. My vocabulary is far less than expansive. Hell, I can't even spell. What I do have, however, is a great memory coupled with the ability to tell the truth. A life like mine has no need for embellishment in order to entertain. What I lack in writing skills I make up for with perseverance, perspective and tenacity. I am seriously surprised I'm still alive.

First and foremost, I am a chef. I think like a chef, I talk like a chef, I act like a chef, and I probably write like a chef. I love everything about cooking great food and creating beautiful plates. I have dedicated my life to the culinary arts. Cooking and my children are the two things that saved me from myself. You may find what you're about to read painful; it hurts when I read or write it because it happened to me.

Why do people like to experience other people's trauma, pain, and tragedy? When I think back and try to remember the first book that made an impression on me, I immediately remember that it was *Helter Skelter* and that I was in the fourth grade. It was filled with graphic photographs that turned my stomach. Reading it sickened me, yet I still kept reading. Another book in that same year, *Jonathan Livingston Seagull*, made me feel great. I finished it in a matter of hours, all seventy-two pages of it. So, when I think back, why don't I remember *Jonathan Livingston Seagull* as the book that made an impression? Are we wired to keep exposing ourselves to the filth and pain in this world?

In the late eighties, I was an executive chef of a beautiful resort in Sedona, Arizona. During the winter the tourism dropped off and I found the place a little boring. I started taking night classes to become a certified EMT to pass the time. After joining the volunteer fire department I was constantly amazed that, upon arrival to a bad car accident, there was always that one guy who had gotten out of his car, climbed down a muddy embankment, and jumped two fences not to help, but to witness the carnage. Every time, the same thing would come out of his mouth, "Oh, God! I wish I hadn't seen that!" Why would he go to so much trouble to get down there?

We have to look when we see bad accidents. I have always been curious as to why. For some unknown reason, we all seem to be interested in the pain of life. Mostly other people's pain. I'm guessing it has something to do with our evolution, survival of the fittest. We need to take inventory of what has hurt other people and avoid it ourselves. To sum up what I am trying to share with you in my writing, it boils down to just a couple of things: First, life can be crazy, hard and painful. Trying to avoid that pain with drugs, well, it not only doesn't work, it's just a special kind of stupid. Second, no matter how hopeless it seems, you can beat addiction. Last, I survived.

I once discussed telling my story with a very successful and accomplished writer.

"Todd, you can't. People love a happy ending and you don't have that yet."

Why do I need to have a happy ending? I asked myself. I have had a happy existence. I have spent my life learning to put the past behind me and move forward. When I think back, it's the happy times that I remember the most. Does this place me in a retrogressive state of denial? Although we all are guilty of choosing to remember the traumas, tragedies and pain in life, that's just part of a good sense of awareness that is critical to assuring they don't become reoccurring issues. If you can keep a positive attitude, you're able to forget about the painful moments while looking back. You can strive to see the good in life.

As you read this, I hope that I am able to bring you into the *Jonathon Livingston Seagull* parts of my life, as I rip you through the *Helter Skelter* of it all.

Chapter 1

IT WASN'T UNTIL A YEAR after I first started smoking pot, in the summer of the eighth grade that I found some friends my own age to smoke with. Mike Gardner was my best friend. We would score a joint, grab our skateboards, and ride the bus from Bountiful to Salt Lake to go to a park that had an empty swimming pool. To get in, we'd climb on the roof of the changing room and hop down. Walkman hadn't been invented yet, so we would just sing our favorite Kiss songs out loud as we skated.

I got us both jobs at Sandwich World. Microwaves were the new big thing, and this sandwich place would slap some cold meat and cheese on a bun, zap it, and people thought it was miraculous.

One time when we were both stoned, Mike forgot to put a bottom bun on a hamburger and the customer burnt his hand when he picked it up to take a bite. He was about ready to slug us both in the face but we couldn't stop laughing.

Another time, I was in the back slicing meat and Mike was working the register. Mike came stumbling to the back, laughing hysterically.

"I can't wait on that lady. You have to."

"No way, man! It's your turn to work the register."

"No, Todd, please. Please, you have to do it." He just couldn't stop laughing.

I threw down my towel and called him a freak as I went out to take her order. Then, right when I was reaching to take her money, I noticed a long tampon string dangling out of the unzipped fly of her polyester pants. I hurried and turned my head, only to see Mike still laughing his ass off in the back. That was it. I just lost it right there. She totally freaked out.

"What in the hell is wrong with you boys?"

"I'm sorry. We just can't wait on you today," I said, trying to catch my breath.

When Mike heard me say that, he busted up laughing loud from the back. This, in turn, made me bust up again, and the lady stormed out of the place. Twenty years later when I saw my first episode of "Beavis and Butthead" working at the fast food place, I swore that Mike Judge had to have eaten at Sandwich World when Mike and I were working.

We had the coolest boss in the world. His name was Tim Pendleton and he was all of nineteen or twenty. His dad, Sy Pendleton, owned four or five Sandwich Worlds across the southwest.

We had a killer connection too. Tim would sell us quarter ounces for fifteen bucks. He and his roommate would work in the mornings and go home when Mike and I would come in at three or four. At nine, he'd drive back to Bountiful to lock up the shop and give me a ride home. I never felt cooler. He had this bitchin' Hemi Cuda that was all tricked out. Lighting up the tires and a joint simultaneously, we'd fly down Main Street listening to Nazareth's "Hair of the Dog".

After a few months, Tim didn't care much about Sandwich World anymore. All he was concerned with was obtaining more high performance parts for his Cuda. So, he gave me a key and we were locking up at night, ourselves, and walking home—no more cool rides.

One payday, Tim's roommate came in and cleaned out the till. "We don't have your paychecks. We're bailing out of state. Here's a bag of weed and Tim's dad's phone number. Just give us a couple of days before you call him and he'll pay you. He lives in Las Vegas, so be sure to dial one first. He's going to kill Tim when he finds out that we bailed with all of the money."

At first I agreed and wished them a safe trip, but, after thinking a while, I decided it was bullshit. That was my money Tim was taking. I still had my key, so the very next morning Mike and I opened up the store and started to sell sandwiches. Our plan was to just stay open long enough to get the money they owed us. Then it was just too easy, so we kept running it. After a couple of weeks, Tim's dad started calling the shop.

"Tim just left. Call him at home," we would say.

A few days later we were going to open up and there were these guys with suits inside of the shop. I told Mike that it had to be Tim's dad. We never went back to Sandwich World.

Back at my house, we counted all the money we had stashed. We had twenty-eight hundred dollars, fourteen hundred each. I thought that it made perfect sense. I was fourteen and I had fourteen hundred dollars. My mom was gone to Mexico with one of her boyfriends for a couple of weeks, so I went right down to Craig's Yamaha and bought a brand new Suzuki RM 250.

When my mom got home, she gave me a leather jacket she had bought in Mexico. I thought it was just perfect for my new bike. When she asked me whose motorcycle was in front of the house, I told her it was mine. I told her that I had saved up all of my money from Sandwich World (which was the truth) and paid cash for it. She demanded to see the receipt. When I showed it to her, she threw a fit—not because of the safety issues, but because I had that much money and I didn't give her any of it for rent or food. We were still on welfare. I thought that this was messed up. Fourteen-year-old boys should not have to pay rent, no matter how broke their mother is. So, for the first time, I felt true freedom. I could just hop on my bike and wheel away from her as she screamed at me.

That year, I got over a dozen tickets for driving without a license. I was on a first-name-basis with the juvenile court judge and I completed hundreds of hours of community service. I scrubbed every toilet at every school in the Davis county school district, but I still had my bike and I rode it every day. By that point, I had gotten a lot better at sneaking through the neighborhoods on my way to hit the dirt.

Meanwhile, school had started. I was finally in the ninth grade. No more getting stuffed in my locker or having my books knocked out of my hand as I walked the halls between classes. It was my third year at Millcreek Junior High and I was as old as any other kid there. In fact, it was a great new start because I had my dirt bike to brag about. I still had to go to the office every Monday to pick up the free lunch tickets they gave kids whose parents were on welfare, but it wasn't as embarrassing as grade school when they would just hand them to you every day in front of all of your friends.

I was in the cafeteria with Mike eating lunch one day, when he told me that he got a new job washing dishes at a local Mexican restaurant called El Matador. He told me to come to work with him that day and that he would try to get me on. I wasn't going to wash any dishes, but I went down there to see if I could get a job cooking.

The kitchen manager was interviewing me when I told him that I had been the night manager of Sandwich World. He started laughing at me and reminded me that I was only in ninth grade. I thought to myself, *Dude, I owned Sandwich World for a few weeks*. It didn't really matter that he was laughing at me, though, because he hired me as a prep cook. Mike only worked there a couple of weeks but I stayed on all throughout the school year.

✧ ✧ ✧

There were only a handful of guys who smoked pot at Millcreek. They were Mike, Rob Hershey, Greg Swidnicki, and me. We never smoked at school because the school was ruled by Mormon jocks. Drugs in general were very uncool there, so I always took a few hits off my pipe as I walked from school to work. Mark, the kitchen manager, would shake his head at me every day when I walked in because my eyes were so red and glossy. He didn't smoke, but I did a good job for him so he would always have me peel onions first thing. This way, I had a good excuse for the red eyes in case the owner noticed. I thought that this was mighty considerate of him. After I got my first check, I never went back for free lunch tickets again. I remember this as a great accomplishment on my part.

I dropped my first hit of acid that spring. The high school kids that lived behind me were having a party; their parents were out of town. They asked me if I had ever dropped before. I told them I hadn't. They would turn me on, they said, but I had to promise that I would stay there until I came down. I thought just hanging out with high schoolers was pretty cool in and of itself, so I agreed. However, deep down I was really scared. All I knew about acid was that after Art Linkletter's daughter dropped, she jumped out of the window of a tall building because she thought she could fly. Also, the people that committed the Manson murders all said that they were frying at the time.

I hadn't even started to feel anything yet when a couple of the other guys started laughing hysterically and acting like dumbasses.

I hope I don't start acting like that, I remember telling myself. Then, I mentioned to the guy who gave me the hit that the moon and stars looked really cool. He agreed and suggested that we climb on top of the roof to get a better look.

"You don't think you can fly, do you?" I asked.

"No, dipshit, why would I think I can fly?" he replied, laughing.

We climbed onto the roof and just stared at the clouds, moon, and stars for about six hours. We talked about how fucked up it was, growing up in a small Mormon town. Later, I went home and no matter how hard I tried I couldn't fall asleep. After I finally did crash, I woke up at four o'clock the next afternoon feeling more wiped out than I ever have in my life. I felt like I had traded every ounce of energy in my body for one hit of acid.

During that time, the house was always empty. All of my older brothers and sisters had moved out and my little sister had gone to live with her dad. My mom was never home. I pretty much spent all of my time at school and work.

When my mother *was* around, she loved to fight. She was married five times to five different men and she fought terribly with all of them. After all of the men left her, she started fighting with my older brother and sisters. It wasn't long until they all moved out. This left my little sister and me for her to fight with. Eventually, my little sister decided she couldn't take it anymore, so she went to live with her biological father. This, of course, left me alone with mom.

Once I was the only sparring partner she had left, I tried my best to recognize her cycles, which revolved around pills. My mother had been taking Black Beauties every morning and sleeping pills every night for years. I can remember both bottles being on her night stand for most of my childhood. I didn't understand it then, but I now know (from my own experience) that you can't make your body go up every morning and down every night with artificial stimulus without it taking its toll on those around you.

First thing in the morning she would wake up and pop a couple of Black Beauties, but it would take an hour before they would kick in. That was the worst hour of my life. I woke up every morning to a blood-curdling scream across the house.

"Todd, get your ass out of bed! If you make me late for work I am going to beat your ass," she would screech from the kitchen table where she would drink her coffee and put on her makeup.

The trick was to stay completely out of her sight, never saying a single word, during the first hour of the morning. She was so wicked. She would wait for me to get out of the shower. I had hot coffee thrown on me at least twice a week. That was the worst, not because the coffee burned, but because it would keep me in her range for another ten minutes while I changed. I would always try to get halfway out the door, and yell back to her.

"You're fuckin' crazy!"

She would then blast out of her chair and chase me two doors down the street. The confrontation would always end with her throwing her hairbrush at me. I knew that all of our neighbors felt so sorry for me. After the Black Beauties started to kick in, she would try to find me walking to school to offer me a ride. I was usually crying, so I'd just ignore her and cut through someone's backyard. I went through most of junior high with swollen eyes and coffee stains on my clothes. Some of my first period teachers tried to talk to me about it, but I always felt like somehow it was my fault so I shut them out.

In twenty years of raising my own kids, while simultaneously doing drugs, I never hit them nor threw anything at any of them. Yet, I am certainly guilty of allowing my children to shoulder the blame for my addiction, just as I shouldered the blame for my mother's addiction. I guess that is all that children know how to do.

I feel bad for myself when I think back, but I feel even worse for my kids. I always told myself, *We're not on welfare. I have never made them live with a stepdad. I never beat them or constantly fought with them. I must have evolved out of the shit I had to put up with as a kid.* It was just a lie. It's impossible to do drugs without distancing yourself from those who love you. Children will always shoulder the blame, and for that I am so sorry.

After school, I would stop by the house on my way to work to change clothes. One day, my mom started getting big manila envelopes addressed to Sharon Black #48. The return address was from Happy Ads, a local free newspaper. Soon, I was so curious that I couldn't stand it anymore. I steamed an envelope and peeled it open. It was filled with tons of letters from sick men telling my mom all of the disgusting things they wanted to do to her and her best friend. Each letter was addressed to Fun Loving Brunettes, #48. I tore out of the house and raced down to Kentucky Fried Chicken, where I knew there was a Happy Ads stand. I found ad #48. It read, "Two single, fun-loving brunettes looking for a great time. We're up for anything." This had to be some kind of mistake, so I thought of every possible scenario to justify the ad. When I realized that it was very true, I spent the rest of the walk home crying and thinking, *My mom is a whore.*

I was too upset to go to my shift at El Matador. Instead, I waited until my brother got off work. Then, I called him.

"Go get a paper. You won't believe what mom is doing."

"I don't need a paper to know that mom is a whore. She's been one her whole life. You need to get over it, save your money, and get out of there as soon as you can… just like I did." Then, he hung up. I was devastated and he didn't even give a shit. I put all of the letters back in the envelope and never said a word about it again.

A few days later, I woke up at two in the morning to a bunch of loud moaning and giggling. I slept in the basement and my mom's room was right above mine. The headboard of her bed slapped against the wall. Upstairs, there was a suit coat draped across the kitchen table. I picked it up and there was a wallet in the inside pocket. Inside, the face of the man who was fucking my mom. I thought about taking his money, but I didn't. I just went downstairs and cried myself back to sleep while plugging my ears.

The next morning, I wouldn't even look at her. I ran to school without even getting ready. Then, just before lunch, I was called to the office. She was there.

"Hi honey, mama's going to surprise you and take you out to lunch," she said all sweet in front of everyone in the office.

"Oh, that's so nice!" they all cooed, knowing nothing about why she was really there. When we got in the car, I still wouldn't look at her or say a word.

"Todd, I know why you're upset and I understand. When I was your age, one day I walked down the stairs and caught Grandpa screwing his cousin Louise, your grandma's best friend. It made me feel just like you do now. So I understand, honey. Where do you want to have lunch?" I never answered her. I didn't say a word to her for days.

A couple of weeks later, one of the guys who answered the ad flew my mom and her best friend to Las Vegas, but when he was done fucking them he bailed without paying. They should have noticed that he only bought them one-way tickets. She spent the next day calling her kids trying to get a way back from Vegas for her and her friend.

✧ ✧ ✧

School was almost out and I was getting sick of El Matador. On one of the last days of school, I watched a Disney movie called Johnny Tremaine. In the movie, Johnny walked into Paul Revere's silversmith shop and said, "I want to be your apprentice and I will work for free." So, that very day, I hopped on a bus and rode to the Hotel Utah in Salt Lake City, where I had heard they had some famous French chef.

In the restaurant, I asked the hostess if I could speak to the chef. The hostess asked if I had an appointment; I told her no. She told me to sit down and that she would check. A few minutes later, she escorted me back to the largest kitchen I had ever seen. There were lots of cooks and they weren't speaking English; it was French. She sat me down in the chef's office. As I looked out the window into the kitchen, I tried to guess which one was the chef. Finally, after about ten minutes, the oldest and shortest man walked into the office.

When he spoke it was so loud that it made me jump. It was so fast, with the thickest French accent, that I couldn't understand a word he was saying. In fact, now that I think about it, I'm not so sure he was even speaking English. I didn't want to look stupid by asking him to repeat himself, so I just jumped up and put out my hand.

"I am Todd Hall. I want to be your apprentice, and I will work for free." I was every bit as loud as he was. He looked me right in the eye and tried to hold back a smile.

"What did you just say?" he said, even louder.

"I am Todd Hall and I want to be your apprentice. I will work for free."

"That's what I thought you said. Sit back down," he grabbed my hand. "How old are you?" I thought to myself, *This is the end. I'm dead. He'll never hire a fifteen-year-old.*

"Fifteen."

"Fifteen. I don't know if I should hire an apprentice who's already fifteen. By the time I was fourteen, I had already graduated from my apprenticeship."

What a trip! I wasn't going to lose this because I was too young... I was going to lose it because I was too old!

"How did you hear about the apprenticeship program?"

I hadn't heard about any program. "I just watched a movie today where some guy walked into a place and said the same thing I just said to you, and he got a great job." He just laughed.

He had six apprentices, he told me, but one was leaving. I could take his place. My new boss pulled out a logbook, a manual for culinarians, and all kinds of paperwork from a nearby cabinet. He walked me down to the personnel office and told a lady that I was his new apprentice. She was to get me a locker and sign me up for the college courses that were starting next week. Then, he said one last thing. "If I find out that I don't like you, I will fire you. Make sure I like you."

"I will."

Roget Cortello, my chef, is to this day one of the greatest men I have ever met. Four years later, I would graduate from my apprenticeship under his direction. At the age of nineteen, I was, and still am, the youngest person to have ever graduated an American Culinary Federation apprenticeship.

The year was 1977, and this new job just rocked my world. Not only was my world changing, but the whole world was changing. Gay people proudly waited on tables, and there was a new drug on the street called cocaine. The Rolling Stones, my favorite band, had just released their album "Some Girls" and sold out to this new kind of dance music called disco. Everything around me was different, except my home.

Every day, all six apprentices would march out of the kitchen in a single-file line to take our break at exactly four-thirty p.m. We walked past security to a van parked right in front of the Mormon temple and smoked out while listening to the Grateful Dead. I loved my new friends. They were all in their mid-twenties and they treated me as if I was as old as they were. I tried as hard as I could to act the part, thinking about every word before it came out of my mouth. This, in turn, led me to say very few words at all.

◎ ◎ ◎

I was so glad when school started because I could finally take driver's education and get my license. Riding the bus to and from work every day was a pain in the ass, and I already had a lot of cash stashed so I could buy a bike that was street-legal. In March, on the day I turned sixteen, I got my license and bought a brand new Yamaha RD 400. It was a six-speed, two-stroke street bike for racing.

Shortly after, I went to a company party on a Saturday afternoon and Candy Alexander, one of the accountants in the executive office, asked me to take her for a ride. She had sandy blonde, curly hair and a bottom shaped like a perfect kernel of popped popcorn, but she was married to one of the room service waiters and was at least thirty. We rode around Memory Grove and she rubbed my chest the whole way as she held on. I took her back to the party and left a short time later.

A couple weeks later I was totally broke, so I went down to the offices to see if I could get my check a day early. A lady told me that I had to ask the payroll accountant, Candy. I thought, *Nice, she'll give it to me for sure.* When I asked Candy, she told me to come back at seven-thirty and she would have it ready for me. I was working then, so at seven-thirty I split from the restaurant to get my check. When I got to the offices, all the lights were out. I thought she blew me off. The door was still open, so I went in anyway and yelled for Candy.

"Candy, are you here?"

"Back here," she yelled. She was in a cubicle way in the back with only a desk lamp on for light.

"Hey," I told her as I arrived to her desk. She didn't say a word. Instead, she stood up, wrapped her arms around me, and gave me the most awesome tongue kiss that I had ever had. When we finally came up for air, she still didn't say a word. She just pulled down her pants and panties, and then she pulled down mine, right there in the office.

"Hurry," she whispered, strained. I never, in all of my life, thought I was going to lose my virginity in the executive offices of the Hotel Utah with my shoes still on. I was done in less than a minute, but I kept going until she took the grip off of my ass. She got dressed fast and told me I had to get out before the cleaning crew came. I rode the elevator up thirteen floors back to the restaurant thinking that I just experienced the greatest thing that ever happened in my life and I couldn't tell anyone about it. No one would ever, ever believe me. Not to mention she was married.

As soon as I stepped foot in the kitchen, the restaurant chef, Jimmy, yelled for me.

"Todd!" I jumped a foot. He looked right at me. "Where have you been? You look really guilty."

"I just went to get my check early."

"Someone's waiting for you on the phone."

I picked up the phone and it was Candy. I had forgotten to get my check.

"What time do you get off?"

"Eleven."

"Meet out front then and I'll give it to you."

When I got off work, she told me to hop in her car. She drove me up to the state capital and we did it a few more times. What a night.

The next couple of weeks at work were weird. I never told a soul about Candy, but when I went into the cafeteria all of the girls from the front office would wink and giggle at me. *What the hell! She told everybody.* She had told everybody, but it turned out that she had an "open marriage" so her husband didn't care. In the kitchen, Roget still called me "The Boy", but in the hallways I felt like I was starting to become a man. I was on top of the world and full of confidence. The first year of my apprenticeship, Candy taught me all about sex.

It's funny when I think about those days now. All I remember is the food, and it was the bomb. The food that was served at the Hotel Utah in the late seventies was as good as or better than anything I have seen to date. Learning how to cook there has been the gift that has kept on giving throughout my entire culinary career. Most of the chefs were European, and it was exactly like learning to cook in France. One thing about the Mormons is that they can afford to hire the best, and they did. My training was regimented, complex, diversified, and the kitchen brigade commanded respect. Even if we were stoned a lot of the time.

Chapter 2

I GO TO BED AT NIGHT wondering if all of this writing is a waste of time. *I don't need to relive this again. So, why am I doing it?* I think to myself.

I am doing it because I have had a tough go of it. Drugs make your life hard. Wait, let me rephrase that. I was given a hard life and I used drugs to make it even harder. I am writing in hopes that if there is even one other person out there who has made his or her life as hard as I have, then they can read this and know that they are not alone. Also, I believe that we teach best what we need to learn most. In that case, I guess that I am writing this for my own benefit, whatever that may be.

I was nine months into my apprenticeship when the Conference buzzes starting infiltrating the kitchen.

Conference is a four or five-day period held annually in the spring. Essentially, Conference amounts to vast amounts of Mormons from across the world converging in Temple Square to eat, drink, and listen to their leaders speak. The hotel would do over a thousand meals a meal period in this time alone through four different outlets: a coffee shop called The Crossroads, banquets, room service, and a gourmet restaurant at the top of the building appropriately named The Roof. We would start prepping four days in advance for the five-day conference, totaling nine days of continuous fifteen-hour shifts. I'm still intimidated just thinking about it.

On the first day of Conference, I was scheduled to flip eggs on the breakfast line at four-thirty a.m. even though I had closed The Roof the night before and, of course, gone out with the other apprentices afterwards to drink beer. I had gotten home just in time to hop in the shower and go back to work. My only comfort was that when I hit the line, all of my friends were there, every bit as burned out as I was. That morning, we were all lined up in a row and I, being the newest and youngest, was in the corner at the end. Hodgi, the executive sous-chef, walked down the line, inspecting us and our stations before the guests arrived. Then, in order of seniority, he walked up to each apprentice, placed something in his hands, and whispered a word or two in his ear before moving on to the next. When he finally got to me, I was so curious I couldn't stand it! He took my hand and placed four white cross-tops in it. In nine months, I had smoked a lot of pot, dropped acid maybe three times, and tried a line of coke twice with these people, but I had never seen speed in the workplace. I did as I was told and swallowed all four of them right there. Hodgi whispered in my ear that he would have a few more for me just before we started lunch.

I don't know if it was the Mormons, old people, or just an older style of eating, but back then people had twenty different ways to eat their eggs. By this point, I had already completed the mandatory three months of egg flipping for my apprenticeship, and I liked to think that I was good at it. Yet, what happened in the next few hours was utterly amazing. At exactly six AM, six hundred Mormons lined up outside the coffee shop. All of them wanted breakfast. I had learned to work three or four pans simultaneously, but now I was working seven. I don't know if it was the cross-tops or my fear of slowing down the line, but I was flying. The eggs were basted, shirred, soft-poached, hard-poached, over-easy, over-hard, hard-boiled, soft-boiled, three-minute, and scrambled. I was rockin' out more eggs than I had ever seen in my life, and flying just as high on speed at the same time. The result of all six of us having the same dose was astounding. We worked together like a well-oiled machine. From six to ten p.m., the wheel was wrapped with tickets. Not one of us said one unnecessary word or even thought about stopping. Not one of us went to the bathroom. Not one of us had a smoke. We just rocked, for four straight hours.

The other cooks had set us up for lunch in the back. At ten-thirty, Hodgi came around and gave each of us two more hits, and we did it all over again. At three o'clock, we shut down our stations, went outside to the van, and smoked joints, trying to take the edge off. No one even thought about trying to eat. We just went upstairs and started prepping our stations at The Roof to get set up for dinner.

I wonder if all of these Mormons know how fucked up their cooks are right now, I thought to myself.

We started to clean up at eleven p.m., and I was still flying. We went to Shane's house after work. Shane was Roget's first apprentice. He was the golden boy and my new best friend. I was cracking open my first beer, still feeling totally amped out after the most amazing day of cooking in my life, when Shane gave me a Quaalude.

"Where did you get this?"

"Hodgi gave me six. One for each of us."

I hadn't even had three beers before I passed out on the couch. Next thing I knew, Shane was waking me up at four o'clock the next morning, telling me to get in the shower. All I could think was that I sure as hell hoped that Hodgi had more speed for me when I got to work because I was wiped out and still groggy from the Quaalude. Of course, he did. We did this for five days straight. By the fifth day, I was turning into a miserable prick. I was experiencing the onset of sleep deprivation, I had not eaten much, and I was exhausted. I kept thinking that all of these fuckin' losers were exactly like my mom. They took pills to get going every day and took more to come down at night. Now, they were trying to make me that way too.

The only difference was that when Conference went away, so did the speed and the Quaaludes. I didn't see them again until the next year.

I'd spent spring break and my seventeenth birthday working. By the time I headed home the Sunday before school was due to start again, I hadn't been home in a week. I remember thinking on the way there, *All I want for my birthday is more than three hours of sleep.*

When I walked through the front door, there were some birthday cards on the kitchen table. A film container filled with pot from my oldest sister Kris sat on top of the cards. Suitcases were flung open and scattered across the living room. As I stood in the kitchen and took stock of the house, my mom walked out and told me my little sister Dawn had moved back in. Her dad had been raping her. Dawn was fifteen.

"Why did you ever let her go there in the first place, mom? You knew he used to rape Cindy." As if my fury meant anything to my mother.

Cindy is my second-to-oldest sister. When I was seven years old, my bed was against the same wall that her bed stood against in the adjacent room. Sometimes, late at night, I would hear her whisper.

"No. No, please not now," I would hear through the heater vent as Charles E. Workman, my stepfather, would try to quietly slide into her bed and rape her without waking anyone. He did this to her for years. My mom knew it, but didn't do a damn thing to stop it. I've often wondered whether my mom had gone to Cindy's school and taken her out to lunch just to tell Cindy that she knew how she felt.

I was worried about Dawn coming back to live with us for many reasons, but most of all I was worried that she would have to listen to my mom screwing the men she brought home at night. I didn't want it to strike up any bad memories. Later, in 1996, a Phoenix newspaper would do a profile on my life, with one paragraph reading that I was "raised by a good Mormon mom." Boy, did they get that wrong.

◎ ◎ ◎

I guess now is as good a time as any to run through the "Dad du Jour" timeline. In the early 1950s, my mom first got pregnant, at age sixteen, by a man named David Bagshaw. She thought that Ted Vanders was better looking, however, so she had sex with him and a few weeks later she told him that he was the one that had gotten her pregnant. Ted did the right thing and married her, and they had a baby every year for the next four years. The first born was my sister Kris, then Cindy, then Nick, and then Tracey. I have heard two stories from my older siblings about why Ted left. The first story goes that Ted found out that Kris was not his biological daughter. The second story says that my mom was screwing around on him. They are probably both true. At any rate, Ted split and never returned once to see his kids. He never even called. I have seen a couple of photographs of him and he looked just like my older brothers.

Years ago when I asked, my sister Cindy told me that later mom got a new boyfriend named Jack Breckenridge. He was a physician's assistant at the Salt Lake County Hospital. Cindy said that she cried and cried when Jack left. My mom once told me that one day the FBI knocked on her door looking for her boyfriend, Jack. He immediately ran out the back door, never to return. The FBI told my mom that he was wanted for theft and distribution of prescription drugs from other hospitals out of state, and that he had a wife and kids in Oklahoma. His real name was Richard Griffith.

When he left, my mother was pregnant. When I was about twelve years old, my sister Cindy told me that she had walked in on my mom with a bunch of coat hangers inside of her during that time. When she asked my mom what she was doing, my mom replied that she and Jack had been taking drugs; drugs were going to make her baby deformed and she had to get it out before it was born. During that same week, my mom painted the entire house with lead based paint all by herself, hoping for a miscarriage. A few months later, I was born in the same hospital where my biological father had worked. Because he had stayed in touch with some of his workmates, he found out and sent my mom flowers. He called her from Hawaii on that day and it was the last time anyone ever heard from him.

I have never seen a photograph of him. I don't even know what ethnicity he is or was. The only thing I know is that, according to my mom, he used to do drugs and stay up all night reading cookbooks. If that's true, I find it ironic that when I was studying to be an EMT, I would do drugs and stay up all night reading medical books. So I guess if I wanted to, I could blame my addictive behavior on genetics. If I believed that it matters why one does drugs.

After Jack, my mom married an asshole named Charles E. Workman. He had a pitted face from acne and I couldn't stand him to touch me. He tried to tell me when I was four years old that he was my real dad. I had already figured out that this didn't add up. I told him that I hated him and not to ever say that he was my dad.

He used to beat all of us kids with a belt when he wasn't fucking one of my sisters. He hung the belt on the wall of our room just to remind us of what we had coming. I have always had a keen sense of smell and late at night I could smell Old Spice aftershave and cigarettes. I would look up from my bed just in time to see him strike a match and light a cigarette in our bedroom doorway. My eyes were not adjusted to the light of the match, and it would appear as a spotlight on his acne-pitted face for just a second, as he stood next to the belt hanging on the wall in the pitch black of our bedroom. This image has been forever branded into my memory.

Charles was also a Jehovah's Witness, and he would take us to church every Sunday. Once, he was "dis-fellowshipped". He wasn't allowed to talk to anybody in the congregation for a year, but he still kept going every Sunday. I guess he thought it would make all of the evil things he was doing okay if he just kept going to church.

Being a Jehovah's Witness in a Mormon town was one of the hardest things I have ever had to deal with. I still think that what they put their kids through is totally fucked up. We weren't allowed to stand up for the pledge of allegiance or celebrate any holidays, and grade school kids are cruel. Every year after Christmas break, some kid would always scream, "What did you get for Christmas, Todd?" knowing already that I didn't get anything.

My mom was married to this prick for eight years. I watched him beat her with the receiver of a telephone, and back then telephones were heavy. I watched him throw her out of the plate glass window in the living room. By the time I was eight or nine, I realized that all of the time at church and bible study was nothing more than insidious posturing to make up for two of the most self-indulgent and vulgar people I have ever known: my mother and stepfather. I would watch their uncontrivable exhibitions of hate and abuse with disregard for anyone but themselves, and I would think to myself, *They deserve each other but we don't deserve them.*

One night, Charles got drunk and kicked my mother out of the truck in Farmington. It was in the middle of winter and as the truck pulled off, all six kids just looked at our mom on the side of the road through the window of the camper shell. He never went back to get her, and we were thirty miles from home. So, she hitchhiked back to my grandmother's house. We would have to go stay at a motel or at our grandma's house at least once a month because of him beating my mother, or us, or God knows what, yet she still wouldn't divorce him.

When she finally did divorce him, she got remarried to the manager of the Denny's where she was waitressing. She had only been divorced for a couple of months when she remarried. This guy was named Mike Hall. He was only twenty-five and she was at least thirty-six or seven. By then, my older sisters had dropped out of high school and had been coming and going as they pleased for quite some time. Mike tried to put a stop to that and they both moved out almost immediately. I liked this guy. I had never had a father figure that I could respect, and, besides, he gave me my first Christmas. He had just got done with two tours of Vietnam as a medic in the Marine Corps. He wasn't loud or strict like a drill sergeant, though. He was pretty quiet and I thought he was cool. He would never talk about Vietnam, no matter how many times I would bring it up. My mom would constantly pick at him for everything, so he would take me fishing every night after work to stay away from her.

One time my mom's car was broken and he wouldn't fix it. So, when she came home with her car fixed without having to pay, he asked her how she did it.

"I had to screw a mechanic. I knew you wouldn't fix it," she told him right in front of me. I was maybe eleven then.

On the opening of goose hunting season, Mike took my older

brother Tracey hunting with him and his friends. Nick and I had to stay home. I was so pissed. Late that same night all of my sisters and their boyfriends came over to the house. I could hear them talking all night but I couldn't hear what they were saying.

The next morning my mom wasn't there and Cindy told me I didn't have to go to school. I wanted to go to school and I was getting ready to go anyway. Then, my mom came home and told me that there had been a bad car accident and my older brother Tracey was dead. I asked if Mike was alive, and she said yes but that he was in pretty bad shape at the hospital. I asked her if I could go to school that day. My mom was furious at me, and demanded to know why I wasn't crying. Why in the hell would I want to go to school when something like this had just happened, she wailed. I just got up, hopped on my bicycle, rode to school, and told everybody that my brother had just died. I was so nonchalant about it that no one believed me. Eventually, a teacher got wind and I was sent to the office while they called my house. Then I was told that I had to go home, and I was not to come back until next Monday.

I had no idea why I didn't cry. I didn't even cry when I was alone reading the obituary. I didn't cry at the funeral. My uncle told me I was a fucked up freak. I got pissed off when a bunch of people that never even met Tracey got up and tried to talk about him. I remember thinking, *If all of you guys loved Tracey so much, then where were you when we all needed you the most?* I loved my brother. I played with him every day and we had been through so much together. Why didn't I cry? Looking back, I think that I had been exposed to so much bullshit that I had finally just become numb. Maybe it was that I wasn't capable of feeling anything, anymore.

Mike never beat me or my mom. I did watch him pour a bottle of honey on her when they were fighting once. He called her the queen bee.

She was so much more wicked when she was trying to hurt someone. One time, she grabbed the gas can for the lawn mower and poured it all over the curtains and tried to set our house on fire. To stop her, Cindy grabbed the garden hose and started spraying mom and the curtains.

Mike finally left her after about three years. One thing he did do was legally adopt Nick and me so we had legitimate last names. There was no custody battle; my mom surrendered custody of me without saying one word. I had to go testify at their divorce. Mike won by default because my mom was screwing her married lawyer and Mike's lawyer found out about it. They called my mom's lawyer on the stand and he told the truth. I knew something weird was going down when the judge told the bailiff to get me out of the court room. I thought to myself, *Dude, trust me, I have heard far worse than this before.*

I went to live with Mike the day he left the house. No one was going to leave me there. As I walked out of the door of the courtroom my mom said, "Well, I'm glad he got custody," just like a catty spoiled brat that didn't get her way. Not that it would last. I didn't know it back then, but Mike didn't like being tied down with a young boy that he had only known for a few years. My brother came to visit after a few months and told me to pack my things. I was going back to mom's.

When I got back to my mom's, I found out that my little sister had gone to go live with Charles E. Workman.

Chapter 3

I WAS EXHAUSTED FROM Conference but I just lay in my bed that night thinking, *Dawn has been through enough*. I wasn't going to let mom put her through any more. I started planning our exit strategy.

The hotel had settled down and my oldest sister Kris had invited me to go camping with her friends over Memorial Day weekend. I had just traded my street bike in for a new Honda XR 500, a kick-ass dirt bike that was street legal. I was certain they had made it just for me. The thought of riding my new bike while camping was awesome, so I asked Roget for the weekend off.

I met a whole different kind of people that weekend. They were all Vietnam vets, and most of them were at least thirty-five or older. A professional drug dealer named Vern Chavez was my favorite. He would become a great friend for years to come. I could buy pounds of Panama Red from him for five hundred bucks and split it with everyone at work. It would end up costing us about thirty bucks an ounce, not a bad price at all. Here was my exit strategy, staring me right in the face.

Vern had brought with him an orange box full of peyote buttons for everybody to eat while camping. They were dried up and hard as rocks, so, being the chef, I suggested that we boil them in water and drink the juice. Everyone agreed and I went to work. I was totally stoned, though, and forgot to watch the pot. The liquid evaporated and soon the buttons were burning tar in the bottom of the pan. I thought I would be in trouble, but everyone just laughed and dogged me about what kind of chef I was. We ended up scraping the pan and rolling up little balls of the black tar.

Since it was my fault, they told me that I was going to have to be the guinea pig and try the burnt peyote first. I already knew it would taste like shit, so I just swallowed it. I then hopped on my bike and was only about a hundred yards away on the hillside when I got so high I couldn't even think. I just laid my bike down on the ground and sat there and tried to figure out how I was going to get back to camp. I could see camp, I could hear everyone laughing, but I couldn't figure out how to get there. After a while, I figured out how to walk back, and everyone asked me where my bike was. I couldn't talk so I just pointed at it up on the hill. They all just busted up laughing. And I went behind a tree to throw up. I was so high for so long that it was well past dark before I was able to speak again.

I went home from that camping trip and told Dawn I had found a way for both of us to move out. I started selling quarter ounces of pot for thirty bucks at school and work. It only took me a month of selling quarters to get together enough money to rent a three-bedroom house with Mike Gardner, who had dropped out and was working with his dad installing glass in buildings. We had to have looked at a hundred houses before we found someone to rent to two seventeen-year-olds in Bountiful, Utah.

Dawn and I went to school every day, and I had a booming business selling pot. It paid all of the bills plus bought food and clothes. I could spend my paychecks from work on my new girlfriend, Stacey.

It was getting too cold to ride my bike to work so I rode the bus. One time I left my backpack on the bus, and it had thirteen quarter ounces in one of those fake oilcans designed for stashing shit. I called my mom from work and asked her to go to the bus station and pick up my backpack for me. She went with my grandma only to discover the cops were waiting there to arrest her. I guess they figured out the oilcan. She called me at work, just screaming.

"Don't you ever send me to go pick up your dope!"

She had lied to the cops and told them I still lived at home. As the next day was Thanksgiving, she swore she would bring me in first thing on Friday Morning. They made a copy of her driver's license and let her go. I told Roget that I needed a couple of days off for personal reasons. I spent all day of Thanksgiving skiing and worrying about my future, and first thing on Friday morning we went down to the Salt Lake County Sheriff's office. I was taken inside of an office with a detective. I was glad when he told my mom to wait outside.

He asked me to explain myself. I couldn't stop thinking about how nice the pot plant in his office was. I was never able to get mine that big. Anyway, I just told him the truth. I said that my mom was a raving fucking lunatic, and I had to support my little sister and myself while going to high school, taking classes for my apprenticeship, and working simultaneously. I only earned twenty-five cents above minimum wage, and that just wasn't enough to pay the bills, so I started selling pot at work to make ends meet. He asked me where I bought my pot. I told him some black guy that rode the same bus as I did.

He said that he had gone through my backpack and found homework from high school, homework from an accounting class at the University of Utah, and my apprenticeship logbook. He even read about how tough Conference was. He said he was impressed and that he couldn't believe he'd found thirteen quarter ounces of pot in a backpack of someone who appeared to have their shit together more than his own kids.

Then he pulled out my logbook and got the telephone number to the

American Culinary Federation in St. Augustine Florida, and put his phone on speaker. I was shitting my pants when I heard them answer.

"Thank you for calling the American Culinary Federation, how may I direct your call?" He asked to speak to someone in charge of the apprenticeship program. When they got on the line he told them his name, rank, and whom he was with.

"What would happen to an apprentice if they were convicted of a felony possession of a controlled substance with intent to distribute?"

"They would not only lose their apprenticeship, but they would be barred from the American Culinary Federation altogether."

"Thank you." He hung up the phone. I couldn't believe what happened next.

"See this rolodex? I am putting your name right here. If I ever hear of you again, I am not only going to nail you for what you've done, but I will nail you for thirteen bags of weed as well. Do you understand me?"

"Yes sir." He threw my backpack at me and told me to get out of his office.

"Hey Todd, just keep working hard and you will get through all of this," he said when I stood up.

"Thank you. May I have my oilcan back?"

"No you can't, but I am sure you'll find another one," he replied, laughing. To this day I still have never been charged with an alcohol or drug violation. I have been charged with many other violations, but never drugs. I have no idea why.

For the next few months, I was making good cash selling weed. Work was great and, for the first time in our lives, Dawn and I were happy. I decided to splurge. I bought a gram of coke from Hodgi for eighty bucks, and I took it over to Vern's to share. I just about shit when he pulled out a needle. He told me that it was a waste to sniff coke, and that it would ruin my nose and sense of smell. I wouldn't be a very good chef if I kept sniffing it. So, right there in his kitchen with a telephone cord wrapped around my arm, I shot up my first syringe of coke. The first thing I said was, "Hey, I can smell it and wow, I can taste it too." I then experienced the most wonderful feeling of my life. I said, "Oh, man, thank you so much." I loved it, I loved everything right then. I had to go throw up, but I even loved that. I was seventeen.

Shooting up coke was just too hardcore to even tell anyone about. In the next few years I only did it a few times, and that was only when I was at Vern's and there was coke around, which was not that often. It was 1979 and my biggest worry was Skylab falling on top of me. This wasn't too much to worry about at all, considering the last seventeen years. A new band had just rolled out, called The Knack. I bought their album and Dawn, Stacey and I would all dance to "My Sharona" in the living room of our happy home.

Chapter 4

I LOOKED AT HIGH SCHOOL differently than most of my friends did. I never cut class unless it was my day off from work and there was fresh powder to ski on. During my junior year of high school, the counselors and teachers started to become very cool. There had been a newspaper article, "Three Apprentices Honored," of which I was one. I had four semesters of college credits under my belt with good grades. I was already on Vo-Ed, a program where you left early every day to pursue your career.

Rulen Homer was the vice principal of Bountiful High School. My first year he was a total dick, but he became very cool after he found out about my apprenticeship. He allowed me to have my first period as a study period in the library to get caught up in my logbook and homework. He could not imagine why I hung out with all of the burnouts when I seemed to have so much going for me. He did not understand that they had been my friends for years, and were the bread and butter of my business.

I would usually get Monday and Tuesdays off work. Sometimes on those days, Kevin Graham and I would skip school and go skiing. I would place a hit of orange Microdot on my alarm clock and set it for five-thirty AM. I would be so tired I would just take the hit and go back to sleep. Bam, right at six-thirty I would be awake and ready to have a killer day on the slopes. Soon, I would hear Kevin pulling up in the driveway cranking AC/DC, and we'd be out of there.

Tuesdays were the best days to ski on acid, especially if it was snowing. You could jam down the slopes without having to worry about knocking some little kid into next week. One time, Mike and I were just flying and he hit a little girl and knocked her right out of her skis. She was screaming bloody murder. Mike was picking her up and trying to quiet her down when this great big guy skied up to Mike and slugged him in the face so hard that it knocked him over and busted his goggles. It was the kid's dad. I just got the hell out of there.

Our friend Greg Swidnicki had just inherited thirty thousand dollars. First he bought a brand new 280 ZX, then he traded it in for a new Triumph Spitfire. After a month, he traded that in for another 280 ZX, and after another month he traded it back in for another Spitfire. He did it one more time and finally ended up with another 280 ZX. That Halloween at about midnight, Mike and I turned a corner and saw Greg's third, new 280 ZX perfectly upside down on someone's front lawn. He was dressed like a pimp and his girlfriend was dressed like a whore. It was one of the most hilarious things Mike and I have ever seen. Greg was happy to see us.

"Dude, can you believe how strong this car is? That roof should be totally caved in right now!" he called out first thing, holding a half empty fifth of Jack in his hand. We gave his girlfriend a ride home and, I have no idea how, but Greg got the car towed out of there without the cops ever showing up. He really is one of the luckiest guys I have ever met. After he got his Z fixed he was just about broke. What a fool.

Greg's older brother Mishadoll was far smarter with his thirty grand. His girlfriend had moved to Venezuela with her parents and when he went down there to visit her, he noticed that they didn't have any motorcycles on the road bigger than 400cc. He got the great idea to go home and go down to Craig's Yamaha and buy two Yamaha 850cc Midnight Specials. He left them in the crate and personally flew them down to Venezuela to have them assembled and sold for twice as much as he had paid. When he arrived in Venezuela, customs confiscated both bikes and he spent Christmas Eve, Christmas, and the next day in a South American jail. He never stopped to think there was a reason for the absence of big bikes in Venezuela.

After attorney's fees and fines, and, of course, the price of both bikes, he was pretty much broke as well. You have to hand it to Misha's entrepreneurial spirit, though. Misha turned out to be a lifelong friend and one of my apprentices. He worked with me at different resorts for the next ten years.

The middle brother, Mark Swidnicki, took his thirty grand and only bought a Les Paul guitar and a Marshall amp. He gave the rest of his cash to his mom and they both went in fifty-fifty on a rental property in Hawaii. Twenty-five years later, Mark has a few rental properties in Hawaii. He hasn't worked a day since he was eighteen. At age forty-five, he just smokes his weed and plays his guitar. And gets checks in the mail.

By the end of winter, our trusty vice principal Rulen had just about had a gutful of all the burnouts. Our numbers were dwindling. In the beginning of the year there were more than a dozen of us burning bowls before class in Smoky Hollow, a cool little creek across the street from the school with lots of trees. Its official name was Millcreek, but we dubbed it "Smoky Hollow". By then, there were only about six of us. A couple of guys had gotten their girlfriends pregnant and had to quit school to get a job and get married.

Rulen walked up to me one day with a proposition. He told me he would give me a full English credit for the next year if I could get those guys to attend class every day and read one book cover to cover. He told me four of the six were going to get kicked out of English anyway, so it was their last chance. I jumped on the opportunity. He gave us a break room with a couch and a couple of beanbag chairs for second period, and the book I chose was *The Hobbit*. I told the guys they would love it because the only thing hobbits did all day was smoke their pipes and eat seed cakes, just like us.

My first problem was that a couple of the guys could hardly even read. I have no idea how they ever made it to junior year of high school, only able to read a dozen words a minute. My second problem was that every time someone would read slow or mispronounce a word, all of the others would start laughing and make fun of him. I was even guilty. When Bob Thompson said, "I don't need help reading any book," I spouted off, "Hey Bob, remember last Saturday night when we got pulled over and the cop asked you what year you were born, and you said, 'Ahhh, either sixty-two or sixty-three, I can't ever remember'? The cop thought you were trying to be a smartass. I had to convince him that you really didn't know. So don't tell me what an academic scholar you are." Everybody busted up laughing because they were all there that night. It made Bob feel bad, though—which made me feel bad.

So we came up with a rule that no matter how bad someone butchered the book while reading out loud, nobody could say anything. If anyone laughed or made fun of him, the rest of us got to slug that person in the shoulder as hard as we could. A couple of rounds of that, and no one ever said another word. They actually looked forward to our reading time. Rulen would try to sneak up on us and open the door real fast to catch us fucking off, but we weren't. We were really reading the book. The guys liked the book so much that instead of just making bongs in ceramics, they were making Golem bongs or Smog the Dragon bongs. I had a good time in that hour, and we actually finished the book by the time summer break came around. I think a couple of them even went on to read *The Lord of the Rings*.

◊ ◊ ◊

I survived another Conference and Dawn and I had a great summer. Life was so much better without the fighting. No one screamed at anyone else and everyone was kind and considerate. What a concept. Dawn and I finally started to see how other people lived. I had really started to move up at the Hotel Utah, too. Three apprentices had quit, and I now had the third highest ranking seniority of the apprentices. It was fun teaching people twice my age how to cook.

One day, Roget got in a couple dozen fresh, whole king salmon. I loved to clean salmon. When I first started my apprenticeship I was butchering the shit out of them, so Roget made me clean every salmon in the whole hotel until I got good at it. That was over a year before and I had cleaned a couple of salmon every day since. I was a very proud eighteen-year-old fishmonger.

I had broken my arm riding my skateboard recently, so when I walked by and offered to help Roget clean all of the salmon he said, "No, no, you will get your cast all smelly, you go up to the Roof and set up your station, but send down both of the new CIA externs."

"CIA" meant the Culinary Institute of America. We got a couple of those guys in every year. All of them could tell you a lot about cooking food, but most of them couldn't cook that well because they just didn't have any time on the line. Some of them actually thought they were chefs. I was always jumping in and bailing them out. Cooking is every bit as much dexterity and timing as it is formulation of ingredients and methods of procedure. No, in fact, it's a lot more dexterity and timing than it is recipes and methods. Most guys coming out of the CIA were at least twenty-five and thought they were Paul Bocuse himself. I always enjoyed bossing them around.

I went upstairs and said in a serious voice, "Hey, both of you, Chef wants you downstairs right now."

The first two years of my apprenticeship, Roget would always say, "You're lucky you get to learn from me. If you had to go to the CIA, your parents would spend twenty thousand dollars and you still wouldn't be a chef." At the time, I had no idea what he was talking about. But I had learned that things in the kitchen would go a lot smoother if you just didn't ask Roget what he was talking about.

I didn't know that the CIA was a culinary school. I had envisioned myself trying to become a spy, instead of a chef. I imagined getting into some kind of trouble and my parents having to spend twenty thousand dollars to get me out of spy jail. I had no idea why he kept saying it. When I met my first extern, a light went on in my head and I said, "Oh, that's what in the hell he was trying to tell me all of these years." You have no idea how many things that Roget taught me about food that I wasn't able to grasp until I had a lot more time under my belt. Even to this day I'll be cooking, I'll finally figure something out, and it will dawn on me that Roget was trying to explain this to me twenty years ago and I couldn't comprehend it yet.

The nuances and subtleties of cooking go far beyond what most chefs ever realize. The externs made it downstairs and started to screw up the salmon, which pissed Roget off. He finally said, "A sixteen-year-old boy with a broken arm can clean salmon better than both of you." One of them was stupid enough to try to argue with him, so he picked up the phone and told Jimmy the restaurant chef to send down The Boy. Roget never once called me Todd. He would schedule The Boy, he would yell at The Boy, and he would tell others how good The Boy was starting to become. To this day, when he speaks about me to someone else, he refers to me as The Boy.

I walked into the kitchen and Roget told me to show these two chefs from New York how to clean salmon. I knocked out five fish in less than ten minutes, all of them perfect, feeling so cool I could float. Then Roget said, "I told you a sixteen-year-old boy with a broken arm could clean salmon a lot better then you." I spouted off, "Chef, Chef, I am not sixteen anymore, I just turned eighteen." He looked at me like, *You know better than to argue with me.* So I hurried and tried to recover by adding, "But you sure were right." He questioned me as to what, and, scrambling, I muttered that this was going to make my cast smell. I went back upstairs and finished setting up my station.

We had a culinary competition coming up in a few days at the Salt Palace. All of the chefs, apprentices and externs could enter to claim a golden platter trophy and bragging rights. There were two categories, one for apprentices and externs, and one for chefs. Roget was really cool about stuff like this. He would buy you anything you wanted to work with, but you had to create it on your own time. I learned a long time ago not to get Roget involved in your project because he wouldn't help you at all until you were all done; then he would look at the final product and tell you that it was totally fucked up. Then he would just throw it away and tell you to start it again.

I had the purchasing department buy me a fresh, fifteen pound Florida gulf Red Snapper. I poached it in a *court bouillon, chaud-froid* it by covering it with a white aspic, left the head and tail on it, and elegantly decorated it without Roget ever seeing it. I raced it over to the Salt

Palace. I came back after judging and saw that I'd received first place in the Apprenticeship category. There was my snapper with the round golden plate next to it. I was so excited I went to a pay phone and called Roget. When I told him I had won first place, he asked me if I was sure and then told me he would be right down.

I hopped on my bike and rode to my mom's house, and told her and my grandma they had to come see. When I got back, my fish was not only gone, but my golden plate was in front of someone else's entry. Roget and Max, Roget's best friend, were standing there speaking French. I had learned enough French to know what The Boy sounded like, and I knew they had something to do with this bullshit.

The judges walked up to me and began apologizing, "We're sorry Todd, but Roget and Max called it to our attention that the fish was not cooked all the way through, so you've been disqualified." Then Roget walked up, charmingly greeted my mom and grandmother, and said, "Oh God, that fish was stinking so bad, we had to throw it away. The judges noticed that you didn't cook it enough. If you had showed it to me before you left, you could have fixed it. What in the hell is wrong with you? You know how to cook fish! You do it every night!"

Heartbroken and furious, I told him, "The longer that I cooked it, the more of the beautiful red color it was losing, and I know that it didn't stink because I was just here. The judges never would have cut into it and noticed that it wasn't cooked all of the way if you and Max hadn't started to poke at it."

Roget raised his eyebrows, "Maybe you're right, but you still don't deserve to win unless you really deserve to win." They both walked away and went and got a beer.

I could not believe that my own chef would go so far out of his way to fuck me up. Thirty years later, I realize that Roget's lesson that day was not about how long to cook fish, but that you should never think that you can get away with something when you know it's not right. I knew the fish was undercooked, but I chose presentation above a cardinal ruling of cooking, and it jumped up and bit me in the ass in front of my family. Do you know how many times I've gone out to dinner at a place where the chef has chosen presentation over the basic principles of cooking? A lot.

Another lesson I learned that day is that it's a hell of a lot better to have Roget throw your work away in the kitchen than it is to have him throw it away at the show.

Chapter 5

MAX CALLED ME LAST WEEK and told me he would be in Scottsdale and wanted to see me. I took him out to dinner at Vincent's on Camelback with my children. After dinner, I got up to have a smoke and when I got back, everyone quit talking. So later when I asked Chelse what was up with that, she replied, "Oh, he was telling us a story about some fish that he and Roget threw away at a food show. He said for us not to mention it because you were probably still pissed off, thirty years later." Max was right. Standing on the curb at Vincent's, it pissed me off just thinking about it. I had won first place.

I had chosen to take Max to Vincent's because both Max and Vincent were just about as French as you could be. Max was staying with another French chef who was a friend of his, Jean Paul. Jean Paul used to be the executive chef for United Airlines. He'd purchased a couple of nice homes in the United States years ago, and now he was retired and living in one of them. When I picked Max up, he looked as debonair as always. He had to be at least seventy, at this point. He wore a classy, dark sports jacket with a tuxedo shirt and a French silk scarf. It had been dark for hours, but still Max had a pair of shades propped up on his full head of salt and pepper hair. He wore the shades up there throughout dinner and the rest of the night.

He was with a beautiful lady who was visiting him from France. She didn't speak a word of English, and, unusually for Max, she was close to his age. They were both drenched in cologne and perfume. It was starting to make me nauseous, so we had to ride to Vincent's with the window rolled down in February. I don't know, but I think the overuse of body fragrance has to be a French thing.

At the time, I was the executive chef at Continental Catering, a premier upscale caterer that has been around for over twenty years. When we arrived, my children were already there and had gotten us a corner table for six. Vincent was meticulously trained in France, and in the eighties he had this valley all to himself. He worked at La Français just outside of Chicago before coming to Scottsdale. He's friends with Wolfgang Puck and everyone else in the wide world of food. One time, I was at his place when Wolfgang was doing a dinner there. I saw Wolfgang's wife Barbara, so I walked up and said, "Hi, aren't you with Wolfgang?" She answered, "No, he is with me."

I had ordered veal sweetbreads for an appetizer, an heirloom tomato salad with fresh mozzarella, and a rare rack of lamb. There is nothing I enjoy more than eating. Especially when another great chef is cooking for me. Vincent is an incredible chef and I have to thank him for his kindness and professional courtesy towards me as long as I have lived and worked in Scottsdale.

The sweetbreads were good. You could tell that they had been properly soaked, peeled and pressed before serving. The veal glace was dark, rich and the perfect consistency, with a beautiful shine to it.

In my world, you have to have exciting, cool food that screams "Nice!" right when it hits the table. Our server came to the table and grinned. "We have some wonderful Champagne, compliments of the chef."

You can tell good Champagne just by looking at it. It's all in the size of the bubbles that are racing to the top for air. This was fantastic Champagne. The bubbles were tiny. I thought, *Now that Vincent knows we're here, I'll get to show Max some really cool food.* Tomatoes really suck in February, however; therefore, I realized that my Caprese might very well suck. You have to use organic hothouse, vine-ripe, or heirlooms. The trick is to just buy great tomatoes and don't let anybody do anything to screw them up. To me this seems very simple, but more chefs serve crappy tomatoes than ones who don't.

Vincent had stellar tomatoes, but you couldn't tell by looking at them because you couldn't see them. He had buried the tomatoes, cheese and basil in a huge pile of microgreens. Now, microgreens are great, but I use them to accent and enhance a plate. Never as the featured item. I ate them anyway just to see if eating a handful of microgreens was good. It was ok.

The salad had perfectly ripe tomatoes, and the Maître D' said that the cheese was made in-house. A lot of chefs make their own fresh Mozzarella. I never learned how to do it, but I have always wanted to. Vincent had used superb olive oil, too. That's another super-secret trick that most chefs just don't seem to be able to pick up on. Great olive oil is expensive for marinades, dressings, and to sauté with, but if I'm just going to pour it on food I always use very expensive oil.

Max and I had been discussing food all night. I told him I had a dinner to do for the CEO of Wells Fargo bank in a couple of days. He asked me if he could help and I said, "Sure."

Chapter 6

WHEN I GOT BACK TO the Hotel Utah, Roget had already put the word out to everybody not to say a single word to me in regard to the food show. He could be kind like that sometimes. I guess he figured I had been embarrassed enough for one day.

A couple days later, Dorothy Hamill was in the hotel for the Ice Capades. You would have thought she was Mick Jagger by the way Roget was going off. She ordered a Seafood Louie salad. I haven't thought about this salad in years, but in the seventies it was on every menu. I wonder what happened to it. Anyway, Roget told me to make a perfect Louie and a fellow apprentice Tom Pirro jumped on my station to try to hog some glory. Roget had gone to his office to get this book that he had famous people sign whenever he fed them.

Just as Roget got to her table with the book, we served the salad. Right after she signed it, she took a bite and quickly spit it out. We had served Dorothy Hamill rotten crab. Roget walked back to the line and sweetly asked, "Who made the salad?" He knew that if he acted pissed off, none of us would admit to it. Tom Pirro quickly answered, "I did, Chef." I spouted off, "We both did, Chef." Roget then grabbed two tablespoons and loaded them up with crab.

"Eat it. Now." Tom smelled it first and protested, "No way, Chef, it's rotten." Roget screamed, "*Eat it. Now!*" He scared me, so I hurried and took the whole spoon in my mouth. I chewed a couple of times before I gagged and threw up in the garbage can.

To this day, I have never served any kind of seafood salad without smelling it first. Years later when I was at the Princess, I tried to do the same thing to one of my cooks. They went to Human Resources and I almost got fired. Tom Pirro got fired right on the spot for not eating the rotten crab. Tom got fired at least once a month. Roget would say, "After you're done with your shift and cleaning up, you're fired." If you didn't finish your shift and do a great job cleaning up, then you really were fired.

The rotten crab lesson was nothing more than Roget teaching me that I have to take responsibility for failure, learn from it, and move on. Just like many of Roget's lessons, I didn't understand the gist of it until many years later.

✧ ✧ ✧

There was this ski bum who would come down to Utah from Alaska every winter to ski. In the summer, he was the chef of a restaurant in Anchorage called Elevation 92. His name was Chuck Wiley. Chuck skied every single day, seven days a week, and drove a Porsche. Shane, the first apprentice, was the first one to take me skiing, but Chuck was the one who really taught me to ski. In fact, Chuck took an interest in my career, my personal life, and me.

Chuck used to tell me, "When I was your age, Todd, all I cared about was making go-karts out of lawn mower engines. Don't listen to those waiters. They may give you a hard time now, but you're going to be making ten times as much as they do in just a few years." One time, I stole a bottle of gin from the hotel and Chuck found out about it. He was so disappointed in me that I never stole anything from anywhere I worked ever again. It broke my heart when he told me, "You know, Todd, I really liked you, but now whenever something's missing I'm always going to wonder if it was you that took it. How can you like someone like that?"

Chuck is the only person I ever told that I had shot up. Instead of dogging me for it, he confided in me and told me that he had tried it also. We talked about being able to taste it and smell it, about how it was the best feeling that you could ever feel. At the same time, he told me that it was just too good. I should never do it again because very few people that keep shooting up can ever stop. I listened to Chuck and I never shot up again. Well, at least not until fifteen years later, when my son died.

Chuck then told me that he had a gram of coke in the glovebox of his Porsche. I don't think he really had any coke in there. I think he was testing me to see if I would break into his car and steal it. I would never do something like that; he just didn't know it yet.

The first time I ever heard of Scottsdale was from Chuck; he would go there to visit his aunt. He would ask me to watch his apartment and feed his cats. Chuck has been in Scottsdale for as long as I have, now. I have never understood why we weren't as close of friends in Scottsdale as we were in Utah.

Chuck was the chef of The Roof during the last year of my apprenticeship. Prior to that, Jimmy Ferri was the chef of The Roof. He had been with Roget since France. He graduated from the Cordon Bleu. I mean *really* graduated from the *real* Cordon Bleu, not like today where every single culinary school says that they're "Cordon Bleu Accredited". Talk about selling out.

Jimmy was a funny little man. He was a no-nonsense kind of guy at work, but he still smoked pot outside the work place. I remember that every Saturday night, the kitchen crew and I would go over to Jimmy's apartment and watch Saturday Night Live. We could never really watch the show because everybody was always arguing about food. I just sat and listened to every side of every argument and took it all in, to be used at a later date. Roget taught me everything about food; Jimmy made sure I listened.

One thing about great chefs: if they ever went out of their way to teach you how to cook, they will always pop in later for a free meal at the least expected time. Fifteen years after the last time I had seen Jimmy, I walked into my dining room in Sedona and there he was, sitting all by himself. He said, "I heard that you were cooking some pretty cool food. Show me." I did.

The food at The Roof was phenomenal. Roget and Jimmy had been running it for about ten years before I even started my apprenticeship. It was the crown jewel of the hotel. Every cook in the hotel aspired to be up there, but there were only five shifts a night. Two pantry, the grill, middle and sauté. Jimmy always worked sauté, and Bruce, his sous-chef, worked sauté on Jimmy's days off. Bruce worked the middle the rest of the week.

Bruce had been Jimmy's sous-chef for over ten years. He was a man who commanded respect. He was a speed freak. Not the drug, actual speed. Cars, dirt bikes, crotch rocket street bikes, it didn't matter. If it went fast, Bruce was on it. He had a 260 Z that he kept racing tires on, that was fast as hell. He used to take Shane and me on what he would call "high speed cruises". The Z was a two seater, so we would put a beanbag in the back and tie the hatch halfway down. That's where I would ride. Bruce was an excellent driver, but I really hated going on those drives. I seriously thought I was going to die.

I remember the first time I ever had Veal Oscar at the Roof. The veal was simply soaked in heavy cream and lightly dredged in flour. Then, it was sautéed in half good olive oil and half clarified butter. It was so good that I had Jimmy make me one every night. The Roof used white asparagus and Dungeness crab legs, complimented with the most perfect of Béarnaise sauces. To this day, I will fix myself this for dinner, even when it's not on the menu I am preparing.

The Roof had the same classic French menu that most gourmet restaurants had at that time. The difference was that we only used the best ingredients. Dishes were painstakingly prepared with the greatest care and concern possible, and every single plate of food was top-full of love from the person that prepared it. The crew on the Roof was so tight; no one would even think about talking smack about someone else. It just wasn't tolerated. There was no need because we were a family. There wasn't one single man on that line who was married or had a family outside of the line brigade. We left work every night after deciding where we would all meet later. It was Shane's house most of the time. He had a killer stereo, a ping-pong table, and a huge yard.

The core group of my high school friends ended up at Shane's house just about every weekend. Mike Gardner was always over there. There was always someone who would buy beer for you, and there was a lot of great weed to smoke.

I truly believe that the most important developmental time for a man is his adolescence. It's no secret that I had a totally fucked up childhood with no father to speak of. What I failed to get as a child, though, I was paid double in my teenage years. Chuck, Jimmy, Roget, Shane, Bruce, and Adolph were the best role models that any boy could hope to emulate while figuring out how to be a man. Sure, we smoked pot, and even dropped acid a couple of times a month while skiing, but the daily dedication to our love of food and each other was unparalleled by the greatest of perfect Mormon families.

Chapter 7

THE LAST YEAR OF MY apprenticeship was totally different than the first two and a half years; everything changed. Hodgi started to deal coke more and more at work. He got John Nolan (the director of food and beverage) hooked so bad that he was outside the hotel in his BMW waiting for Hodgi to get off every single night. John had a master's degree from Cornell in hotel management. He got fired and a couple of years later he decapitated himself flying down a canyon in a car accident. Hodgi was fired shortly after. Within a couple of years, he was pulled out of Lake Powell, drowned.

Shane had just graduated. Roget wouldn't let you work with him any longer after you graduated. He just scheduled you somewhere else, and he didn't even ask you where you would like to work. He sent Shane to Stanford Court Hotel. My best friend at work was now gone. Chuck had gone back to Alaska for the summer, and Jimmy kept needing surgery on his leg. Finally, Jimmy announced that he was going to retire from cooking and teach. After Jimmy left, they called Bruce the acting chef of The Roof. We all just assumed he would get the job. After all, he had been doing it two days a week for over ten years. A month or so later, Chuck was back. I wondered what was up with that; the ski resorts weren't going to open for another couple of months. Then, Roget told us they had hired a new chef for The Roof. Chuck. Awesome, Chuck was my friend and a great boss. We all felt really sorry for Bruce, but he didn't really seem to mind that much.

I knew Roget had made the right decision, even though Chuck did ski every day. Chuck was more interested in food than Bruce was. Chuck would always buy the latest issue of Food and Wine or Cooks Magazine, and give them to me after he had read them. Bruce was always talking about cars and bikes and how fast he could go. Chuck was always trying to teach himself how to evolve with the latest cooking trends. I would read something like "nothing browns in the presence of steam" and Chuck and I would stand on the line and discuss all of the different applications of the principle. For instance, if you don't pat all of the water off of your sea scallops before you start to sauté them, they will be overcooked way before they ever caramelize and turn that beautiful golden brown. Or, if you're a shoemaker and you use frozen chicken breast, the skin will never crisp until all of the water evaporates.

Bruce would just stand there and listen to us and then say, "Both of you guys should become professional food detectives. No shit, nothing browns in the presence of steam. Everybody already knows that." That's the problem with Bruce and most chefs: they just don't think hard enough about what they're doing. You don't just do things because it works and people like it. You take it a step further and figure out exactly why it works from an elemental standpoint. Cooking is chemistry applied to the laws of physics in an artistic format. I believe that it would serve one well to learn as much about chemistry, physics, and art as one could. Then, after years of line time, one could call him or herself a chef. That's why Chuck got the job as opposed to Bruce. He was constantly trying to figure out *why* things worked the way they did.

Bruce and I had the same day off so he, Stacey and I rented some horses and went riding. When I went into work the next day, Chuck called me aside and told me, "There's been a bad accident, it's Bruce. The doctors say they don't think he's going to make it." Bruce had just bought a brand new Ducati, an Italian racing bike. He was flying down Wasatch Boulevard at speeds in excess of one hundred and twenty miles an hour when a car flipped a U-turn right in front of him. They say he impacted at over one hundred miles an hour. I went to the hospital the next morning and he was in a coma. He was black and blue from head to toe. It made me sick to my stomach. He had broken just about every bone in his body.

Chuck made me the acting sous-chef. At any other time, this would have been the greatest point of my career, but it was for all the wrong reasons. Bruce was in a coma for a few weeks and in the hospital for a few months. He did make it, although he was never the same.

✪ ✪ ✪

Mike Gardner had gotten his girlfriend pregnant and moved out, so it was just Dawn and me in the house when Stacey told me she was pregnant. I was barely nineteen years old. On one hand, I was the most successful apprentice chef in the nation. On the other, the biggest fuck-up on earth. That was according to Stacey's parents, as well as Roget. He was so pissed. He was getting ready to send me to London to work with Anton Mosimann at the Dorchester. He had already started to make the arrangements.

When he found out, he called me into his office and just screamed at me for not using a rubber. "When I was your age in France," he bellowed, "a blowjob was good enough! We didn't have to be greedy and try to screw every girl we dated!" He made me feel like shit. He hollered at me for over an hour in some kind of weird half-English, half-French language, although I understood every word.

Adolph told me that I was Roget's favorite and best apprentice.

Because he got me at such a young age, he was able to mold and develop my cooking skills better than any that had gone before me. Roget glared at me every time he saw me for about a week, and then didn't talk to me for about two. He had big, international plans for me and I just ripped them right out from under him.

Two days a week on Chuck's days off, I was calling all of the shots at the best restaurant in Utah in one of the top hotels in the nation. At the age of nineteen I was still the youngest person in the restaurant, but I was in charge. There were waiters that had worked there for fifteen years and they respected my authority because I had earned it.

I would be off when Chuck would come back, so we wouldn't see each other for four days a week. He would come in from skiing, take a look at the sauté station, see two boxes of shrimp that needed to be peeled and deveined and a case of snow peas that needed to be picked and cleaned, hurry up and go downstairs to pick up all of the food for the restaurant, and try to get back up to do all of the work. When he would pull out the boxes of shrimp and open them, he would see that I had already peeled and deveined them. I placed them back in the box to trick him. The snow peas, too. When we processed food, we normally placed it in food containers when we were done. I would put it back in the box so that Chuck would have a pleasant surprise during a hectic night. On Chuck's days off, I would always try to prepare a nightly special that was better than the ones he prepared. That way, when he came back in, the waiters would tell him how good it was. I was working my ass off, and for good reason. I now had a family to support.

On one of Chuck's days off, the General Manager of the hotel, Stuart Cross, walked into The Roof kitchen and wanted to speak to Chuck. When I told him Chuck was off that day, he got all perturbed.

He told me he wanted me to make an order of veal scallops *meuniere*. We weren't even set up yet, but I pulled out the stuff and whipped one up. He took one bite, and then discarded the plate. He looked at me carefully. "I will be in for dinner tonight with Robert Lawrence Balzer, the food writer and critic for Travel Holiday Magazine. He will order veal scallops. He always does. Make sure that you do it just as you did. Don't try to be creative, just do it like that." He walked away.

First of all, if you tried to change anything on The Roof menu, Chuck, the servers, and other cooks would shut you down before you ever plated. I would never dream of it. In any case, I was nervous. The Roof had received the award of excellence for over ten years. They had each and every year's certificate posted on the wall right when you walked in the dining room. If I fucked this up, then everybody would know for years to come, because it would be the only year out of succession that they didn't receive the award. The Roof was the only restaurant in the state that had this award. I did fine and once again we received it.

The following day I was in the dining room having lunch. The restaurant was only open for dinner and I was the only one in there. This little old man came in with a camera and started to take pictures of the Temple down below. He turned to me. "This looks exactly like a restaurant in France which looks down on the Cathedral Notre Dame."

I was incredulous, "Wow, you have dined in France?"

He nodded, "I get paid to dine all over the world."

I knew right then that he was Robert Lawrence Balzar. I introduced myself and told him I was one of Roget's apprentices. "Nice to meet you, Todd," he said as he shook my hand. "You are very lucky to be here, you know. Roget is one of the greatest chefs in the world. By the way, could you tell me the name of the chef that prepared my meal last night?"

"Actually, Mr. Balzar, I did."

He paused for a moment, "I thought you said you were an apprentice?"

"I am. I'm getting ready to graduate. I am acting sous-chef because it's the chef's day off."

"How old are you?"

"I'm nineteen."

He cracked a huge grin, "That's Fantastic! Congratulations, Todd." I didn't know it then, but Robert Lawrence Balzer would be giving me many more awards in the years to come. Later in life I would ask myself, *Was the food that good, or did I get it just because he knew that I was one of Roget's apprentices?* I decided that the food was just that good.

That fall I finished high school, graduated my apprenticeship, got promoted at work, and got married. All within a few months. To this day, it was the busiest time in my life. The local newspaper donated the entire front page of the food section to the graduation of my apprenticeship. The headline read, "Who is training the great chefs of Utah? At such an amazingly young age." They had a great big picture of me holding up some apple bird I had just carved. Today, apple birds are cliché. Back then they were the shit, though, and it took a lot of practice to get good at them.

Stacey moved in with Dawn and me. I quit selling pot and would never keep more than a quarter ounce at one time in the house. I would still be a middleman and pick up a couple of pounds and drive them down Parleys canyon to someone's car to make a few hundred bucks on the deal. But I never had Stacey with me. I was responsible now. I had grown up. I had to.

I made a promise to myself that no matter what happened between

Stacey and me, I would never leave any child of mine. My children would never have a stepdad as long as they lived. Nor would they ever know the taste of powdered milk, the embarrassment of food stamps, or what it feels like to have a welfare Christmas. I have been able to fuck up just about every single aspect of my life, but I was able to keep that promise. I kept it not only to myself, but also to all four of my children. Certainly, my greatest accomplishment on the face of this earth.

After about six months, Bruce was able to come back to work, even though he still wasn't himself. He would work the middle when I was on sauté, which was weird. Bruce had lost his sense of taste and smell because of the brain damage. He would make me taste every pan of food he made to ensure it was balanced. I would rather cut off my left arm than lose my sense of taste and smell.

When I got shot in the chin fifteen years later, I thought about Bruce, and what it would be like if I couldn't taste anymore. Most people would be worried about dying. To me, that would be dying.

◊ ◊ ◊

One day, I went downstairs to check my schedule. I had Monday and Tuesday off; Wednesday at The Roof; and Thursday, Friday, and Saturday all at Le Parisien. I asked Roget, "So, you want me to go help out Max this weekend?" He shook his head, "No, you are the new chef of Le Parisien." Just like that. No job interview, no discussion of my salary, nobody even cared if I wanted the job. I was just kicked out of the nest and it scared me. Le Parisien was a well-established French restaurant, and I was the new chef at the age of twenty. I was so surprised I could hardly appreciate what a great opportunity it was. All I could think about was that I would have to leave my culinary family.

Chelse was born now. I ultimately came to realize that work was meant for providing an income, and home was where you received your love, guidance, and direction. I was very grateful for the surrogate family at The Hotel Utah. Now it was time to move on.

Le Parisien was a trip. It was too cold to ride my bike, so I would catch a bus from Bountiful to Salt Lake and get off at the Hotel Utah to ride my skateboard six or seven blocks to Le Parisien. Max had concerns with his new executive chef riding a skateboard to work. He got over it. In fact, he told that story to my children over dinner last month.

The first thing I learned at Le Parisien was that just because you graduate an apprenticeship and someone hires you as a chef, doesn't mean you're a chef. Le Parisien had been open so long that the cooks had a status quo and they pushed back on any change. Jack, who was actually a friend of my sister's, would get blackout drunk every night and come in wiped out. Todd had worked there over ten years and was sous-chef, but he worked as a roofer all day and showed up tired and slopped the food up. I went in there acting like a big shot, and, in just a matter of weeks, I alienated the entire crew against me.

Pretty soon, they wouldn't tell me when we were running low on food staples. They wouldn't point out that I had made a scheduling error and there was an uncovered shift. I needed them a lot more then they needed me. For now, anyway. I eventually built a new crew of cooks who wanted to learn and took their job more seriously. I have learned over the years that hiring people who hold a personal code of ethics and work hard have a way of causing the longtime slackers to fire themselves. Their work just simply looks terrible next to work that looks great.

I wasn't allowed to change things too much. Max had been open for twenty-five years and he had his market pegged: whole Dover sole from the English Channel, shrimp *scampi*, beef *bourguignon*, chicken *coq au vin*, and *escargot*. It was real, classical French food, but more peasant style. The Roof was definitely classical gourmet.

Chapter 8

MY AUNT DELORES AND Uncle Larry asked Stacey and me over to their house for dinner one night. I had lived in the same town as them for years, but rarely saw them. They were staunch Mormons. My Grandfather had told me that my great-great-great-grandfather was Isaac Morley, one of the first Mormon missionaries ever. And his grandson was William Morley Black, Brigham Young's right hand man. William Morley Black had six wives, thirty children, and sixty grandchildren. Can you imagine coming home late from work and having six different women bitching at you for it? No, thanks.

Anyhow, they called me to dinner to ask if I would take the discussions from the Mormon missionaries in their ward. "The discussions" is the term used to describe the teachings and history of the Mormon Church. My aunt guilted me about the pot I left on the bus, and explained to me that if something like that happened now I could lose Chelse. She told me it was time to give up my evil ways and focus on becoming a good father and husband. Finally, she said, "You, Todd, of all people, should know the importance of having a father because you never did. Do you want Chelse to have the kind of hectic childhood that you had?"

That was it. She got me with that one. I agreed to go over to their house every Tuesday night for the discussions. The missionaries were very cool. One was a little old lady, and the other girl couldn't have been more than nineteen. My age. I, of course, took the opportunity to name drop. "I know your prophet, Spencer W. Kimball. He lives on the tenth floor at the Hotel Utah and he always uses the service elevator. I have ridden up with him a hundred times, and he always smiles and talks to me on the ride. I've fed him a lot!" I asked them if they knew about the underground tunnels that go from the Lyon House to the church office building to the Hotel Utah and then over to the temple.

On my last discussion they asked me if I believed that Joseph Smith was a true prophet of God. I had never met the man and I had no idea. In fact, I had a hard time believing that they were the only true church with exclusive rights to God. I looked deep in my heart and knew that this was not the case. I believed then, and still do now, that we all have an exclusive and inherent right to God, no matter what religion we follow. But, never the less, I said yes. Because they wouldn't quit asking me until I did.

My uncle baptized me a couple weeks later. I drank my last beer and smoked my last joint the day before. It was some killer Thai weed that I had gotten from Dale just for the occasion. My baptismal joint. Stacey had grown up Mormon, so she didn't have to put on the white polyester jumpsuit and get dunked. The very night that I was baptized, I ran into Bob Thompson at Slim Olsen's when I was getting gas for our 1965 VW Beetle. Stacey and I had bought it for three hundred and fifty dollars in the parking lot of Kmart because she had been afraid that she would go into labor and have to ride to the hospital on a dirt bike. Bob waved me over, "Dude, let's get a twelve pack and go smoke out." It was so tempting, but I told him no.

I followed all of the Mormon rules, and, trust me, that's not easy. Giving up pot and beer wasn't that hard, but coffee? My God, was that a bitch. I would promise myself I wouldn't have any, but I would feel so tired in the mornings. I would always slip back into my evil ways and stop at 7-Eleven to get a cup. I can't believe how guilty I felt doing that. I would walk into the store all paranoid that someone from my ward would walk in and catch me in the act. Now looking back, I would rather live my life stoned all the time than to have to put up with that kind of guilt again… and from all things, *coffee*.

Now, I realize that it wasn't the coffee at all that was bad. It was the brainwashing. I read The Book of Mormon every day on the bus as I rode to work. That's a tough book to understand and get a hold on. Dr. David Lewis, the coolest Mormon I ever met, was my home teaching companion. He was an obstetrician, and thank God, because he had seven kids. Who could afford to pay someone *else* to deliver that many babies?

I would teach cooking classes to all of the ladies in my ward at Le Parisien. They would tell me how many dinners they had to fix that night, I would buy all of the stuff, and every Tuesday we would make salmon *en croute*, beef Wellington, or chicken *cordon bleu*. I would charge them fifty dollars for the class, mark up all of the food they took a few times, and, by the time they took the dish home to finish it off themselves, I would make as much money selling my talent as I would've made selling pot.

After a few months of this, Doctor Lewis said to me, "Todd, I cannot tell you how much I enjoy our Tuesday night dinners. If you ever want to get your own restaurant, come and see me. I will have no problem backing you." I was only twenty and I knew I was way too young and inexperienced. Max was a genius in my eyes and he worked constantly just trying to keep Le Parisien in check.

Our bishop made Stacey and me Sunday school teachers. We were teaching six and seven-year-olds. The cutest little girl asked me a question when I was teaching a class about Joseph Smith finding a big stack of golden plates in the ground. She so innocently asked me, "Brother Hall, do you really believe that happened?" Wow, what a responsibility. There was no way I could lie to this sweet little girl. The truth was, I didn't believe that what I was teaching had happened. So, instead of lying to her, I distracted her.

That day, I walked into the bishop's office and said, "We got to talk." I told him that I could not be responsible for teaching children things I don't really believe. I told him, "You are all a great bunch of people and I have been going to this church based on that alone. I still have a lot of questions in regard to your doctrine, and until they're answered I don't think I should be teaching anybody."

He told me to just relax and my testimony would come in time, and if I really wanted to be released from teaching Sunday school that he would do it. I told him I thought that would be best, and, besides, I wasn't worthy because I was still drinking coffee. I had been a Mormon for a little over six months. It was the cleanest I had been in six years, but I really wasn't that dirty in the first place.

Then, I came home one night from work and the house smelled like pot. Stacey was stoned. She tried to deny it, but I busted her. I had finally decided that was it. We weren't going to be those Jack Mormons you would always see in the liquor store after they got home from their mission. We were going to do this right or we weren't going to do this at all. Apparently, Stacey didn't want to do it any more than I did, and besides, all of my high school friends were calling me up and saying, "Brother Hall?" I would say, "Yes?" and then they would make a great, big, loud fart sound over the phone and hang up. I knew exactly who it was. I had heard that sound a million times before. Every time someone would say something stupid.

It was good to feel guilt-free and normal again, whatever that is. I quit teaching the cooking classes, but Doctor Lewis was still our friend. He would have us over for dinner once in a while.

Chapter 9

MAX OWNED RENTAL PROPERTY and he was having a dispute with one of his tenants. They then accused him of molesting their eight-year-old boy. The police knew that there was no merit in the accusations, but the press had a field day. It was big news in Utah and it was on TV and in all of the papers. I never believed for a minute that Max would do something like that.

When we were at Vincent's for dinner, I about died when Max brought this up with my kids. He didn't mention what he was accused of, but he did say that he missed out on the whole Nouvelle Cuisine fad because of it. He really wanted to do this dinner on Tuesday with me for Wells Fargo so he could see what it was all about. Like I cook Nouvelle Cuisine. Anyway, I picked Max up on Tuesday afternoon.

I was preparing a five-thousand-dollar dinner for eight people. When we pulled into the garage of their five-million-dollar home, my partner Dan Ingles had the truck unloaded and the kitchen set up.

I had made these really cool little Asiago Cheese baskets to put some sautéed sea beans and a sea scallop in for my first course, but they were all busted up. I'd figured this might happen during transportation because they were so thin and delicate, so I'd loaded some cheese on the truck just in case. I showed Max how to do one, and told him to make ten more. He was so shaky and intimidated that he kept making ugly baskets, so I kept throwing them away. What a switch; the apprentice was now teaching the master. After about twenty baskets, I was finally able to find ten that I would serve. I got all of my *mise en place* together, and we were good to go. I'd plate up a course in their kitchen, go into the dining room and explain it to them, and then go back out to the garage where we had all of our equipment.

They loved the sea scallop and sea beans in the cute little basket; I had garnished the top with some crispy lotus root chips. The next coarse was *Caprese*. I made a tower with heirloom tomatoes and water buffalo mozzarella from Italy, drizzled it with velvety-smooth, aromatic, pricy olive oil, and some barrel-aged, twenty-five-year-old balsamic from Modena. I took a two-inch copper pipe and laid some perfectly rectangular *gaufrettes* on it. *Gaufrettes* are potatoes that have been sliced like ruffles except both ways so they look like netted potato chips. When you bake the *gaufrettes* on a copper pipe they are all uniform half circles, just like Pringles. I placed one of these on both sides of the tower and it looked like the whole thing was encased in a delicate, crispy potato net. I then took just a touch of chiffonade of fresh basil and micro-greens, placed it on top of the tower, and sent it out.

Next I had a candied ginger blood orange sorbet. This was a pain in the ass because earlier that morning the ice cream machine broke, so I had to stand there holding a drill on the top of it in order to make it spin. I lined the rim of a martini glass with some orange sugar crystals and topped the sorbet with some slivers of candied ginger.

At this point, Dan had been stirring some porcini risotto for the last forty-five minutes. I took the risotto and placed it in these little shoestring potato cups I had made back at the shop, and then placed one *osso buco* on top. These veal shanks were so small; they had to have practically come from aborted calves. They were only two inches in diameter, with the shank bone, and no more than three ounces total weight. I braised them with a rich burgundy, *mirepoix* vegetables, and just an essence of fresh thyme. The veal shank made a perfect little lid to my risotto cup. It not only looked really cool, it kept everything hot. I then opened a can of fresh truffles, held my slicer above each plate, and piled on the truffle slices. I used all but one truffle on just eight plates.

I went back out to the garage; I had made some homemade *lavash* that was still raw. I cut the *lavash* into two inch strips, formed them into a cup, and held the seam with a giant paper clip. I tossed some organic baby field greens in some fresh lime juice with just a touch of sugar, kosher salt, fresh ground pepper, and that nice olive oil. When I took the *lavash* out of the oven, I hurried and placed a small handful of the dressed salad into the *lavash* rings. The cracker bread was still warm when it hit the table.

For a cheese plate, I had this little machine from France that made beautiful rosettes out of Tête de Moine, translated "Monk's Head". It's an unpasteurized cow's milk cheese, and there are only ten cheese dairies in Switzerland that still make it. I added some Tallaggio, the Italian's answer to brie; a little Stilton, all nice and yellow; and a small wedge of Cowgirl Creamery Mount Tam. A wedge of apple and a couple of grapes, and we were done.

For dessert I had made some little tiny bird's nests out of spun sugar. I piped a little raspberry *coulis* on the bottom of the plate, set a hazelnut toffee pyramid on it, and placed white chocolate truffles in the nest to look like eggs. Dan scraped some fresh vanilla beans and whipped up some cream, and I placed just the smallest dollop next to the pyramid. Finally, I randomly tossed on three kinds of fresh berries, and *voila!* We had a great dessert. I received a standing ovation when I went to go say goodnight to the guests. This is really why I cook; it is better than the paycheck.

My ribs were killing me from a dirt bike accident a week ago where I broke a few of them. I was so excited about how well the dinner was going that I didn't realize how much pain I was in. For someone whose doctor had told them not to work for at least two weeks, I had really overdone it. I went out to my truck, took a couple of Percocets, and grabbed a handful for Dan. I had way too many, plus that was a perfect tip for Dan. As always, he had been an invaluable partner.

We packed up and I drove Max home. On the ride, he asked me about my brother Nick, who was also a chef. Nick had died a few years before at the age of forty-six. He had been diagnosed with fatal alcoholism. I think he committed suicide by drinking himself to death. Whatever it was, he is certainly dead now and I am the last surviving man in my family.

It was great to be able to show Max what I do; it is so different than what he and Roget had taught me twenty-five years ago. He took pictures of every course and e-mailed them to Roget in France. Roget's only reply was for Max to be sure to tell The Boy that he's way too fat. But I knew that my food was beautiful and Roget would expect nothing less.

Two weeks after our dinner in Scottsdale with Max, I received a call telling me Max had died. He had been diagnosed with terminal bone cancer. He knew he only had a short time to live, and made a point to come visit and cook with me during his last month alive without telling me anything about his illness. What an honor that was.

✧ ✧ ✧

The bad press in regard to the molestation had really taken its toll on Max and Le Parisien. We were only doing half the amount of covers that we used to. I guess everybody in Utah didn't believe in Max the way that I did.

I had been there almost a year when another chef commented, "Boy, someone with your kind of talent should be in Texas right now. Dallas and Houston are both booming." My sister Cindy lived in Dallas and that sounded like a pretty good idea. I was totally bored with Le Parisien; it just wasn't stimulating me anymore. I had never lived anywhere but Utah. I started mailing my resumes to hotels in Dallas.

Chapter 10

IT WAS 1984. There was this new girl on the music scene who called herself Madonna, and everyone was playing "Like a Virgin". Fourteen countries had just boycotted the Olympics in Los Angeles. It was as good a time as any to get the hell out of Utah.

Cindy was so excited that Stacey, Chelse and I were coming down to Dallas. She had taken my resume to this enormous hotel with a thousand rooms and fourteen restaurants, called The Loews Anatole. I had three or four telephone interviews with this guy named Morris Salerno, the area director of banquets. Morris offered me thirty-five thousand dollars a year to be a sous-chef in charge of banquets. I accepted. It was ten thousand more than what Max was paying me.

We flew to Dallas and Cindy picked us up at the airport, gave us a car to use, and let us live with her. Cindy's husband Eli was the personal escort for Prince Turki from Saudi Arabia. They had a real nice home and Cindy had done very well for herself, considering where she had come from and what she had gone through. Dawn went to go live with my oldest sister Kris and her boyfriend. She ended up graduating from Bountiful High.

When I showed up at the Anatole, I had a meeting with Morris. I have never seen anything like the Anatole in my life; this place was a city. I had no idea what I had just gotten myself into. I met Morris in the lobby. The moment he saw me, he looked so upset, and I couldn't figure it out. Then he growled, "How old are you?" I told him I had just turned twenty-one. He narrowed his eyes, "Oh fuck." That really pissed me off.

My age wasn't on my resume. I was hired for my experience, not my age.

"Look, I moved my whole family down here. You at least owe me the opportunity to try."

He nodded his head and looked me in the eye, "You're right, this is my mistake."

Morris took me into the banquet kitchen. I have never seen a kitchen like this in my life. It was a big, empty room and way in the back you could see row after row of cooking equipment. But most of all, it was a big, empty room. Your voice would echo when you talked. There were black electrical cords hanging from the ceiling about every four feet. Hundreds of them. There was a refrigerated cold kitchen on one side of the room that had to have been twenty yards long.

"Where is everybody?" I couldn't stop glancing over his shoulder at the cavernous space.

"They don't have any functions for another two weeks."

"And how many cooks am I responsible for?"

"Forty-six, and you're younger than all of them," he still looked pretty on edge.

"It doesn't really matter, Morris. I have been younger than everybody my whole career, I am quite used to it by now." He lightened up, took me to Human Resources to have me fill out my paperwork and get my ID, and then took me to security to have my keys issued to me. Then he told me not to come back for two more weeks. Thinking of my family, I told him I needed to work. I needed money.

He just laughed, "Oh, you're going to have plenty of chances to work, Todd. In any case, you're a salaried manager and you will be paid for the next two weeks just as though you were working."

He then told me that all twenty-two chefs from the different restaurants and outlets were having a barbeque next Saturday afternoon. He would be calling me with the address. It was mandatory that I attend, and I should bring my wife. Little did I know that in just a few weeks that great big empty room would be so crammed full of hot boxes and speed racks that you'd barely be able to walk through it.

When I got to the barbeque, I realized they had a couple of famous chefs working there. Dean Fearing was the chef of the Veranda, an exclusive private club at the Anatole. Takashi, he had been the chef of Buckingham Palace for fourteen years. His restaurant, Mistral, was my favorite. Takashi didn't have any menus. Dinner started at six-thirty and you got whatever he felt like preparing for you. Then, they had Ann Lindsey Greer; she had designed the restaurant on top of the tower called Nana Grill. Ann had just written a book titled *The Cuisine of the American Southwest*. Nana Grill was the first restaurant that I had ever heard of that was serving Southwestern cuisine. I was certainly in good company.

When I finally started working, it was a bitch. We would do anywhere from a thousand to five thousand meals a day. We ran six five-man crews with a supervisor on each one. Then, I had a floor supervisor. It was not uncommon to need to make one hundred or one hundred and fifty gallons of Alfredo sauce or demi-glace. I preferred to make these sauces myself. The sauce is as important as the featured item.

I was intimidated with a crew of this size at first, but it's just like rock climbing: you never look down, only up, and make sure that every move is a wise one. I started looking at the five-man crews as one man. I would pretend that instead of feeding three thousand, we were feeding three hundred. Well, a party of three hundred is cake. If it were three hundred, I would have one guy sear off the filets. I would have one guy clean, blanch, and shock the vegetables. I would have one guy prepare the potatoes and I would have another guy do the sauce and garnish. So, when we were doing three thousand, I would pretend that one guy equaled one crew.

The only thing different was I could not tie myself down with the actual preparation. I would go from crew to crew, answering questions and stopping them from doing tasks incorrectly.

Nothing is worse than a really fast crew. They can fuck things up at twice the speed of a normal crew. If someone overcooked the baby carrots in this operation, it wasn't like any other operation I had worked before. There were three main issues. One, if they overcooked the baby carrots, chances were good that they overcooked a hundred pounds of them. Two, back then you could not buy baby carrots already peeled, so we had to peel them ourselves. A hundred pounds equals three five-man crews, peeling for over an hour. That's over fifteen paid hours of carrot peeling. The labor cost far more than the carrots themselves. Three, if you'd think you could just run down to the storeroom and requisition another hundred pounds of baby carrots, you'd have another thing coming. Plus, the chances of getting them peeled in time for dinner were slim to none (even if the storeroom did have them, which I promise you, they didn't). I wasn't paying attention and someone overcooked the baby carrots once. It didn't happen again.

The Anatole went from hard to really hard as soon as the 1984 Republican convention checked in. President Regan and Vice President Bush were staying at the Anatole. In fact, everybody that was anybody was staying there.

We were doing over five thousand meals a day; I was working from five to nine p.m., twenty-one days straight, without a day off. The total bitch was that the Secret Service would not let us park our cars anywhere near the building. Our lot was now a half a mile away. I only made that walk once, then that very day I split from work for an hour and bought a skateboard.

The following morning, someone put seventy-two sheet trays of paned bacon in two rotary reel ovens and then went to the restroom. I walked into the kitchen to find smoke billowing out of both ovens. It took so long to unload those ovens that by the time we were done, the bacon was really burnt. Suits were never in the kitchen in the morning, but that morning the breakfast was for the president of the United States. Sure enough, who walked in? Morris with the executive chef, Van Atkins.

The executive chef of the Anatole had so many outlets to worry about that I rarely saw him in the banquet kitchen. They both walked up to four 40-gallon trash cans just top-full of burnt bacon.

Van looked at me, "Who doesn't know how to cook bacon?" I looked over at the sea of tall white hats, all twenty of them trying to pan bacon as fast as they could.

"It takes a couple of different people to burn that much bacon. Not sure who they are yet." I really wasn't sure who they were; I always preferred to place responsibility on all of us together. After all, we were a team.

"I thought we were done burning shit after the baby carrots," Morris muttered. I didn't even answer that.

Van changed the subject, "Todd, we're not down here to check up on the president's breakfast party; we're certain that you have that fully under control. Actually, you're the only one who can settle a small wager between Mr. Salerno and myself. Can we step into your office?"

"Sure," I replied.

As soon we walked in my office, they both busted up laughing.

Morris reached in his pocket, pulled out twenty bucks, and handed it to Van. I had no idea what was going on.

Van tapped the skateboard, "Todd, at four-thirty this morning, I was taking that long walk from my car to the hotel. Now, I just moved here from Las Vegas, and it was still dark and I was worried about being mugged on my way in." *It's funny he should mention that because I felt the same way yesterday. That's why I went and bought a skateboard*, I thought.

He continued, "I heard a faint sound creeping up behind me. It was *ker-plunk, ker-plunk*, and it was getting faster and louder as it approached me. Then, *Whoosh!* Someone brushed up against me going fast. I was certain that it was our new banquet chef. So when I arrived, I told Morris here, 'Your new banquet chef rides a skateboard to work. Are you sure he's old enough to drive?' Morris assured me that you drove because he had seen your car. I bet him twenty dollars that you still rode your skateboard to work, and there you have it." He gestured grandly to the upside down skateboard on my desk, displaying the union jack on the bottom. I had planned to hide it but the cooks were burning bacon, so I just threw it down on my desk and ran into the kitchen.

Almost instantly, everyone in the hotel knew that the new banquet chef rode a skateboard. I didn't care — in fact, I started to ride it in the halls to the storeroom to check on my food. That is, until a Secret Service agent confiscated it and told me to pick it up in security.

The last time a president stepped foot in Dallas, Texas, he was shot. You could not enter the kitchen unless your Hotel ID was displayed on your chest, and then every hour I would be issued a whole bunch of little, round, colored stickers. I was told to go to each and every person on my crew and personally place the color corresponding with the current hour on his or her nametag. By the time I was finally done with all twenty of them, it was time for the next color. This went on for a week. It was a real pain in the ass.

Then, there were five or six agents standing next to every single pot of food we were cooking, making sure that no one was putting poison in the food. If it was a buffet that meal period, every hotel pan of food that was intended to go in a chaffing dish had to be sniffed by a dog. Those dogs were amazing. They would stick their noses right next to a big, beautifully roasted prime rib, but never even touch it. I would look into the eyes of those dogs and I could just tell that they wanted to say "fuck this" and run off with the meat. But they never did. Like someone was really going to place a bomb in a prime rib. They would even place the dogs on hydraulic lifts and raise them to the ceiling of the ballroom, to have them sniff the chandeliers before a function.

God has a way of balancing things out. One morning as I was skating through the parking lot, a twenty-dollar bill blew in front of me. I picked it up, continued to skate, and another twenty-dollar bill blew in front of me. I figured, *Shit, I'm going to start walking.* I passed row after row of black Suburbans, all belonging to the Secret Service, and then I looked on the ground next to the driver's side door of one of them. There was a great big stack of bills. Six hundred and eighty dollars had fallen out of some agent's pocket the night before. I felt like it was proper payment for the pain in the ass that these guys were. I bought an expensive camera for Stacey's birthday that we ended up pawning several years later one night, when we just had to get some more coke.

In a matter of five days, I had fed every single president of the United States since Lyndon B. Johnson, with the exception of Jimmy Carter. One morning I was told by Morris to go to the top floor in the Atrium and prepare omelets in a private suite. Gerald Ford was there with

Howard Baker and Bob Dole. Pretty cool. George Herbert Walker Bush was the headliner at every function that Regan didn't attend, and he brought George W. with him.

With two days' notice, Nancy Regan asked Morris if we could do a pop-up luncheon for herself and twelve hundred of her closest friends. This was the first time that I got to write my own menu. I decided to have chilled zucchini soup for the first course; a chilled, marinated grilled vegetable platter with a baby artichoke filled with watercress aioli in the center of the plate, for the main course; and a frozen lemon soufflé for dessert. I don't know what in the hell I was thinking when I chose chilled zucchini soup. They loved it and it tasted great, but it still sounds like a strange soup and I have never done it since.

I had chosen three chilled courses for two reasons. One, the only way you can get away with that is if you're feeding a bunch of fancy ladies who never eat when they're together anyway, and, two, we had a lot going on that day already. I couldn't allow this pop-up function to do anything to slow us down; I didn't care whom it was for. By choosing cold food, we could pre-plate everything an hour before the meal and it would still be good. Nancy Regan personally thanked me for a great event. That was a real class act.

We poured the chilled soup into chilled cups, and piped a rosette of nutmeg cream on top just as they were sitting down. I didn't want to do it ahead of time because it would get a scab on it. We were halfway done pouring the soup when Morris looked at how much I had left and started to second guess me by saying we would run out of soup. He told five guys to start cutting zucchini. I superseded his decision and told them to stop and get back to pouring and garnishing soup. I told him, "Look, Morris, I have enough soup. I made it and measured it myself. Just settle down, we'll have enough. Besides, by the time they're done cooking it, it won't be chilled enough to serve for a couple of hours. The function will be over by then."

He didn't say a word, he just glared at me. The five cooks he had barked out orders to, were just staring at him, wondering what to do. He finally snapped, "Fine, just keep pouring soup." We had a gallon, maybe two left, when we were all done pouring. Morris settled down, walked over to me, and whispered in my ear, "If you ever cut it that close again I will personally kick your ass." I just smiled at him.

Morris and I both walked into the ballroom and watched as the waiters served the soup. The entrée was already plated and done in the back. When a waiter walked by us with eighteen cups of soup on one tray, I told him, "If you drop that, you'd better just keep on walking and never come back because both of us will be fired." I was finally able to get Morris to laugh again. He added, "He's not kidding."

When I came to work the next morning, everybody was congratulating me and I didn't even know why. Then, they showed me. A reporter from The Dallas Morning News had attended the luncheon. There was a photograph of my chilled vegetable platter in the paper with a stellar article about how great the food was. They made it sound like I had invented soup. I was very proud; this was the second great piece of press I had received in my career. Van called me his new golden boy and told me that I was welcome to dine at any of the restaurants whenever I felt like it. All I had to do was type up a paper describing my experience. The fact that they valued my opinion was far better than the free meals.

Right after the president and the Republican convention left, the American Culinary Convention checked in. The American Culinary Federation Convention had been held at the Hotel Utah in 1976, the first year of my apprenticeship. I remember the convention had Roget wound so tight that he was a living dickhead the whole time they were there. I had worked on most of the functions. One, in particular, always stands out.

I was working a Caviar Blini Station, making little buckwheat pancakes which would be topped with caviar and served in the ballroom. I looked up to see Shane across the room, carving tenderloin and dancing up and down, pointing to his chef's hat. I looked at him like, *Knock it off! If Roget catches us fucking off during this function, he will kill us.* Roget was in the room talking to other chefs. Shane wouldn't quit, so I finally stopped looking at him.

Then, a waiter just about knocked me on my ass and threw my hat down and started stomping on it. Apparently, while I was making blinis, I had bent over the candelabra on the buffet and started my paper chef's hat on fire. I guess it had been burning for quite some time before it was knocked off.

The day the American Culinary Convention checked in, Van asked me to go to a meeting with the Chairman's Committee. This was cool; we went over all of the functions coming up in the next few days.

We had left the meeting and were walking down the hall when Van asked, "Well, Todd, how does it feel to be on the Chairman's Committee for The American Culinary Federation National Convention?"

"I didn't know that I was," I replied, surprised.

The night before the Grand Ball, I was in the kitchen by myself with only a couple of CIA externs helping me make *terrines* for the event. The *terrines* had been my idea. Chuck had taught me to make them and they were really bitchin'. We only had twenty *terrines* to cook them in (like *cassoulet* and other French dishes, *terrines* are named after the vessel in which you cook them), so I had to do three batches. I was done cooking the first batch and I tasted it. It was good, but just a little flat. I'd thought that the smoked salmon would have incorporated plenty of salt, but it hadn't. I adjusted the other two batches with more salt, more white pepper, and a little more lemon juice.

We had just finished cooking all of the *terrines* when Morris and Van walked in the kitchen to check up on me. I don't know if Van would always go grab Morris before he ever stepped foot in the banquet kitchen or what, but those two were always together every time I saw them. They started to pick at my *terrines*. To make them, I had taken the smoked salmon and laid it out on cellophane in a one-foot by two-foot rectangular layer. Then I applied another thin layer of scallop mousse with a spatula, rolled it into a tube, and froze it. After that, I filled the *terrine* with scallop mousse and squished the tube into it until I thought it was dead center. When the *terrine* was cooked, chilled, and sliced, it would be shaped like a piece of white bread with this killer red pinwheel in the center of it. I served it with crème fraiche and two chive sprigs. Very simple, but very cool.

What happened next made me appreciate what an awesome chef Van was. He had taken bites from a couple of different *terrines*.

"They're different!" he barked out.

"What?"

"They're different. This one tastes different than this one. Why?"

"I had to adjust my seasoning a third of the way through."

"The second one was better than the first one, but it doesn't matter; they both need to taste the same."

"OK, we'll make them again."

"No, they're fine. No one will notice. You just need to figure this out before you do it again."

Morris then told me that I wouldn't be dishing up the Grand Ball.

Are you nuts? I thought to myself.

"You have to bring a suit with you to work tomorrow, and tell your wife to show up here at six-thirty. You both will be attending the ball," Morris explained.

"Morris, no way."

"Todd, the *terrines* are done, the salad is pre-plated, and your crew is good. All they have to do is roast some veal and plate up. They can do that without you. If they can't, you're a poor trainer." Since he put it that way, I couldn't disagree.

Stacey and I were seated at Van and Morris's table with their wives. The *terrine* was great and after I ate it, I excused myself to use the restroom. I bolted for the kitchen. I just couldn't stand it. I was sitting there thinking of the seven hundred ways they could screw this meal up. I walked in the kitchen in my suit and tie, and immediately all of the cooks started whistling and giving me catcalls. I just flipped them all off collectively, ran to my office, grabbed a thermometer, and started probing all of the veal racks to make sure they were cooked right. All of them were exactly one hundred and thirty-five degrees resting. I knew they would be perfect and I felt a lot better.

Someone grabbed my arm hard. It was Morris, and he escorted me out of the kitchen and back to my table without ever letting go. All of the cooks got a real big kick out of that. I had a few glasses of wine after that and I was sitting there, thinking about what an awesome pastry chef we had, when I heard Van's voice come across the P.A system. I hadn't even noticed that he had left the table. He was up on stage.

"We have had a lot of important guests here at the Anatole in the past few weeks, but I want you to know that none of them were more important than you chefs." This was a total bullshit line; the president of the United States of America was a hell of a lot more important than this group of chefs.

"I want to introduce the members of the Chairman's Committee for this year's convention," he continued. I looked up on the stage and there were all of those old-timer chefs standing to the right. I immediately looked at Morris like, *What the fuck, why was I left out?* He knew exactly what I was thinking without me saying a word. He just shrugged his shoulders and gave me some fake ass sad face.

Van not only introduced these guys, he placed a gold medal around each and every one of their necks. I was so pissed I could have spit. I was staring at Van on stage and thinking about what a fucker he was when he said, "Now, I would like to introduce the chef that was responsible for all of your meals this week: Chef Todd Hall." The whole room filled with applause, and Morris started laughing his ass off. They had planned it this way because they knew exactly how I was. When I thought that I was supposed to stand up and walk up there to get my medal, I looked at Morris for direction, and once again he shrugged his shoulders. What a prick. I had no idea what to do. Stacey kept pushing me to go up there.

Van continued, "Looking down at Todd's table, I see that I have a problem that I will have to address with him in the morning. He's drinking a glass of wine and I know for a fact he doesn't turn twenty-one for another couple of months." The entire ballroom started laughing and clapping. Then, Morris stood up and told me to walk up there. As I was approaching the stage, I heard Van say, "Not only that, but this guy rides a skateboard to work." Everybody started laughing again and Van continued, "No, I am not kidding. He really does ride a skateboard to work." I walked up on stage and I got all choked up. Van placed the medal around my neck and gave me a big hug, and that was it. I started bawling. I didn't even say thank you. I just waved. And ran for the restroom.

I don't know if it was the wine, the hours I had worked, or that life was just that good, but I do know that it took quite a few minutes until I was able to regain composure and return to the ballroom. I wished that Roget and Max could have been there, but there were a few chefs from Utah who were, and they both ended up finding out that I was kicking some ass in Texas.

Chapter 11

AFTER BANQUETS SETTLED DOWN, I started to search for a way to serve better food. Takashi would come to work every day at one p.m., and the first thing he would do was pick up his food from the storeroom. He was the shit. He ordered stuff that I had never heard of like turbot, brill, *loup de mer*, and my new favorite fish: John Dory, a.k.a. St. Pierre. I would show up in the storeroom every day at one p.m. just to see what he ordered.

I would spend my nights off in Takashi's kitchen. I would just stand there and ask him not only what he was doing, but also why he was doing it. It was a fun little game to him, because he would never tell me. He would make me guess. If I was right, he would say, "That's correct." If I was wrong, he would say, "No." He would cook anything he felt like for his guests. He would pass me a small plate to try as he went along with his evening. I remember the first time I tried John Dory.

"What kind of fish is this?"

"John Dory. In America, they call it John Dory because it has to be caught on a hook and line in the English Channel and it really fights when you catch it. They named it after a great, bare-fisted prize fighter in the nineteen twenties. In France, they call it St. Pierre because when Jesus was approached by tax collectors, he told the first apostle, Peter, to go to the river and catch a fish. When he did, he found a gold coin in its mouth to pay their taxes with." Then, Takashi showed me the two black spots that were still on this fish today from where Peter had touched it; one on both sides of the body, just below the gills. Takashi knew everything about food.

He was serving it with *Bordelaise* sauce, which was completely out of context, in my eyes. *Bordelaise* is veal stock with a Bordeaux reduction, garnished with poached bone marrow. I had never seen something like this served with fish.

"If you are going to be good, then you will have to read the Escoffier cookbook," he admonished me when he saw my surprise. I had read the Escoffier cookbook from cover to cover each and every year of my apprenticeship. Roget made us. I knew better than to argue with a great chef, though. Roget had taught me that years ago.

"OK," I just replied, like it was some kind of new idea that I had never thought of.

I had a couple of Escoffier books but they were all in Utah. So, the very next day I went to the mall and bought another copy. Sure enough, there was not only St. Pierre *Bordelaise*, but Dover Sole *Bordelaise* and ten other kinds of fish *Bordelaise*. I could not understand how I missed all of this when I had read the book three times. So, I read it again and paid a hell of a lot more attention.

I was going through the process of elimination one night with Takashi and I could not figure out what he was using for a liaison, to thicken a sauce. Normally, we would use roux made with flour and clarified butter cooked at low heat for over an hour. If not a roux, then cornstarch mixed with water or white wine; a slurry. He told me to read page seventeen. Takashi not only knew the Escoffier book, he knew it the way a preacher knows scriptures: by the page number.

On that page, Escoffier stated how much better it is to use cornstarch in place of flour, in roux. Flour is only seventy-two percent starch and its other constituents mask your palate from the true flavor, not to mention you have to scum it for three days to get rid of the impurities. I was blown away with this page because Escoffier himself, the chef of kings and the king of chefs, had written, "It is only habit that causes flour to still be the binding element of roux, and indeed, the hour is not so far distant when the advantages of the changes I propose will be better understood—changes which have been already recommended by Favre in his dictionary."

I am sorry to have to be the one to tell you, Chef, but you wrote that in your cookbook in 1907 and, although you spelled it out for all of us, it's been over a hundred years and Takashi is the only one that I have cooked with who really understood it. No matter where I go or where I work, everyone still uses flour for roux. Or they have sworn off roux altogether and just use reductions, purees or liaisons.

The next time I was in Takashi's kitchen, he handed me a cup of soup. It had a puff pastry dome on top of it and I asked him what it was.

"*Billi bi en croute.*" This soup rocked. When you tore into the pastry, the most wonderful aroma filled the air. It was distinctively mussels and saffron. I had to know how to make soup like this. It not only looked really cool with the flaky pastry dome, it tasted rich and wonderful. I was so excited. I had started our little game.

"Did you use mussel stock?"

"That's correct." Nice, I got one right.

"Did you use cream?"

"That's correct." Two for two.

"Did you use saffron?"

"That's correct." That was a given.

"Did you use roux?"

"No." Bummer.

"Did you use cornstarch?"

"No."

"Did you use cornstarch roux, like on page seventeen?"

"No." What the hell, how did he thicken this soup? Then I thought of it. A liaison, in the true sense of the word. In old-time France, they would incorporate a combination of just the right amount of egg yolks and cream to a sauce at the last minute. I never liked to use liaisons because if the soup you were thickening ever got above one hundred and sixty degrees, it would curdle. I knew I had it now.

"Did you use one of those old-time liaisons of egg yolks and cream at the last minute to thicken the soup?"

"No." I wish he would just tell me! He kept cooking like I wasn't even there.

I decided to start from scratch; I was not leaving the kitchen until I knew how to make this soup.

"Did you use a soup pot?"

"That's correct."

"Did you heat the soup pot by turning on the burner?"

"That's correct."

"Did you place whole butter in the pot?"

"That's correct."

"Did you sauté *mirepoix* vegetables in that butter?"

"That's correct."

"Did you add a bay leaf, thyme, salt and pepper, and maybe even saffron to those *mirepoix* vegetables?"

"That's correct."

"Did you add mussels?"

"That's correct"

"Did you add water?"

"No." Now, we were getting somewhere; if he didn't use water to make his stock, then what did he use?

"Did you add *fume* (fish stock)?"

"No."

"Did you add clam juice?"

"No."

"Did you add lobster stock?"

"No." What in the hell did he use for the base of his stock? It was beyond me. I had used every option I could think of, so I said to myself, *We're going to move on.*

"Did you add cream?"

"That's correct." I took another bite of the soup and could not, for the life of me, think of anything else that I could taste in this soup.

"Is there any other ingredient in this soup that I have failed to ask you about?"

"No." OK, I had it all, but I still could not figure out what he used for a base to his stock, or what he thickened it with.

"Did you use a shit load of cream?"

"That's correct." Nice, I figured it out. He had substituted cream for water when making his mussel stock. If he reduced it long enough, he would not have to thicken it at all. This was ingenious. I had one more question.

"Did you add a shitload of cream and then reduce it until it was the proper consistency?"

"That's correct." Takashi reached through the window of the line, shook my hand and bowed the way that oriental dudes do. Game over.

◎ ◎ ◎

Stacey and I were dining in all of the restaurants at least twice a week. One time at Le Entrecote, the Anatole's premier French restaurant, I didn't want to butcher the pronunciation of a bottle of wine so I pointed to the one I wanted on the wine list. The wine steward brought us a bottle of Chateau Yquem, a two-hundred-dollar bottle dessert wine. I thought that this wine was awfully damn good for only thirty-five bucks. When I got my check I learned never to point again.

I went to the Veranda kitchen one night on my day off to see what kind of food Dean Fearing cooked. I was not very welcome in his kitchen. I asked if I could watch and the cooks looked at me as if to say, "Why?" He was plating a party. He had a piece of halibut breaded in macadamia nuts and he was serving it with *pommes dauphinoise* (layered potatoes with cream). The dish looked very heavy. There were a few carved carrot flowers and some carved leaves out of snow peas. It was a garnish you would use on cold compote salad for Sunday brunch buffet. That was his vegetable. Julia Child said that some of the new chefs handled the food way too much.

I already knew what kind of potatoes he was serving and I had made them a million times, but I was trying to strike up some conversation. "What kind of potatoes are these?"

"*Pommes soufflé.*" *Pommes soufflé* are potatoes that you have to fry in three different temperatures of oil to make them puff up like a fried potato pillow. Dean's were two inches thick, cut into squares, and had been baked in a 200-hotel pan. They were not *pommes soufflé.*

He and his sous-chef were snickering, thinking that I was some clueless kid. It pissed me off, so I was out of there. Just before I left, I shook his hand and thanked him for his time.

✧ ✧ ✧

Van and Morris walked up to me one day with some big news. "Todd, we're opening a new resort in Tuscan called Loews Ventana Canyon Resort," Van started to say, but I interrupted him.

"I don't want to move to the desert."

"Settle down, no one's inviting you." Then he continued, "Randy Pitt is the new executive chef of that property, so we need someone to cover Le Entrecote." I thought I had died and gone to heaven. Me, the chef of one of the finest French restaurants in Texas—no, wait, the nation? What a dream.

"I would love to take over Le Entrecote."

"I told you he would want it." Morris said as he looked at Van.

To Van, a great chef is measured by how many people you have under your direction and how much revenue your outlets produce. To me, a great chef is measured by how tasty and beautiful your food is. Le Entrecote had far better food than banquets. Hell, they only had to feed one hundred and twenty people a night, plus no one really cared if they made any money. Le Entrecote was to the Anatole what a cool garnish is to a great plate of food; it's not the featured item, but it certainly does help to dress the dish up.

Van was surprised I wanted to do it, but he told me I could if that's what I wanted. I was lucky that Randy was still around to train me. I loved this restaurant. They had duck liver, beluga caviar served in little ice carvings, and four-pound lobsters boiled to order. Within just a matter of days I was buying anything I felt like from anywhere in the world. I started to emulate Takashi. I would run turbot, brill, and John Dory for my nightly specials.

I went to a French restaurant in Dallas called Old Warsaw. I always thought that name sounded Polish, not French; anyway, it was a great place with a great chef named John La Font. He had worked with Roget at the Chanticleer in Monte Carlo, so he was real nice to me and let me hang out in his kitchen on my days off.

Chef La Font had jars and jars of black and white truffles he had preserved. He would buy them in truffle season in January and then bottle them just like my grandma would with jam. I bought a shitload of truffles and did the same thing. Between what I was picking up at Old Warsaw; what I had learned from Roget, Jimmy, and Chuck; what I had learned in banquets; and what I gleaned using the process of elimination from Takashi, I was coming up with two or three different specials a night that the servers had never seen before. They loved me because I would charge more for the specials than regular menu items, and they would get more tips.

I was only the acting chef of Le Entrecote. Privately, Morris told me to show them what I could do and they would give me the position within three months. Morris had never lied to me before and I wanted this badly. I made sure I always went to go pick up my food from the storeroom at exactly one o'clock so I could see what Takashi was ordering and show off what I had bought. He was very impressed with my preserved truffles and asked me if he could have a couple of bottles. I was so honored that Takashi was asking me for anything.

We would get a lot of famous people in Le Entrecote. One night, Larry Hagman was in there trying to impress both of the "ladies of the evening" he was with. Back then, he was the star of the most popular show on television. Bo, the maître d', was so smooth. Whenever Larry came in with his wife, Bo would croon, "Mr. Hagman! It is so nice to see you again. It has been a very long time, what has kept you away from us?" Everybody had seen Larry the week before with some very seedy ladies.

Larry just ate that shit up, though, and would always pass Bo a hundred. Anyway, on this particular night he was drunk and loud and demanding to see the chef. I had gone to his table before, always with a positive response.

He was talking so loud it was embarrassing. When I got to the table, he almost yelled, "Chef! I ordered the crepes and I can tell that this crab is frozen! Why aren't you using fresh crab?" You have no idea how bad I wanted to say, *Look, there is no such thing as fresh crab. It's cooked and frozen right after it's caught. Nobody gets fresh crab unless the crab is still alive. Not even J. R. Hewing. Not unless he's standing in Alaska right when they boil it, or eating soft-shell crab during the molting process.*

"I am so sorry Mr. Hagman, we ran out of the fresh crab tonight and I was forced to use frozen. Most people don't notice, but I should have told you prior to being served."

"I knew it." He quieted down, graciously thanked me, and when he shook my hand there was a hundred-dollar bill in it. I walked back to the kitchen thinking, *Hell, I'll lie for a hundred bucks any day of the week.*

◊ ◊ ◊

A couple of weeks later, it had been three months and I was anxiously awaiting the appointment of my new position: The Chef of Le Entrecote. Van's secretary called me and told me that Van wanted to see me in his office. I thought this was it; he was going to give it to me. Instead, he told me that he went to battle for me, but the general manager of the hotel would not concede to having a twenty-one-year-old as the chef of his premiere French restaurant. Van told me that the GM agreed that I was doing a great job, but it was a high-profile position with lots of events outside the hotel and lots of press. He told me they had hired some guy that was working with Wolfgang Puck and he would be there in a couple of weeks. I was more than welcome to go back to banquets if I didn't feel like playing second fiddle.

Soon after, Stacey got in a car accident on the Lyndon B. Johnson Freeway, and it scared the shit out of her. When I saw her, she was furious with me. She hated Texas. I wasn't ever home, I would always spend my days off at other restaurants, and for the past year that we had lived there she and Chelse hadn't spent any time with me. She gave me an ultimatum: she was going back to Utah next week and I could stay or I could go. It was up to me. I wasn't going to let her take my baby girl away from me; I immediately said I'd go with her.

When I gave notice, Morris and Van tried to talk me out of it. "What in the hell do you want to go back to Utah for? There's no good food there." I asked Morris for a letter of reference, and on my last day he thanked me and gave me the letter. As I was walking out of the Anatole for the last time, Morris yelled, "Aren't you going to read it?" I opened the envelope and read the letter. I started to boil.

"Chef Todd Hall was a sous-chef of The Loews Anatole Hotel. Although he was required to work many hours, he never worked one without bitching about it. He burnt twice as much food as he ever served, and when we invited him to the Grand Ball he was a crybaby. *–Morris Salerno, Banquet Area Director.*" Van and Morris just had to yuck it up, one more time. Morris handed me a great letter then, inviting me back to their mecca of chefs any time I wanted. They were a couple of wise guys, but I had learned to love them both. I knew that I was going to miss them and The Anatole.

Chapter 12

WHEN THE JET LANDED at Salt Lake International Airport, I had already lined up a job. My new boss came to the airport to pick us up in a limousine, but he had so many of his drunk friends in it I wasn't about to put my baby in there. Stacey, Chelse and I got a cab to Bountiful. I felt like I was taking a giant step backwards, because I was. I looked down at the beautiful little girl asleep in my arms. I kissed her softly on the forehead and whispered, "You're worth it, baby."

Jim Greaves had owned a restaurant in Bountiful since I was a little kid. He had also just leased the kitchen in a private club called The Fifth Amendment. I was in charge of both.

Jim would wake up at noon and start drinking by one. That made a pretty short day of it. He always had some good weed and we would do blow a few times a month. I remember thinking, *I just went a whole year without doing any drugs at all and didn't even notice.* I was so wrapped up in food, I never went looking for drugs. They certainly weren't around the people I was hanging out with. The whole time I was in Texas, I smoked maybe two joints, sniffed coked once, and did this new drug my sister Cindy brought home from Europe, called Ecstasy. It was like dropping acid after taking a Quaalude. I wondered why so many more people did drugs in Utah than Texas.

Just a few weeks before, I had been serving duck liver to movie stars and presidents. Now all my clientele wanted was extra gravy with their chicken fried steak. What a waste. Stacey and I settled in and got a house, but I worked hard every day thinking, *I have totally fucked my career up.*

Stacey was pregnant again, though, and I was excited about it. Chelse was the light of my life and the thought of having a little friend for her was great. I remembered Doctor Lewis's offer to help me get my own restaurant and wondered if it still stood, even though I wasn't a Mormon. I called him, and it did. So, I started looking for locations to open my first restaurant.

I found a place in the old Elk's building on South Temple in downtown Salt Lake. It was functioning as a restaurant called Cherish, but the owner wanted out. He would sell it to me for seventy-two thousand dollars. I drew up a business plan to open a restaurant that would serve southwestern cuisine, something that no one in Utah had heard of yet. There was this great new dish that was being served everywhere in Texas and everyone was ordering it. *Fajitas*. I decided to call my new southwest restaurant Armadillos; the name just screamed "southwest". I gave Doctor Lewis my proposal and he said, "No way." He told me to try something else.

A few months later, we took a camping trip with my brother Nick and his kids to Logan. I'd lived in Logan Canyon as a kid. Mike had moved us all there when he was the manager of a gourmet restaurant that was just getting ready to open. We'd lived eight miles up the most beautiful canyon in the world. There was no TV reception out there at the time, and we lived in a cool, cabin-like house right below the restaurant.

Every day after school, I'd grab my fly rod or shotgun and walk up and down the river. Mike trapped for muskrats and I would check all of the traps before I went to school and after I got home. You could get two dollars a pelt back then, and Mike would give me fifty cents for every pelt I pulled. Out in Logan, Mike also taught me how to slowly reach my hand under a river embankment and gently caress the side of a brown trout until I could slide my finger in its gill and pull it out of the water. It was a very cool trick, and I would show everyone that would come visit us. Every night, I'd read myself to sleep listening to the Rolling Stones, Creedence Clearwater Revival, and The Beatles.

When we went by the restaurant that we used to live at, it had a "For Lease" sign in the window. I got so excited! What if I could own the same restaurant I had lived at? What if I could teach my kids to fish with their hands in the same stream? I could teach them to run a trap line! I couldn't stand it. It all made perfect sense.

I called the number as soon as we were out of the canyon. It was the same owner as when I was a kid. He agreed to meet with us in Ogden, the next day. Nick was all nervous and kept asking, "Why are we meeting with this guy? We don't have any money." I assured him that Doctor Lewis would come through. The next day we met with Wilford Goodwill, the owner. I bragged about my training and my success in Texas. Nick was the executive chef of the Officers Club at Hill Air Force Base, so I bragged about him too.

Wilford told us he had already leased the space in Logan canyon, but he owned part of another restaurant in Salt Lake that had been open for ten years. He had bought in at twenty-five percent, seven years ago, and every single month it just broke even. It never lost any money, but it never made any money. He had no idea if it was his two other partners fixing the numbers (they were both lawyers), or the employees. But he thought it was just too coincidental that it hit exactly the right number every month for seven years. He offered us a decent amount of cash to go in and take a look.

The restaurant was named Joe Vera's. It was located on Foothill Drive, a ritzy area of Salt Lake at the mouth of Parleys Canyon, and it was bustling. They would sell over three hundred mini bottles of tequila on any given weekend night during ski season. Utah has weird liquor laws. You have to buy your alcohol at the host stand and pour it in yourself... just to make sure nobody gets you drunk but you.

Joe Vera was the man who opened the place ten years prior. He got into some legal trouble, racked up a big bill, and then was killed in a car accident. Two lawyers, Bruce Dibbs and Earl Spafford, took seventy-five percent of the restaurant away from Vera's estate to pay the outstanding bill. They took twenty-five percent each, and sold the remaining twenty-five percent to Wilford Goodwill. The other twenty-five percent remained with the Joe Vera estate.

The kitchen was run by a crew of undocumented immigrants from Mexico hired by Joe Vera, himself. It took me all of three days to see that the amigos were feeding the barrio. No one was taking any cash, but these guys were so good that they knew how to over-order in correlation with how busy they were, and just take the food.

I told Doctor Lewis about the place and that I wanted to buy it from the lawyers and Wilford. I was sure that I could get it for seventy-two thousand. Doctor Lewis went there for dinner and said, "Sure." A few days later, I went and picked up a check from him for seventy-two thousand dollars, and he said, "Todd, if you go bankrupt you won't owe me a dime. If you make it, you need to pay me back the same amount that I would receive if I put the money in money market certificates." I agreed.

In my first meeting with the lawyers and Wilford, I told them that the amigos were pilfering. I presented my check for seventy-two grand and offered to buy it from them. They started arguing and asked me to leave for a minute. When they called me back in, they could not come to an agreement.

In the next few days, I started to offer them amounts for their shares individually. I got Wilford's first for eight thousand. I got Bruce Dibbs for six. I had to sign papers indemnifying each of them against any liability from the restaurant. I now had fifty percent for only fourteen grand. I told Doctor Lewis and he said I was in over my head, and referred me to a lawyer. The lawyer went with me to offer Earl Spafford money for his shares. He didn't want to sell, but he wanted to be my partner. This guy was sneaky and I had a bad feeling about him.

I then had my lawyer track down the Joe Vera estate. He gave me an address and I went and knocked on the door. A soft-spoken Hispanic lady answered the door and invited me in immediately. She had a handicapped son in a wheelchair. She told me about her late husband and how much he loved the restaurant. When he died, the lawyers took control of it, and she had never received a dime since. I felt so sorry for this lady. I told her what I was doing, and then I offered her twenty thousand for her twenty-five percent. I knew she would take less, but I thought she had received a raw deal. Plus, that kid in the wheelchair was breaking my heart. Then she told me that she had already sold her shares of the restaurant two days ago to Earl Spafford for two thousand dollars, and she started to cry. I had offered her ten times that much.

Finally I asked, "Why did you sell it to him for so cheap?" She told me that our good Mormon friend, Earl Spafford, had informed her that the restaurant had acquired a lot of bills that she was legally responsible for and he didn't want her to go through any more than she already had. So, he offered to bail her out for two grand. I was so pissed and I apologized to her for bothering her. As I left, she said, "You seem like a nice boy. If you do end up getting the restaurant, could you please not change the name? It makes us think of Joe whenever we drive by." I assured her I would get the restaurant and I would never change the name.

I asked Earl to have a meeting with my brother Nick and me at the restaurant; he agreed to meet us there that afternoon. I had my lawyer sit in. I offered him ten thousand dollars for his twenty-five percent again. He said no.

My skin felt prickly and hot just sitting in the same room as this guy. "How can I get ahold of the Joe Vera estate?"

"After Joe died, his family was deported back to Mexico. They were all here illegally." The lie was as smooth as a two-hundred-dollar bottle of wine. That was it. I just couldn't stand this scumbag another minute.

"You lying motherfucker, you walked into her house two days ago and ripped her off right in front of her handicapped son." My brother and my lawyer started to yell back at me in stereo.

"Todd, Todd, Todd, knock it off."

"I will not put up with this kind of profanity." Spafford spat, as he got up and headed for the door.

That day he called my lawyer and said he would sell his fifty percent for twenty thousand dollars, but I had to indemnify him from any liability from the restaurant. I bought it. I made payment arrangements with Doctor Lewis for fifteen hundred dollars a month. A week after I borrowed the money, I paid Doctor Lewis a year and a half's worth of payments.

"Todd, you will need this if things get tough." I told him that I still had a lot.

Nick and I started running Joe Vera's. Nick's wife Shelly thought he was an idiot for quitting his job with the Air Force to go work with his little brother. I continued to lease the kitchen at the Fifth; the only difference was that I prepped all of the food at Joe Vera's and restocked the Fifth when I went home.

I brought in Misha and a couple other cooks I had working for me at the Fifth. I could have any burnout high school student make chicken fried steak, and I had a couple of them. I also fired all of the original kitchen workers. I did not want to have to wonder which one of them was ripping me off.

Now, you would think two great chefs would have no trouble running a simple Mexican restaurant. We fucked this place up every way possible into next week. No one wanted something they had never heard of, like fajitas. They wanted the exact same enchilada they got last year when they were here skiing. The beans weren't the same, the rice wasn't the same, the burritos weren't the same, and people were pissed about it.

Once I changed the menu, they were pissed before I even served them. Joe Vera's had not changed their menu in ten years and everybody was just fine with that. We went from doing between seven and eight hundred dollars a night to three or four hundred.

"Dude, we have to do something," Nick would say at the end of every night.

The night I admitted failure was when I was working the line with Misha. Keep in mind that I lived two doors down from this guy for ten years. I was the one that got him into cooking in the first place. Things were so bad that night, I tried to blame it on Misha.

"Fuck off, Todd." He didn't even stop working the line to say it.

"That's it, you're fired."

Misha just laughed as he rolled a steak burrito. "Oh, NO way. I am not letting you off that easy. You've been fucking this place up since I started. You made me quit my job to be a part of this circus. I am going to stand right here until I get to watch this fuckin' place bury you."

We both just kept on feeding people without saying a word. Misha was right. I had fucked this place up, and I had no one to blame but myself. I laugh about it now because that is the most awesome response I have ever heard to the words, "you're fired". Misha was cool then and he is still cool now. Last I heard, he was the chef for the TV show, *Touched by an Angel*.

The next morning, I came in and asked a lunch waitress if she knew where all of the kitchen guys that I had fired lived. She did. That day, I drove around with her until I was able to get every one of them to come back. For more money, of course. I had thrown away all of the old menus, but they all knew everything by heart. I had to pay for printing, but I didn't have to worry about what to write.

In two days the kitchen was organized and clean, the food was exactly the way it had been for the last ten years, and everyone was happy. Especially our guests. It took about three months to make up for the damage that the great Chef Todd Hall had done, but our numbers finally hit where they were. In fact, they went up considerably over the following ski season. I realized then what Mrs. Vera was trying to tell me; whether I paid for this place or not, the restaurant would always be Joe Vera's. It would never be Todd Hall's. Restaurants are like that; they're very loyal to their creators.

Chapter 13

I ENDED UP BEING GREAT friends with all of the kitchen amigos. They didn't really need either Nick or me to run Joe Vera's. I had learned my lesson, so I just let them do what they wanted and in return they gave me lots of money.

Stacey gave birth to a beautiful baby boy; we named him Parker Allen Hall. I got sick of living in Bountiful, so I rented the highest house on the mountain in Summit Park in Park City. I was bored, so I picked up a couple of more kitchens in private clubs. We got the Elks Lodge in Bountiful and the Club Cabana in Salt Lake. Now I had something to do. I hired cooks to make fish and chips and burgers and spent my days delivering food to three places. Computers were the big rage and I was the first one in Utah to have direct order entry with Sysco, a major distributor of food products.

Shane had moved back to Utah and was working at this new ski resort called Deer Valley. Shane came in one day and told me about a guy who was looking for a private chef for two weeks. Shane could only do it once a week on his day off. Nick and I drove up to Deer Valley and talked to the guy's personal assistant, who had arrived a few days ahead to set everything up.

The guy's name was Kutayba Alghanim, his assistant told me. Everybody just called him Mr. K. He was very wealthy and from Kuwait, and I was told that he was the third richest man in the world.

"Mr. K needs a private chef for breakfast and dinner every day. How much do you charge?"

"Six hundred and fifty dollars a day, plus the cost of food." Nick just about died. He thought I had just screwed this opportunity up.

"Fine, it's a deal. His private jet lands on Friday; be here at four."

When I got there, Mr. K hadn't arrived yet, but his staff had. He had twenty-six security personnel and four or five assistants. They had rented three luxury homes right on the ski run at Silver Lake Lodge in Deer Valley. The guy in charge was Fahti. I told Fahti that my brother-in-law worked for Prince Turki from Saudi Arabia.

"Do not mention that in Mr. K's presence."

"Why not?"

"You must be very careful about everything you say." *Oh, great.* Fahti continued, "It will go a lot smoother if you just come up here and cook exactly what he wants, when he wants it, with minimal conversation. Breakfast must be ready at five-thirty every morning. If you're late, he will not invite you back. We will pay you cash every night. If you do well, he will invite you back for the following day. If not, then we will find another chef. It is not uncommon to go through three or four chefs on a trip like this.

"Mr. K's oldest son is Omar. The next son is Waleed, and his eight-year-old daughter is Samar. Someone tried to kidnap Samar a couple of years ago, so keep that in mind and don't try to take her for a walk or anything stupid like that. The children will get anything they want, whenever they want. But, usually, they want to eat the same thing their father wants to eat. They all should have been here an hour ago. I have no idea where they are."

"What am I going to fix them for dinner tonight?"

"Mr. K will come here and meet you. Your first meal will be tomorrow's breakfast."

"I was asked to start tonight." Fahti reached in his pocket and pulled out a great big wad of cash and handed me six hundred and fifty dollars.

"Is that what you're worried about?" he asked.

"Exactly."

Some British dude came over, introduced himself, and wished me luck. He was the navigator of Mr. K's yacht.

"How many people does Mr. K travel with?" I looked around at the enormous, perfectly stocked kitchen.

"Sometimes on these short trips, as little as thirty-five or forty. If it's a long trip, it can be as many as fifty or sixty. Most of those people are security, valets, and drivers."

"Why so much security?"

"When you have three shifts a day with five people per shift, five days a week, it works out to be that many."

"So, I'll be feeding about forty people a night?"

"You think he pays a private chef to cook for us? Not even. You'll be cooking for no more than five or six people a day, depending on who he flies in." The navigator was chuckling now.

Meanwhile, Fahti was frantic. He was placing ashtrays all over the house with a packed box of Marlboro Red cigarettes and a folded-open book of matches next to each ash tray.

"Wow, he must smoke a lot."

"Constantly," The navigator answered. "And the man has never lit a cigarette in his life."

"What? Someone just runs over and lights it for him every time he picks up a box?"

"Yup, and since the day he was born someone has always dressed him. His children have been dressed since the day they were born, too."

This was really starting to sound ridiculous to me; I guess my cultural exposure was limited.

Then, Fahti came to me. "I forgot to tell you something. No matter what he says, never disagree with him. Also, when you enter the same room as him, never turn around and walk away. In fact, never allow him to ever see your back. Just walk out of the room backwards."

"You guys are just messing with me," I laughed. They both shook their heads.

"No, we're not. You need to do this."

"In his country, it is considered rude to turn your back on someone, no matter what," the navigator explained.

Then, the chief of security came over and asked to see my car. After he took down my license plate number, he asked to see my driver's license and registration.

"Why? Are you going to give me a ticket?" He gave me a dirty look.

"Look, I suggest that you leave your smart ass comments somewhere else if you want to be invited back here. I have a job to do, just like you do. Now get me your registration." After writing my registration information down, he handed it back to me. "If you plan on using any other vehicles I will need to see them today as well." I called Nick and told him that he needed to come up and show security his Bronco.

All around us, security was installing miles of cable and closed-circuit cameras everywhere. Everybody had a radio. These guys were every bit as pissy as the Secret Service was at the Anatole. As we were standing out front, three black Suburbans pulled up to the house. I thought it *was* the Secret Service. The security dude told me to go wait inside.

Everybody in the house started running around crying, "They're here! They're here!" Then, they all lined up right at the door and stood at attention as Mr. K walked in. Fahti had told me to wait in the kitchen until he came and got me.

I tried to listen to what they were saying, but they were speaking in Arabic. I heard my brother-in-law speak Arabic all of the time when he was on the phone in Texas. I always thought it sounded like they were clearing their throat and getting ready to spit. It was a half hour until Fahti finally summoned me in to see Mr. K. As soon as I stepped into the room, everybody started speaking English. Even the kids began speaking English to one another. This group really had some manners.

Mr. K was a roly-poly man with a smile from ear to ear. If I had billions of dollars, I guess I would be smiling too. He was gracious, polite, and easy to talk to.

"I am sorry we are late," he began, shaking my hand. "We got hungry during our flight from New York and we had to have the pilots land in Kansas City to go to McDonald's. We all really love McDonald's." Can you imagine how much it costs to land your jet and take off again, just so you can settle your Big Mac attack?

"Where were you trained?" Mr. K asked.

"I did a formal French apprenticeship under the direction of Roget Cortello." His smile widened.

"Great! Then we will have *pillared du veau* for dinner tomorrow night. You know what it is, don't you?" I had no idea. I have never cooked that before, but I knew enough French to know that *pillared* meant "grilled" and *du veau* was veal.

"Yeah, it's grilled veal." He smiled even more and told me that he wanted it served with *pommes frites*. French fries.

"Not just French fries, I want McDonald's French fries. Hot and crispy."

"Sure, what kind of vegetables would like?"

"No vegetables, just a Caesar salad, veal, and fries for six."

This was going to be the easiest six hundred and fifty dollars I had ever earned. I thanked him, told him how nice it was to meet him, and he introduced me to his children. Then I very carefully walked out of the room backwards.

Back in the kitchen, Fahti told me that every morning they ate the same thing for breakfast. Twenty-four croissants fresh out of the oven filled with beef sausage, no pork, with a small fruit platter and some natural yogurt. If we were even one minute late, we could never come back. Then, he got pissed off.

"Why did you tell him that you could serve McDonald's French fries? This will be your first and last meal here."

"I'll just go to Mc Donald's and buy a bag of fries and cook them here."

"That's what every chef says that he plays this trick on. No matter where we are in the world, not one of them has ever done it. Good luck." I waited until they were out of the living room and I went out to the deck to check on the grill. It was almost brand new. Gas. Nick pulled up so I ran down and told security that he was the guy who would be delivering breakfast every morning. They did the license and registration thing with him too.

When Nick was done, he walked over to me.

"So, let's go meet this guy."

"Dude, don't ever walk in there unless you absolutely have to. It's fuckin' nuts."

We went back to my house in Summit Park and smoked a joint while I gave him the rundown of all of the rules. Then I looked up *pillared du veau* in the Escoffier book. It wasn't just grilled veal.

You have to take seven ounces of veal tenderloin and pound it until it's at least twelve inches in diameter. This makes it so thin you can read the newspaper through it. Then, you place it on a hot grill for just a second, flip it, roll it up like a burrito, baste it with fresh anchovy butter, squeeze fresh lemon juice on it, and sprinkle it with fresh chopped parsley.

It seemed pretty simple, but to get the veal that thin was a total pain in the ass. I ended up placing it between two pieces of parchment paper and rolling it with a pastry pin to get it just right. I was glad I only had to make six of them.

I did all of this at Joe Vera's, then I went to McDonald's get the fries. I was kind of worried about what Fahti had said, but I wasn't too bothered. When I got there, I asked if I could buy a bag of raw French fries, still frozen. The girl sent over her manager and I told him what I wanted.

"No way, we can't sell our fries like that."

"Look dude, I'll give you a hundred dollars for a bag of fries, just give me a receipt and the fries."

"I can't sell you a bag of fries for a million dollars. I'll get fired." That was my final answer.

Out in the McDonalds parking lot, I sat in my car, thinking. *Fahti was right, I can't buy them.* I knew that if I tried to make them myself I would never pass them off. This guy landed his jet for these fries and he knew enough about food that he'd catch me. Just then, a McDonald's employee emptied the garbage in the dumpster. He looked like a high school kid. I ran over to him.

"I'll give you this hundred-dollar bill if you go back in there and steal me a bag of French fries."

"No way! You probably work for McDonald's and you're just seeing if I steal."

"Dude, do I look like I work at McDonald's? I am a famous chef and I need those fries. Do you have any idea how much weed you can buy with a hundred bucks?" He started to snicker.

"How can I just walk out the back door with a bag of fries?"

"It's easy. My cooks do it to me all the time. Just take a bag of fries and throw them away when no one is looking. Then, hurry and put an empty box on top of them, and take out the garbage."

"Alright, but you have to pay me first." I agreed.

"If you walk out the front door and blow me off, I'll come back here and kick your ass. If you return empty handed, you give me the money back." Ten minutes later, he came out with more garbage and handed me the fries.

I was so proud. When I got to the house, I showed my fries off to Fahti and he was impressed.

"Every time anyone else tried to buy the fries, McDonalds wouldn't sell them. How did you get them?"

"I had to pay some kid a hundred dollars to steal them for me. I couldn't get a receipt." Fahti busted up laughing.

"You are going to do very well here," he said as he reached in his pocket and handed me a hundred dollars.

The meal seemed so simple I couldn't understand how it could have impressed them. When Mr. K yelled out, "Bring me the chef!" I walked up to the table. "This is outstanding, Chef, I am very pleased. You know, in order for *pillared du veau* to be great, you must have a great butcher."

"I cut and pounded the veal myself," I replied.

"I am impressed, and these fries, they're even better than McDonald's."

"Thank you sir, but actually they are McDonald's." I then walked out of the room backwards. When I got out of the room, Fahti was waiting for me in a frenzy.

"Hurry! Go back in there and tell him he is right. They are better than McDonald's."

"You have got to be kidding me."

"No, no. You have to go back now, hurry." I went back to the table and Mr. K looked up at me.

"Excuse me, Mr. K, but I blanched the fries in some really good olive oil, and I don't think McDonald's does that." He was so happy and winked at me.

"I knew they were better," he told his guest as I backed away.

"That was a close call," Fahti whispered.

After they were finished with dinner, I was summoned again to discuss what we were going to have for dinner the next night. I rattled off all kinds of totally gourmet stuff.

"Chef, do you know what I really want?"

"What's that?"

"*Pillared du veau* with *pommes frites*, exactly like you did it tonight. I have been looking for someone to do it the way they do in France for years. So, we will have it again." I nodded, "Fine." Fahti told me I did a great job, handed me eight hundred bucks for my fee and the food, and told me not to be late in the morning. I told him I am not a morning person, but my brother Nick would be here at five-fifteen with the breakfast stuff. He nodded and gestured vaguely in the direction of the dining room.

"Oh, and there will only be five for dinner tomorrow."

"Why?"

"One of the guests said that Reagan was a bad president and Mr. K is good friends with President Reagan." Sure enough, that dude was eighty-sixed from the ski trip by the next morning.

I split the cash fifty-fifty with Nick. When he went to do breakfast, Fahti just took the stuff at the door and Nick never went in. I had to go get another bag of fries. This time I told my fry connection I would be back in an hour and I wanted three bags for a hundred bucks, just in case this guy wanted fries every night.

He not only wanted fries every night, he wanted *pillared du veau* every night. I made it five nights in a row. I was in like Flynn with these cats. It got to be easy money. By the time they were getting ready to leave, I was hanging out with the kids. Mr. K liked when I would play backgammon with Samar; that way he didn't have to. And, of course, I always let her win. It was Waleed's birthday coming up, and I asked him what he wanted.

"A ride on the space shuttle."

"What did you get last year?"

"A Testarossa." What a life.

Mr. K left me one of the luxury homes for three days as a tip. I never saw any of them again.

Chapter 14

NICK AND I WERE WORKING at Joe Vera's one day when a waitress told us that three guys in suits would like to talk to us. Most the time when you hear that, they want to bitch about something. We both walked over to their table and the leader stood up.

"Hi, we're from Zion Securities. Do you have a moment to chat with us?"

Anyone in Utah knew that "Zion Securities" meant the money side of the word, "Mormon". Zion Securities owned Zion's Cooperative Mercantile Institution (ZCMI); Zion National Bank; both newspapers, The Desert News and The Salt Lake Tribune; KSL Television and Radio, and just about every piece of land and building in the whole state. At the time, Zion Securities was the twelfth largest corporation in America.

"Sure, we have time to talk. How can we help you?"

"I'm Kent Money and I'm the president of Zion Securities."

"Wait a minute, you're the president of Zion Securities and your name is Kent Money?" I interrupted. Everyone at the table chuckled.

"Yes, I am, and yes, that's my real name. Anyway, these are two of my property managers. Let me introduce you to Jim Walton, and Kent Gibson." President Money continued, "We're not here just for lunch. In fact, we have been here a few times for lunch already. We just acquired a property that has a couple of restaurants in it and we wanted to know if you folks would be interested in running one of them?"

"Running the restaurant or leasing the space?"

"Both. If you sign a five-year lease, we will absorb any costs of getting it back open, as long as any F, F, and E remain the property of Zion Securities."

"What are F, F, and E?" Nick asked.

"Furniture, Fixtures, and Equipment," I answered. "Nick, didn't you read the lease we signed for this place? What these guys are proposing is that they will set us up with a working restaurant if we sign a five-year lease. Then, they're going to make us secure the lease with our personal property, like this restaurant for example, or our cars or homes."

"No way!" Nick instantly replied, but Mr. Money interjected.

"Todd's absolutely right. You will have to sign as a corporation, but in this case it's a little different. Most of the time we ask for personal guarantees, but we won't require those in this situation. We just bought the building a few weeks ago. It's to our benefit to get one of the restaurants back open as soon as possible so we can start leasing the office space."

"What building?" I asked.

"The old Elks building on South Temple." I about fell off my chair! That was the same building for which I did my original proposal for Doctor Lewis. The restaurant in Logan canyon.

"What restaurant? Cherish or Confetti?"

"Cherish. We're turning Confetti into office space." I started laughing. I couldn't believe it.

"Can you gentlemen excuse me for a minute?"

I went into my office and pulled out my Doctor Lewis file. Sure enough, I still had the proposal for Armadillo's. Right on the first page, it said that Armadillo's would occupy the space that is now called Cherish in the old Elks building.

I showed Mr. Money and he snapped his head up at me in disbelief. Then, he passed it around to his colleagues, and they stared at one another with long, meaningful glances. I could just tell they were saying, "This is the Lord's work," telepathically.

"Doctor Lewis put you guys up to this, didn't he?" I asked.

Mr. Money shook his head. "Doctor who? Todd, the reason we decided to approach you folks is because I live right on the foothills and I have been coming here for years. I have always received good food and service at a reasonable price. I do have to say that it's quite uncanny that you created a business proposal a year and a half ago, for the same space we are asking you to lease. If you were going to consider leasing from us, the first thing we would have requested from you would be a business plan exactly like this."

This was too good to be true. I couldn't change a thing at Joe Vera's, but I was going to get my dream restaurant, Armadillo's, without having to borrow a penny from anyone. I was starting to think it was the Lord's work myself, and I wasn't even Mormon anymore. I still had concerns, however. I told all three of them that a "good Mormon" named Earl Spafford had just screwed me and I still had a bad taste in my mouth. Mr. Money called it to my attention that they were not asking me to invest a penny in this new restaurant. All they wanted was my crew, food, and talent.

We ended up getting the space, and they really did put a lot of money into it. Zion Securities paid for china, glassware, equipment; the works. Then, Kent Gibson informed me that there would be an amendment to the lease. They were building the Eagle Gate condominiums next door to the restaurant, and the Prophet Ezra Taft Benson would be living on the top floor. They didn't want me to use my liquor license at the new restaurant.

"No way!"

Kent tried to pacify me. "Todd, look, we've already gone so far with this—we can't back out now."

"Kent, you knew where the Prophet was going to be living before I ever met you. You should have been straightforward and told me the very first day you proposed the deal. Forget it. I'm sorry."

He called me back the next day. "We're prepared to forgive the rent for the first six months if you open up without your liquor license." At five thousand dollars a month, this equaled thirty grand. I asked him to let me think about it. In the end, we just used our beer and wine license. We sold out to the Mormons on the mini bottles. In Utah, there are two kinds of licenses: one for beer and wine and another for mini bottles.

We opened up Armadillos that spring. It was pretty busy at lunch, but we couldn't get people to go downtown to Temple Square at night for dinner. You can't really make any money on lunch. People eat the same amount of food at lunch as they do for dinner, but you can only charge half the price. They did love the fajitas, though.

My brother hired one of his friends to cook with us. His name was Ted Sockal, and he was a part-time coke dealer and a full-time cook. He had just about everyone in that restaurant hooked like a tow truck.

Chapter 15

ONE MORNING, THE MANAGER of Joe Vera's called and told me that immigration had just hit the restaurant and deported all four cooks who were working.

"How much did they fine us?"

"Nothing." I was surprised. That left me a crew of three. Rico, one of my remaining guys, told me that the others would be in Mexico that night and back across the border by the morning.

"How long until they're back here?"

"The problem isn't getting back across the border," Rico informed me, "it's the checkpoints on the way back to Utah. They always get caught at that place where they ask you if you have any fruits or vegetables with you today."

"What should I do?"

"Start driving to Arizona now and call us when you get to Phoenix. We will tell you where to meet them."

Nick and I hopped in his Bronco, picked up an eight ball, and headed to Arizona. Nick whined the whole ride down.

"They're going to take my truck and we're both going to end up in jail for interstate transportation of illegal aliens."

"Relax. Get another line ready and turn up the stereo," I replied.

The sun was just rising when we hit Black Canyon City, about forty miles north of Phoenix. I got all excited because I could see the silhouettes of the saguaro cacti. The only time I had ever seen cacti before was in cartoons. They actually looked just like they did on Quick Draw McGraw!

Stacey had just flown down to Phoenix the day before with the kids to see her mom. I called her and asked where her mom lived. She was all freaked out and wanted to know why I was in Arizona.

I stopped by for just a couple of minutes and used the phone at Stacey's mom's house to call my cooks in Utah. They told me to meet the guys at a Circle K in Mesa in an hour.

"What's a Circle K?"

"It's just like a 7-Eleven," they explained, and gave me the address. I gave Stacey and the kids a kiss and a hug and told them I would see them in a couple of days back in Utah.

We got to the Circle K and sure enough, there were all four of my cooks sitting on the curb by the pay phone. I was amazed; I thought it would be a lot harder than this. We headed back up I-17 and the whole time I was thinking about the fruit and vegetable dude. I knew the checkpoint was just past Flagstaff. I took a real hard look at it on our way down. It started to rain by the time we got to Flag, and then I got an idea. I knew better than to tell Nick; he would just say that it wouldn't work. I stopped at a gas station, bought a Phillips screwdriver, and loosened the little screw on the windshield wiper just enough to make it wobble. I tested it and it was perfect.

"What in the hell are you doing to my truck?" Nick eyed me suspiciously.

"Get me another line ready, it might be our last." I should never have said that. It just made him more paranoid. He didn't want to get me another line.

"You have had enough."

"Look, I have been driving sixteen hours and I have another twelve to go. Get me another line." He did. We drove from Flagstaff to the checkpoint for over twenty miles in the rain without using the wipers. Nick was freaking out.

"Fix the damn wipers and turn them on!" Our cooks always thought we were crazy, but now they knew it for certain.

I turned on the wipers right when I pulled up to the check point. Then I jumped out of the truck and approached the guard.

"Hey, do you have a Phillips screw driver? My windshield wiper is loose." He was all happy to help and reached into his pocket.

"Yeah, I have one right here on my pocketknife." *What a Boy Scout.* He told me to turn off the wipers and I did. Then, he tightened down the little screw and told me to try it. He never once looked at the four amigos in the back seat. Nick was just sitting there shaking and sweating like Barney Fife from Mayberry.

"Hey, they work great now, thank you so much!"

"No problem, happy to help. Have a safe trip!" I was just pulling out and rolling up my window, when I heard him yell.

"Hey, come back here!" I looked in the mirror and saw him waving me back. Nick started to freak out again.

"Shut the fuck up. Now." I muttered. I put the Bronco in reverse, and rolled my window back down.

"I almost forgot to ask you, do you have any fruits or vegetables?" I started laughing.

"No, sir, I don't."

"Thanks," he yelled and banged on the door.

"No, thank you!" I split.

Chapter 16

THAT SUMMER THE DEVIL herself walked into Armadillo's. Her name was Irene Roadbush and she was with the Internal Revenue Service. In her hand, she had papers stating that I owed her over eighty thousand dollars in back payroll taxes. I used a payroll service and they paid my payroll taxes every pay period. Not to mention, the taxes were accrued in 1974, 1975, 1976, and 1977. I was twelve years old then. It must be a mistake, I told her.

"You indemnified the people who accrued taxes from any liability from the Joe Vera Corporation," She replied.

Those bastards. All of them knew about these taxes. That's why they kept arguing when I originally offered them the seventy-two grand. This was probably the legal trouble that Joe Vera got into that allowed these pricks to take over the restaurant in the first place.

"I am no tax attorney, but I am smart enough to know that you can't sell someone your tax liability."

"No, we are pursuing the previous owners just like we are pursuing you. You own the corporation and you indemnified all of them from liability, so we are going to pursue all of you until one of you pays. I have set up a payment plan according to your quarterly earnings statement. It's fifteen hundred dollars every week."

"You mean a month."

"No, I mean a week."

"That will kill us, we will never be able to do it."

"You did well over fifty thousand dollars a month with just one restaurant last quarter."

"That was in the winter. We drop in half when the skiers go home, plus, Armadillo's is not making a dime. What happens if I don't pay you?"

"We will take away your federal tax ID number as well as your state sales tax certificate, meaning you can't buy or sell anything legally." Then she told me she would be there on Monday morning for her first payment and walked out the door.

We kept up the payments and proceeded to get broker and broker. The broker I got, the more coke I sniffed, the more alcohol I drank, and the more pot I smoked. I had sniffed so much coke, my teeth ached. I went to a dentist and he knew what was up right away. He kicked me out of his chair and told me that my teeth were fine, but I had a hell of a drug problem. I moved out of the three-story house in Summit Park and rented a small place from Max in the Avenues. We kept up the weekly payments through the fall, but we were starting to get in debt with our purveyors. The power bill alone at Armadillo's was five grand a month.

Kent Money came in for dinner one night by himself; I knew he could tell I was spun on blow. He noticed a beer bottle on the table next to him and freaked out. He told me that I had violated the lease agreement by serving beer. I told him that the lease said I could not use my liquor license. It said nothing about my beer and wine license.

"You knew what we meant, Todd."

"Kent, we have been serving beer and wine here for over six months. I did not know what you meant. You have many buildings with many restaurants and you should know by now how the liquor laws work in this state." He agreed and replied that he would have Kent Gibson call me in the morning.

Kent called me in the morning and offered to pay our power bill for the next five months if we quit selling beer and wine. When I relayed the phone conversation to them, Nick and the entire Armadillo's staff said, "No way." I was the president of the corporation, though, and ultimately I went against all of their wishes.

"Look, it's only a matter of time until the power gets turned off anyway. If we get Zion Securities against us, they will somehow find a way to kick us out within thirty days."

So, we stopped selling beer and wine. Some alternative newspaper wrote an article about how we had sold out to the church. It was mid-October. Things were tight, but we only had thirty more days until the ski resorts opened. With a reasonable ski season, we would be fine until next summer.

God must have been pissed at me for doing so much blow because it was the driest winter on record for twenty years. The ski resorts still weren't open by Christmas break. In fact, they didn't open until the second week of January. By then, we had missed two or three payments to Irene Roadbush.

We were shut down and they auctioned off all of the equipment we owned at Joe Vera's and Armadillo's. Every chef in town was there buying my shit for pennies on the dollar. They were a pack of hyenas laughing at me.

I packed up all my computers, stereo equipment, ski equipment, and anything else I had bought that was valuable. We went to go pick up a U-Haul, but when we got back someone had broken into the house and stolen everything. It must have been pretty easy for them because it was all packed up and ready to go. I am sure it was some disgruntled employee that I owed money to. All that we had left was our furniture and beds.

The following day was our last day of bankruptcy court. Right after, we drove to Arizona to live with Stacey's parents. It was just like that Grateful Dead song, "When life seems like easy street, there is danger at your door."

The year was 1987. Chelse was about to turn four years old and Parker had just finished his first year of life. There was this new band called INXS, and we listened to the tape the whole ride down to Arizona. I was seriously jonesin' for some blow. I began to think that every time I started doing coke, things went really bad. No, I decided, it was just a coincidence.

Chelse was in the back seat trying to teach Parker how to talk. They were both so cute and I loved them so much. Stacey was a trooper through all of this, too. Most wives would have left their husbands after such nonsense, but not Stacey. She just stood right by my side and kept loving me. And I loved her.

Chapter 17

WE GOT TO PHOENIX AND I got a job as the banquet chef of the Registry Resort for eight bucks an hour. A far cry from the Anatole. A couple months later, I saw an ad in the paper for a restaurant chef's position at the Scottsdale Conference Resort. I interviewed with Heinz Neuhauser, the executive chef. He hired me for thirty-two grand a year as the chef at The Palm Court—not too shabby. The Palm Court only fed about fifty people a night and they let me do whatever I wanted. International Conference Resorts owned the Scottsdale Conference Resort; I never knew why they called themselves "International". They only had four resorts and they all were in America.

The owner was a guy called Mr. J; his real name was Richard Joaquim. Mr. J reminded me of Mr. K because he ate the same thing for dinner every night: Boston scrod. He was definitely an Ivy Leaguer, but eating the fish from your alma mater every night was taking it just a little too far.

Mr. J had an awesome audio and visual department, and he would let me take my dinner specials down to the photo room and have them shot on 8x10 chromes. I was starting to collect a great book of food photos that were magazine quality. I could spend all day dicking around with one or two plates and no one cared.

Mr. J told me he was opening a new resort called the Barton Creek Conference Resort in Austin, Texas. He wanted me to write a killer menu for the final night of the grand opening event. He was all excited because Cab Calloway was the entertainment that night. I had no idea who Cab

Calloway was, but I wrote a menu and flew down to Texas with my crew. He put all of us up at the Four Seasons. One of my cooks, a guy called Jo Buck, brought an eight ball with him. This was the first time I had done coke since I'd lived in Arizona.

We would prep all day, then sit at a table with Heinz and twenty other people and drink all night. One night, I got back to my room and I was starving. They had twenty-four-hour room service, so I ordered an omelet. I was in nothing more than my tighty-whities when I pushed the room service cart back out the door and it slammed behind me. *Shit*, I was locked out of my room in my underwear. I ran down to the elevator where there was a house phone and called the operator. I told her there was an emergency in room five hundred and fifty-three, send the night manager. The manager was there with security in just a couple minutes.

"What's the emergency?"

"I locked myself out."

"Who is in there? What's going on?" I thought, *What a dumbass. If someone was in there, I wouldn't have had to call you.*

"I am by myself and in my underwear."

"So, what's the emergency?"

"Listen, if it were you standing here in your underwear, in the hallway, I am sure you would call it an emergency. Now, please, just open my door. Shit, I used to have nightmares like this when I was a little kid and you're just making it worse." He started laughing and unlocked my door.

My menu for the final dinner was Takashi's *billi bi en croute*, asparagus salad with lobster aioli, a cinnamon grapefruit sorbet, and a roast rack of veal filled with prosciutto and chanterelles. I had taken the prosciutto, sliced it thin, laid it out on cellophane, sautéed the chanterelles, deglazed them with Marsala, and then poured them onto the prosciutto with some Boursin cheese. Then I rolled it all up nice and tight and froze it. I poked a hole in the center of the veal rack with my sharpening steel, and shoved the frozen prosciutto log in the hole. When I roasted and carved the rack, there was this killer center with ham and mushrooms and cheese.

The night of the dinner, Mr. J flew Stacey down to attend the event. Stacey was sitting next to the laser man during dinner, and when I walked out to check on her I caught them making goo-goo eyes with each other. This pissed me off, but I had a lot going on. After dinner, they had a laser show. The laser would hit an ice carving and reflect just like a disco ball. I was dishing up dessert when it started. Mr. J came running into the kitchen, grabbed my arm, took me to the dining room, and pointed to the wall. "Stacey is a doll" was written in laser. When I looked up at the laser booth, Stacey was in there kissing the laser man.

Mr. J didn't make a scene, but his voice was ominous. "Get control of your wife." I ran up there and grabbed Stacey. I scared the hell out of her because she was still in the laser man's arms. She shuffled to the kitchen with me while I finished with dessert.

Mr. J had arranged horse and carriage rides for our transportation that night. We both got in without saying a word. We were almost up to the hotel when I just started screaming at her. Someone behind me walking down the street yelled, "What's going on?" My voice echoed back in the courtyard, "It's none of your fucking business!" Then I heard *click*, and I was handcuffed and pulled out of the carriage.

They arrested me for being an asshole. They didn't book me or fingerprint me, they just put me in jail for six hours to cool off. I remember thinking, *This is because I did coke.*

Stacey was up all night partying with my cooks and doing coke. She told everyone I was in jail. No one even tried to get me out. We got the first flight out of Texas the next morning.

When I went back to work, I was fired; I didn't even ask why. This was the first time I had ever been fired. Roget would fire you all the time, but you could always come back. I was never invited back to the conference resort.

Chapter 18

AFTER I GOT FIRED, all I had was a cool book of photos of my food. Honestly, it was much better than a resume. I was still new to Arizona, so I started to ask people who the best chef in Scottsdale was. Everybody told me, "Christopher Gross at Le Relais," so I drove up to Pinnacle Peak and Pima. It was miles away, out in the dessert, back then. Chris was a little distant and aloof at first, but after he had taken a look at my photos, he told me my plates looked beautiful. He didn't have any work for me, but he gave me Steve Ast's number.

The Scottsdale Princess Resort was currently under construction and Steve Ast was its food and beverage coordinator. Steve was fascinated by my time at Joe Vera's. It was clearly on his mind as he flipped through my photo book.

"Can you make Mexican food look the way the plates look in your book?" he asked me.

"Sure, but we would have to work on it for a while in order to get the plates clean and precise." *Pretty cool idea.*

We put on hardhats and he took me on a tour of the resort. La Hacienda, the restaurant he was considering me for, had not even been started yet. Steve stepped over a pile of cement bags and gestured toward the huge expanse that would become my kitchen. "La Hacienda is going to be a five-million-dollar restaurant that will serve gourmet Mexican Cuisine. It has to open with four stars." There wasn't a four-star Mexican restaurant anywhere in the world. Not even in Mexico.

Steve Ast was like that. He wanted something that no one had ever accomplished before. I asked Steve how old he was; he told me thirty-five. I said to myself, *I am going to be where he is when I'm thirty-five.* I had eleven years to get it done. Seven hours later, I was hired.

Steve introduced me to the corporate director of personnel for Princess Hotels International, as well as the general manager of The Scottsdale Princess. They offered the position of Chef De Cuisine of La Hacienda for forty thousand dollars a year. I was the first chef they had hired for the new resort. They had not even decided on the executive chef, yet. After I accepted the position, Steve told me that I would be flying to Acapulco to do research and development for La Hacienda's menu for a couple of months.

Steve was adamant on not serving what we, in America, call "Mexican food". He flew me to Los Angeles to go to the Mexican consulate to get an FM3 work permit. Do you have any idea how hard it is for an American to get permission to work in Mexico? I was in that consulate for five days, filling out papers and standing in line while Mexican officials talked down to me.

I used the restroom only once in the consulate building, and it was the sickest thing I had ever seen. First of all, it didn't have any stalls; just a bunch of toilets sitting out in the open with guys on them, taking a crap. Next to each toilet was a pile of shit-covered toilet paper. These disgusting men were wiping their asses and throwing the toilet paper on the floor instead of flushing it down. I never stepped foot in there again, not even to take a piss.

After five days, I still didn't have my permit. Steve told me to fly back to Scottsdale. I told him that I had one more meeting that afternoon. If I didn't get the paperwork, I would be back in Scottsdale that night. I got my permit at that meeting and flew to Acapulco the following morning.

✲ ✲ ✲

The Aeroméxico flight to Acapulco was so bumpy that all of the beers on the beverage cart bounced off and rolled down the aisle. *Very convenient.* All I had to do was reach down and grab a couple as they rolled by. When we landed and went through customs, there was a group of girls welcoming tourists to Mexico. On one side, they were handing out Sol beers, on the other, Corona. I grabbed one of each.

There I was with a couple of beers when I saw, right in front of me, a guy with a sign that said, "Chef Todd Hall". *Busted.* Señor Chopski didn't care, though, he just grabbed my bags and hurried me off.

Señor Chopski was about fifty or so. He had thick glasses that were secured to his balding head with a piece of rubber. His eyeballs were the size of small pancakes when you looked at them through his glasses. The dude had to be damn near blind. His accent was so thick, you could hardly understand what he was saying. It wasn't Spanish; it was German. He gave me the creeps. I had read *The Boys from Brazil* and I knew all about Nazi war criminals hiding out in South and Central America. I was certain that I had just found Joseph Mengele.

Señor Chopski checked me in and gave me a credit card that was good anywhere at the hotel. The Acapulco Princess had the same number of restaurants as the Anatole, and almost as many rooms. Right on the beach, it had three towers built to look like Mayan Temples. Señor Chopski led me to my accommodations, *Casa De Executivos.* It translated as, "House of the Executives". It was right on the golf course. The room was old and musty, and there was a shitty bottle of cheap champagne on ice on a table in the corner. One thing I have to say about Acapulco is that they had great produce. There was a giant fruit basket next to the champagne. The card on the fruit read, *Señor Volknar Holtzner, General Manager*. Great. Another Nazi war criminal.

Señor Chopski told me to get unpacked, make myself comfortable, and meet him in the lobby in ten minutes. I thought to myself, *Wow, a whopping ten minutes. Why don't I just meet you now?* This guy was creepy, though, and I wanted him out of my room.

"No matter what, do not use the telephone. A call to America costs forty-five dollars," he told me before he left.

When I was walking out to the lobby, there was a guy in a Princess uniform sitting on the curb in the hot sun, pounding away at the sidewalk with a hammer and chisel. You could see that he had already removed a couple of sidewalk squares, but he had plenty more to go.

"*Buenos dias*," he called out when I walked by him.

"*Buenos dias*," I replied, but added, "Dude, you need to get yourself a jackhammer." Acapulco was turning out to be a lot more third world than I had expected.

When I met Señor Chopski in the lobby, he whisked me away to tour the restaurants before I had dinner at La Hacienda with the general manager.

"Wow, you guys have a La Hacienda?"

"Yes. That is not why you are here, no?" I nodded and thought, *Who in the hell talks like that?* as I repeated his phrase back to myself.

Señor Chopski took me to all fourteen restaurants for a high-speed tour of thirty minutes. I soon discovered he was always in a hurry. Not only that, but no matter where we went, when the employees saw Señor Chopski coming they would all bow their heads and look at the floor in submission. He would humiliate as many of them as he could in Spanish, as he blew through their area. He told me that a couple of years ago all of the employees started to riot. *Yeah, I wonder why?* It was important, he continued, to keep them in line to make sure that it never happened again. I thought, *That's just what you tell yourself so you can sleep at night.* This guy was a dickhead and he enjoyed every minute of it. When we got to La Hacienda, he introduced me to Chuco, the chef.

The public guest space at The Acapulco Princess was beautiful, but the back of the house was all dark and beat up. Everything looked like it was held together with duct tape and bailing wire. They had five times the number of employees as the Anatole. Everywhere you went, there were armies of amigos. There was no sale system in any of the restaurants, and all of the guest checks were handwritten on paper. When I went to the accounting department a couple of days later, I couldn't believe it: they had at least a hundred Mexican girls adding each and every one of those guest checks on a ten key adding machine. I think the Flintstones had it better in Bedrock.

At the end of my tour, Señor Chopski told me to come back to La Hacienda at seven for dinner and at two the following afternoon to work. As I walked back to the *Casa De Executivos*, that same dude was still pounding away at the sidewalk.

The first thing I did when I got back to my room was call America. Steve was in his office. He was glad to hear from me and glad I was finally at the resort. His voice was tinny through the receiver.

"We've heard mixed reports about the food at The Acapulco Princess, so get out and look at as many other places as you can. Hang tough, don't get sick, and I'll be there in a couple of months to pick you up."

I then called Stacey to tell her I had made it and that I would have to bring her to Acapulco sometime. It was really beautiful. After I said hello to Parker and Chelse, I hung up.

Someone had knocked at my door, I answered it and it was a Corona man, in a Corona uniform, with a Corona truck. He started rattling off in Spanish and I had no idea what he said. Just then, the guy above me, sitting out on his deck, yelled down to me in English.

"This gentleman is the equivalent to what you would call a milk man in America, only he serves beer. He will come by every other day or so and if you place your empty bottles outside of your door, he will replace them with full ones."

"How much?"

"It's about three dollars American per case."

"Hell yeah," I said to the Corona man and he brought me my first case. I was really starting to like this place. The dude above me was about my age, maybe a little older, and from Holland.

"How long are you staying here?" I asked him.

"I have been here for two years."

"I bet that's expensive!"

He just laughed at me. "Didn't Señor Chopski tell you that everyone who lives over here is an executive for the Princess Hotel Corporation? These are condominiums, they're not hotel rooms. That's why you have a refrigerator to put your beer in."

"I better not throw any late night parties around here, then." My new friend just laughed again.

I met Señor Volknar Holtzner for dinner. What a nice man; he was nothing like Señor Chopski. Very quiet, very polite, and well educated. I didn't know it at the time, but Volknar and I would become good friends. Ten years later, Volknar asked me to open a bank account for him in

Scottsdale. He deposited about a hundred and forty-five grand, and the address on the checks was his address in Acapulco. He told me he didn't trust Mexican banks.

La Hacienda was very disappointing. It was just like a Sizzler. There were lots of steaks, baked potatoes wrapped in foil, and some weak ass cauliflower and broccoli for vegetables.

"What's up with this food?" I asked Volkner over dinner one night. "Why isn't this place serving Mexican food?"

Volkner gave a polite little sigh. "It used to have great Mexican food, but all of the American and Canadian tourists complained about it and never come back. We changed to this fare; they love it, and we stay busy." *Leave it to an American tourist to screw up a great restaurant.* "I do not think you intend to serve this type of food at your La Hacienda?"

"Absolutely not," I assured him.

They only had a couple of items on the menu that I was interested in seeing. I had *caldo marisco*, crepes *huitlacoche* and *cabrito*. The *caldo marisco* kicked ass. It was a tomato-based chili broth with whole mussels, clams, and head-on prawns. Outstanding. Crepes *huitlacoche* was a trip.

Volknar explained, "In the rain season this fungus grows on ears of corn called *huitlacoche*. It's very similar to a black truffle."

"No, it's not."

I was chewing this thing and, trust me, the only thing it had in common with a truffle was that it was a fungus and that its color was black. The texture was like yogurt with stringy fibers in it. It didn't taste bad, but it certainly didn't taste good. They served it with béchamel sauce, which is a cream sauce. The black fungus would swirl into the white sauce and make gray goop. The *cabrito* was tough but very tasty. I had had worse meals in my life.

"This Mexican restaurant menu has a couple of items that have a very French influence," I pointed out to Volkner. "Why is that?"

"France has invaded just about every decent country in the world and their food always seemed to stick," he replied. This made sense.

Right then, Señor Chopski ran up to our table all frantic. He started bitchin' at me for calling America. I had no idea how he'd found out so fast. If PBX was anything like accounting, he shouldn't have found out about those calls for another couple of weeks. He acted like he was going to have to personally pay for the call. Volknar said something to him in German, though, and he walked away in a huff.

I apologized to Volknar, "My boss told me to call as soon as I arrived."

"Don't worry about it, but in the future if you want to call America please go to my administrative assistant, Ruby. She will place the call for you. Also, don't worry about Señor Chopski, he gets a little overexcited sometimes."

"You really think so?" I tried not to sound too sarcastic.

Dinner was over and I went back to my *casa*. I had a couple of ice-cold Coronas and decided I would go try out my new hotel credit card at a few of the bars. I ordered a margarita and it came in a martini glass. I took a big swallow and about choked. This wasn't a margarita; I had served hundreds at Joe Vera's. This was straight-up tequila with a squeeze of lime. Whatever it was, though, I liked it and had a few of them.

I was sitting, watching the waterfall in the pool next to the ocean, when something blasted right in my ear and scared the shit out of me. It was Mexican man playing a trumpet with all his friends, a'blasting away. I got the hell out of there.

People were swimming in the pools and I was starting to get drunk enough that I wanted to swim too. I went to the gift shop and bought a suit. I changed in the bathroom and asked my friend, the bartender, to keep an eye on my clothes. Then I thought, *Why would you swim in a pool when the ocean is right there?* So, I ran across the beach and waded out into the waves.

The ocean water was dark and cool. I wasn't out there for more than ten minutes when a Princess jeep pulled out to the edge of the water and shined its spotlights right on me. Loud as fuck over a PA system, they demanded that I get out of the water immediately. I walked up to them and they wanted to see my room key. I told them who I was and what I was doing at the Princess. Then they said, "Señor Hall, if you go into the ocean at night the sharks will surely eat you and we will be in a lot of trouble when your bones wash up on shore." I didn't even think of that. I thanked them, and figured that was enough swimming for my first night.

My credit card was working great, but I was waiting for Señor Chopski to come racing around some corner to tell me I wasn't allowed to get wasted on the card. He never did, the whole time I was there. I always thought they would yank it because I was abusing it, so I was living it up while I could. I was buying people drinks and taking people I didn't even know out to dinner. No one ever said a word.

The next morning, I woke up before the sun rose. I can never sleep well in foreign places. I had a screaming headache and I needed some water immediately. I opened the fridge. Nothing but Coronas. That would never do, so I got a glass and filled it with tap water. It came out hot and nasty, but I knew I had to drink it anyway. I put on my new swimming suit, which was still wet. I didn't care. That was the least of my worries. I walked down to the beach and watched the sunrise reflect over the ocean and the clouds above.

There were already quite a few American tourists staking their claim to the best spots on the beach. I grabbed a great one right on the front line. These people would not only stake their claim, but they would homestead it all day long until dark. Even that early, there was a barrage of cute little Mexican kids all trying to sell you some sort of crap. Their moms would always be hiding in the shadows, watching to see if they made a sale. This got old fast. These kids would just not take no for an answer. I learned that if you didn't even look at them, they would eventually leave you alone.

Watching the surfers made me want to surf. I mean, I was an awesome skier and skateboarder. So, how much harder could this be? The little Mexican kids could do it, no problem. I rented a surfboard from a kid for fifty cents. I paddled out and tried to stand up. I couldn't do it. Most of the white people were just lying on their boards and riding in, but that wasn't good enough for me. I wanted to stand up. I tried every single day for a long time until I finally stood up. But once you're up, it's awesome. I surfed every single day for the next two months.

There were waiters that would walk up and down the beach and take your order. Everybody was having these drinks served in whole pineapples or coconuts. They looked so good, but I thought I had better not show up to work my first day with a buzz. So, I just ordered a coke.

When the waiter brought me the coke, it was still in the bottle. I don't know if it was the beach, or the ocean, or because I was worn out from trying to surf, or even all the beautiful girls wearing skimpy bikinis, but it was the best coke I have ever tasted. I later learned that it was none of the above. In Mexico, they use pure cane sugar to make Coca-Cola. In America we use corn syrup, and sugar is far better than corn syrup. I often thought if we could all get together and boycott Coca-Cola for a few weeks and demand that they make it right, we would have a lot better coke to drink.

I was starting to get hungry, so I asked the family next to me to save my spot. I went to Chula Vista. Chula Vista had the best breakfast in the whole place. They had a scrambled egg burrito with ranchero cheese, salsa *la casita*, and the Princess's signature, homemade chorizo sausage. It was so good that I had the same thing for breakfast every single day for the next two months. *Oh my God, I'm turning into Mr. K and Mr. J.*

I went back to my lounge chair on the beach with a full belly and promptly fell asleep. The mom of the family next to me woke me up at about one, and told me I was starting to get sun burned. She offered me some lotion. Her little girl walked up to me and whispered, "Mommy woke you up because you were snoring so loud that it was starting to make dad mad." I have always loved the way little kids can be so honest. I was glad that they woke me up because I had to get to work.

◊ ◊ ◊

Next to my *casa*, the same man was pounding away at the sidewalk. I asked him if he wanted a cold Corona, he just shrugged his shoulders like he had no idea what I just said. Probably because he didn't. I brought him one, and he was elated. I jumped in the shower and took the sidewalk pounder another beer on my way to work.

It was a lot hotter in the kitchen than it was outside. The first thing I noticed was that these cats were drinking beer at work. *Nice.* They offered me one and I said sure, so they showed me their stash in the walk-in. They had about ten cases of Negro Modelo in the bottle. If I had known about this, I would have had one of those foo-foo drinks on the beach. The next thing I noticed is that there was no air conditioning. This was sick and wrong.

Chuco and I worked for the same hotel corporation, we had the same title, and our restaurants even had the same name. I earned forty thousand dollars a year, and he earned thirty-five dollars a week. I had more money in my pocket then he earned all year. If I worked his job, you'd better let me drink all the beer I want at work.

Every single cook would walk up to me and say, "*Mucho calor.*" I had no idea what they meant. I later found out that's how you say "very hot" in Spanish. I think they were also trying to tell me I'd gotten sunburned.

After working with the amigos in Texas, at the Anatole and at Joe Vera's, I honestly thought that I spoke Spanish. I didn't speak shit. I could only speak Spanish to people who knew how to speak English. We had a real communication problem. Not one person in the La Hacienda kitchen spoke a single word of English. I mostly just watched the first couple of days.

The most impressive thing I saw was that the line cooks did not have any tickets. Everything was called out verbally when the food was ordered, and then again when the table was picked up. If you're not a cook, that might not sound like a big deal. But, when you're feeding two hundred and fifty people a combination of thirty-odd items in four hours, it can get very confusing—even with tickets.

They ran ten-man lines at La Hacienda. About fifteen were in the back and another five were always on break; easily five times more than necessary to feed that many people. They had so many people because it didn't cost them anything. It was the Mexican way. Find a job, make it ten times harder than you have to, and then hire too many people to do it. Just like that poor guy pounding rocks on the sidewalk.

I walked around the kitchen eating everything. Most of it was crap, but some of it was great. It reflected their country: things were either awful or beautiful.

I knew it would take me all of tomorrow to learn to make the five menu items I liked. I had to find a way to learn how to cook some of the things I had been reading about. I had bought three books before I left Scottsdale: Rick Bayless's book from La Fonterra in Chicago, a book by Diane Kennedy, and Patricia Quintana's book, *Mexico the Beautiful*.

The thing is, you cannot learn to cook by reading cookbooks. The person teaching you has to hand you the love in person. I knew the books were in English, but most of the recipes were traditional Mexican fare with Spanish titles. Not knowing any other way to communicate what I wanted to learn, I ran back to my room, grabbed my books, and brought them to Chuco.

Pointing to the titles of the dishes, I asked him if he knew how to make *this*, and I asked him if he knew how to make *that*. He knew how to make everything I pointed to. I asked a waiter to interpret to be sure. He concurred: Chuco could make all of this. The waiter started to walk away, but I called him back. "Ask him where he learned all of it, because they certainly don't serve this kind of food here."

Chuco laughed, "*Mi madre y mi suegra*." That was good enough for me: his mom and his mother-in-law had taught him. Exactly what I was looking for.

After that, Chuco and I would do at least four different dishes a night. He would make big ass batches and I would ask him, "What are you going to do with all of this food, run it as a special?" He grinned and pointed to his buddies and said, "No, we're going to eat it." This was great. Now I was getting somewhere. Sometimes the dish would be just like in the book; sometimes it had nothing in common with the recipe.

Just like in America how every single family makes tuna fish casserole differently, but they all still call it tuna fish casserole.

Chuco's interpretation of these menu items rocked. I liked just about everything he did. His food had this roasty, toasty, earthy flavor that came from grilling or roasting most ingredients before incorporating them into the dish.

I was surprised to see that Chuco used soy sauce as much as he used salt. He used a lot of Worcestershire sauce, too, and he had this other stuff in a black bottle, "Maggi". If you ate it out of the bottle it tasted nasty, but Chuco promised me it made sauces and soups taste better.

Chipotle chilies were my new favorite ingredient. This was the first time I had ever seen them. Chuco used them in everything, and now I do too.

Chapter 19

AT THE END OF MY FIRST NIGHT in the kitchen, my second night in Acapulco, I started to feel queasy. I went straight back to my *casa* and went to bed. I didn't know if it was the heat, the beer, or the sun burn, but I was getting dizzy. As I fell asleep I wondered, *Do I really snore that loud?* I woke up at two in the morning, puking my guts out. I had a high fever with sweats and chills and I just couldn't quit throwing up.

They had a doctor right there at the Princess and I almost passed out walking to his office. Looking me up and down, he didn't seem surprised at all. "It's very normal for first-time visitors to become ill, Todd. It will be three or four days until you feel better. It's usually a one-time issue, however, and it's unlikely that you will experience this again during your time here." It was some small reassurance, at least.

I went back and didn't leave my room for three days. I had no appetite at all, I just ate the fruit in the basket. Señor Chopski came and checked on me. He pushed his glasses up into his pancake eyes. "Eat chilies. It will make you feel better."

When I was finally able to get back to work, I started visiting the markets in the daytime and working at La Hacienda in the evening. The markets were a trip; they were actually pretty gross. They had chickens just hanging out in the sun with swarms of flies around them. You could buy dried crickets, ants, and every kind of chili known to man. The best thing they had was the seafood; they had shellfish of every kind. One thing I learned is that certain types of shellfish are only meant to be eaten at certain times of the year. If you didn't watch the natives and buy what they buy, you could get yourself sick. This was a pretty good rule of thumb for all types of food vendors. Don't follow the tourists, follow the amigos. Eat what they eat.

I would buy all kinds of stuff and take everything back to the kitchen to play with. I started to venture out to the back of the house of the Princess as well. The pastry shop was located on the bottom floor, and they baked all of their own *everything*: breads, desserts, Danishes, croissants; all of it. Willy, the pastry chef, was Danish. He had beautiful cocoa paintings and over one hundred amigos on his twenty-four-hour-a-day staff.

Hanging around the bakery one day, Willy told me a story about when he had first started. "A few years back," he began, "Howard Hughes was living on the top floor of one of the Princess towers. Just about every day, he requested a strawberry Danish, but no matter what I made he scoffed at it and said it wasn't right. I made over twenty kinds of Danish! None of them would do. So, Mr. Hughes had one of his assistants fly his private jet to Louisiana to buy the Danish that he liked." Hands covered in flour, Willy shook his head at nobody in particular. "When they came back with the pastry, it was a regular Danish! The only difference was that they had used a whole cup of this super sweet strawberry filling that tasted like jam. There was twice as much filling as pastry. Who would *like* something like that?"

I knew exactly why Howard had wanted Danish like that. Every time I was high for a few days and came down, I craved sugar like nobody's business. Anyway, Willy started making Danishes like that every day for Mr. Hughes. He loved them and ate them every day until he died. I wonder what killed him, the drugs or the Danishes?

After the pastry shop, I decided to go check out the loading docks.

There was always a lot going on at the loading docks at The Anatole. At least a couple of semi-trucks were always pulling in or out. The Princess was equally busy, but different.

First of all, there was a *federale* there with an Uzi strapped to his shoulder. This was no big deal though, because they were everywhere throughout the hotel. I ate at the employee cafeteria once, because that's where Señor Chopski so graciously took me to lunch that day, and two *federales* sat next to us and plopped their machine guns right down on the table.

Señor Chopski explained, "We let them eat for free so we don't have any more riots."

I only managed to say, "Well, that should take care of it, shouldn't it?"

The loading dock didn't have any semis, but they did have lots of smaller trucks pulling in and out. I stood there and watched an unrefrigerated truck pull up and unload. In the truck there were some dead chickens on top of a goat, and a bunch of shrimp next to a stack of egg flats. No wonder I got so sick. This truck took the term "cross-contamination" to a whole new level. The local ranchers would just slaughter their animals, throw them in the back of the pickup, and sell them not only to the Princess, but all the local resorts.

The director of purchasing walked out to the truck and tossed a couple of dead animals around until he found one he liked. Trucks were backed up for a mile, waiting their turn. Not one of them was refrigerated, and it was hot that day. The purchasing director later bragged to me that they bought their food fresh every day. I said, "No kidding, because it's going to be fuckin' rotten by tomorrow."

I tried to block everything I had just seen out of my mind because I knew I still had to eat at the Princess for another month. I only had to use an egg while cooking a couple of times, and it was disgusting both times. The eggs not only still had chicken shit all over them, but little feathers stuck to them. Plus, the cooks saved the flats that the eggs were delivered in and gave them back to the egg farmer to be used again. I wondered how many generations of chicken shit were on those flats.

I went to the butcher shop. The whole place was refrigerated and the amigos were wearing coats. They were happily cutting all kinds of different meat. The head butcher was very friendly and collectively introduced me to everyone. He spoke English, which surprised me. It took the head butcher a while to tour me around the whole place. Eventually, I saw that the amigos were cutting and marinating some skirt steak for fajitas. I was excited. "Great! I always wanted to know how to authentically marinate fajita meat." The head butcher laughed, "Well, then you should show *me* because I have lived in Mexico my whole life and I had never seen this dish until all of the American tourists started requesting it a few years ago. *Fajita* isn't even a real word in Spanish, it's like that other made-up word, *chimichanga*." I thought to myself, *Aren't all words made-up words?*

"Where does your chorizo come from?" I ate it every morning and it rocked.

"Ah, well, we make three or four hundred pounds of chorizo every Tuesday at seven in the morning. We would be happy to show you how to make it next Tuesday if you would like." *Nice, we had a date.*

I was working in the kitchen one night when Señor Chopski came and got me. He was all excited and had something to show me. We went out to a great big lawn area where there was a party going on with at least fifteen hundred people in attendance. It was an American insurance company, there for a convention.

Señor Chopski wanted to show me the buffets he was so proud of. The first thing I saw totally caught me off guard. They had human skeletons in a pile on the buffet, before the plates or anything! Señor Chopski looked at me all proud, "Isn't this *great*?" He picked up two human skulls and knocked them into each other, making a clack. I was mortified. I had been creeped out by Señor Chopski since the day I met him, but now he was frightening me.

"Why on earth would you put people bones, or any bones for that matter, on a *buffet* table?"

"It's for decoration." He couldn't understand my concern at all.

"I understand they're for decoration, Señor Chopski. My question to you is why anyone would ever want to decorate a beautiful buffet like this with *human bones*?"

"Oh, the bones are not from real people! They're imitation!" He excitedly nodded like I finally got it. I gave it one more try.

"Señor Chopski, why do you want to decorate your buffet tables with *imitation human bones*? Don't you think maybe some candles, or perhaps some fresh flowers would be a little bit nicer?"

"No, No, it's the holiday, and on the holiday we get to use bones." *Glad we cleared that up*, I thought. *They save the bones for the special occasions.*

"What holiday?"

"*Dia de Los Muertos*, the Day of the Dead." I used to think Halloween was kind of a creepy holiday, but this was a lot creepier.

He continued to show me cakes decorated with the grim reaper, accompanied by more skulls and bones. My first thought was, *Nice work, Willy. These are some pretty fuckin' scary cakes.*

Chapter 20

I WAS STILL SURFING EVERY MORNING. I was starting to get good at it, and the longer the ride was, the better. So, one morning, I decided that I was really going to paddle out there. I worked at it for a while and, eventually, I was so tired from paddling I sat on my board for a few minutes to catch my breath. There was a big ship way out to sea, and suddenly I noticed that I was a lot closer to the ship than I was to the beach. In fact, there weren't even any waves big enough to ride back anymore. As I sat there, the people on the beach looked more and more like ants and the ship looked bigger and bigger. What the hell? I was headed out to sea and I wasn't even paddling!

I scrambled to paddle towards shore as hard as I could for twenty minutes straight. When I looked up to see where I was, it was like I had hardly moved at all. It took me over an hour of paddling as hard as I could to finally reach waves big enough to ride in. By then, I was so exhausted I couldn't even stand up.

Collapsed on the beach, I asked some little kid, "Why the hell does the ocean take you out?"

"It happens like, once a week," he told me. "Sometimes the tide drags the tourist out so far he never comes back." *Nice, that is definitely something to keep in mind.* The waiter came by with a wine bucket full of cokes on ice and I drank a coke while I clung to land.

The more time I spent in Mexico, the more I began to understand that the whole country was just one big shakedown. I was completely sick of listening to macho tourists showing off to their girlfriends their great negotiating skills by talking eight-year-old Mexican boys down to ten pesos before finally buying some t-shirt that said, "I Got Stoned in Acapulco".

What really pissed me off was when I went out one night with the guy from Holland that lived above me, and he only paid two bucks for the cab fare into town.

"*What?* Why does it only cost you two bucks? I've been going into town for three weeks and it's always ten bucks."

He cracked up, "You never tried to talk them down?"

"No, why would I?" *Have I been getting ripped off with everything I've bought?* It was just way too much to worry about. I was starting to get homesick.

Sitting on the sand, I watched an American tourist buy pot from the same guys who rented out horses on the beach. After the tourist left, the kid that sold him the weed walked over to the *federale* standing there, and told him which American he just sold the weed to. The *federale* shook down the tourist, and escorted him to the nearest ATM machine. Then, the *federale* returned and gave the weed back to the kid renting the horses.

Even though I saw all of this going on, I still wanted to buy some weed. I had it all figured out. I went to the beach with only two ten-dollar bills and my room key. I wore shorts and sandals, no shirt. With the first ten, I rented a horse. Then I got on the horse and told the kid, "I want ten dollars of *mota*." He told me to get off the horse and talk to him. I said, "Forget it, then." Annoyed, he agreed and came back with a newspaper that had at least a half ounce of Killer Acapulco Gold.

I handed him the ten and tore out of there like a bat out of hell, making that horse run as fast as he could. I turned in between the two towers, across a street and on to the golf course. I kept running the horse on the golf course until I got to *Casa De Executivos*. The dude pounding rocks on the sidewalk thought it was pretty cool that I had a horse and kept yelling, "Beano *caballo*, Beano *caballo*." I tied the horse up to the bumper of a jeep, ran in my room, stashed the weed under the mattress, and ran back out to the horse. My friend upstairs was out on his deck. "Hey, Todd," he called down "Have you given up on the ten-dollar taxis?" He was laughing.

"Yup!" I yelled up, and rode back to the beach.

I wasn't even done returning the sweaty horse when the *federale* came and frisked me. I had nothing but a room key on me. He then asked me were my room was and I said, "*Casa De Executivos*." The *federale* walked away, bitchin' at the horse dude in Spanish. I had enough weed that I was pretty much stoned for the rest of the trip; this definitely helped with the homesickness, and it made the food taste a lot better.

The next day, Señor Chopski started bitchin' at me. Something about riding a horse on the golf course.

"What are you talking about? I wasn't riding any horse on the golf course! How could you even accuse me of such a thing?" I gave him a big, fake-confused look. He went on for a while, then finally shut up.

The next morning, it was finally time to learn how to make chorizo. When I arrived, there were about fifteen amigos all lined up at this u-shaped table. Two guys took four hundred pounds of ground pork butt (or so they said. Who knows what they had ground up?) Anyway, they evenly distributed the pork clear around the table like one great, big snake. Each guy was in charge of his three or four feet of the sausage snake. Then, there was the spice dude. He would start at one end of the snake and evenly sprinkle a particular type of spice all the way along it. He would make a chili powder run, then he would make a dried oregano run, then he would make a salt run, and then a dried chipotle run. All the while, each guy was mixing his part of the sausage by hand. It took them about an hour and a half to make about four hundred pounds of sausage. Then, the head butcher took some of the finished sausage and ate it raw to see if it tasted right. *Raw.*

"Dude, you are so brave, you're my idol. Talk about being dedicated to getting the right flavor," I told him. He offered me some. "Hell no! Are you kidding me?"

He stood there with his hand still outstretched, "I thought you said you loved it?"

"I do. Cooked."

"It's ok like this."

"I'm sure it's just great… but I'll wait until tomorrow when it's cooked inside my burrito."

This whole sausage experience was the most idiotic thing I had ever seen. I could not, for the life of me, figure out why they would do it like they did. So, I went to the head butcher.

"Next week I want to make all of the sausage by myself. And I will bet all of your guys a case of Corona that I can do it in thirty minutes instead of an hour and thirty minutes." The butcher interpreted what I said and they all started to chuckle.

"*No, no lo puedes hacer en treinta minutos.*" The amigos gave one another knowing looks. The bet was on and I couldn't wait for the next week.

My Spanish was getting a lot better. Nothing will make you learn a second language faster than needing it to survive. I was starting to get sick of La Hacienda, so instead of going there at night I started spending my nights in search of authentic, gourmet Mexican food. I wanted food just like the stuff I was reading about in Patricia's book, *Mexico the Beautiful*. All I had been able to find outside of Chuco's kitchen so far was *Mexico, the Sellout to American Tourists*.

I went to the Hyatt, I went to Las Brisas; I went everywhere trying to find real, gourmet Mexican food. Every time I went to a nice place for dinner, the menu was full of the stuff I had learned during my apprenticeship: rack of lamb with Dijon mustard, duck a la orange, veal cordon bleu. Where was all of the nice Mexican food? I would sit at the table and realize immediately that the place was not what I was looking for. I prided myself on classical French cuisine, though, so more times than not I would stick around just out of curiosity.

After a week of touring all the local fine dining restaurants, it was time for the chorizo showdown. I knew I had a job to do, so I wasn't even that hungover. Before I ever stepped foot in the butcher shop, I snagged a Queen Mary. For all of you people that aren't in the restaurant business, a Queen Mary is a big cart that I guess they used on the Queen Mary. I left my cart outside the butcher shop.

The most important thing was getting the right spices. The spice dude assured me that he had given me the exact amount of spices needed to make one batch. I took the spices and the ground pork, placed it on the cart, and hit the button of the elevator. I was surprised that no one followed me. Maybe Señor Chopski would fire you if you were caught outside your department.

I went downstairs to the pastry shop and asked Willy if I could use one of his mixers for a minute. He said sure. I dumped everything into the mixer and hit the second speed. In ten minutes, it was all mixed up. I packed up and hit the elevator button. I showed up at the butcher shop in fifteen minutes and gave the butcher a handful of raw sausage for the ultimate taste test. I passed. They owed me a case of beer.

I thought they would be happy, but they were pissed at me. I then realized why the dude was pounding rocks outside my door every morning: it was not because they needed the sidewalk, but because he needed the work. If the Princess really needed the sidewalk that bad, they would certainly have bought a jackhammer. If they needed chorizo that fast, they would have put a mixer in the butcher shop. Here I was, thinking that I was a genius, and the fact of the matter was that I was clueless.

Chapter 21

I WAS EXPEDITING THE LINE one night when someone put their arm on my shoulder. It was Steve. Finally, he was there to take me home. I laughed when his first question was, "What's up with that Señor Chopski guy?"

When we sat down to have dinner in La Hacienda, Steve noticed the food just like I had when I sat with Volknar on my first night. "You've got to be kidding me." He poked his spud with a fork.

"What, the baked potatoes are wrapped in aluminum foil?" I asked.

"Yeah! I haven't eaten this in years." He was totally incredulous.

"I know. The Americans who come here won't eat Mexican food. The menus that I've been working on have nothing to do with what they serve here."

Steve was with Raphael, the dining room manager for the new La Hacienda, and his new bride Keeley. They were trying to enjoy a working honeymoon. He was also with this strange, little man named Jim Esposito. He was the corporate food and beverage manager for all of the Princess Resorts.

Esposito had this disease that Roget had told me about, called, "*complexe de Napoléon*" (Napoleon complex). This guy was a one-upper. No matter what anyone said or suggested, he would have to one-up it. If Steve saw a four-tine fork and said, "I like the fork, but can I get it with five tines?" Esposito would say, "No, what we're looking for is a six-tine fork." If Steve suggested we add a black line to the china pattern, Esposito would say, "We need two lines." I admired Steve for his ability to tolerate this guy.

As we were pushing our plates away, Steve turned to me. "We are going to have a tasting tomorrow morning at nine AM. We want to try your new menu." We had been faxing the menu back and forth for months. Chuco and I had made everything on the menu several times, but it still required a lot of prep. I thought, *How am I going to be able to get one of everything, from a forty-eight-item menu, done by nine am?*

Steve continued, "We're going out to different clubs tonight to do research and development for La Hacienda's Club Cabyobyo. I want you to come with us." I asked him to give me a minute.

I grabbed a waiter to interpret for me and found Chuco. "I have to have one of everything on my menu by nine am, and I won't be able to prep tonight because I have to go with them."

The waiter translated, "He says, relax. He will round up the food products tonight, and have the guys come in at seven AM. Everybody will only have to make one plate and they will be ready an hour ahead of schedule." You've got to love Mexico. To get night cooks to show up to work the next morning in America is next to impossible.

We went to Fantasy, Baby O's, and all the other cool clubs that night. I had already been to most of them. At Fantasy, there was a conga line. Of course, we all joined in. If you were at the head of the line, then they would put a hardhat on you, pour 7-Up and tequila in a shot glass, cover the top, smack it on the hardhat really hard to cause pressure, and squirt it down your throat. They appropriately named those things "poppers".

By the time we were all in the cab and on the way back to the resort, I was too drunk to even slur my words right. I started to ramble in this confessional tone, "My new bosses are so cool… we're going to have the best damn Mexican restaurant in the world… and I could have just come down here and surfed every day, but I didn't. I really worked."

Steve shifted his weight next to me, "Well the sun must be pretty bright in those kitchens because you have a real dark tan for someone who didn't surf every day." He paused, then said, "And I have another question for you. With all of those beautiful beaches, why were you seen riding a horse on the golf course?" *Fuckin' Chopski.* I didn't answer. But I did ask Raphael why he kept elbowing me in the gut.

They told me that we were all going to meet for breakfast at eight a.m. to go over the menu. It was three thirty in the morning. At seven forty-five I walked to the pool, still drunk. I had sunglasses on. Like that was going to help. I kept trying to remember all of the stupid stuff I had said and done the night before, but it was just too much to remember. I got to the table fifteen minutes late. Right off the bat, Steve started going off about how eight o'clock meant eight o'clock. I just muttered, "Good morning to you too, Mr. Ast."

When he got up to go to the buffet, Raphael told me that Steve had arrived just barely before I had. I liked this guy Raphael. These guys had to have felt as shitty as I did. When it was five minutes to nine, we got up and walked over to La Hacienda. I about died when I saw that Chuco had a great, big buffet table nicely decorated with one of each item from my new menu. Everything was still steaming hot. Steve couldn't believe it. "What, did you go straight to the kitchen when we dropped you off last night?"

"You didn't drop me off last night. You dropped me off this morning."

I thought I would be in trouble for having it all laid out like this. I had envisioned going in the kitchen, making a dish, presenting it, and then going back to make the next one. It was pretty obvious that I didn't cook all of this food by myself. Actually, I hadn't cooked any of it, but it looked perfect. That was a great start.

Esposito, who had not said a word all morning, tapped a serving spoon with his index finger. "Steve, how is it that we have done tasting after tasting for four different restaurants and banquets back in America with that beautiful new facility, and not one of those chefs was able to finish their whole menu in less than three hours? This guy, who is obviously still drunk, can do it in a foreign country in fifteen minutes." He paused, then grinned. "I like all of it. It looks great."

Steve laughed, "I have no idea how to even answer that, but I like it too. Great job, Todd. Thank you for your hard work. This is exactly what we are looking for. How about you Raphael, what do you think?"

Raphael nodded, "It's beautiful. All of it is beautiful." Steve turned to Raphael, "I want two photographs of each plate before we try any of it." They all took a couple of bites then, but everyone was way too hungover to enjoy any kind of food.

Esposito finally announced, "It tastes like Mexico. This is as authentic as we could ever hope to get." I thought to myself, *Well, you got that right.*

The luckiest morning of my life took a turn for the worse when Steve said, "Todd, show us their kitchen." They all knew La Hacienda was only open for dinner. When they saw that army of cooks in there, they would certainly know that I hadn't cooked any of this. So, I couldn't believe it when we walked in the back. It was cleaner than I had ever seen it the whole time I had worked there, and the only person that was still around was Chuco. Steve's eyes got real big. "You're cleaned up already?"

"Yeah," I said, trying super hard to stay casual. "Unless there's anything else you would like me to show you, I think we are pretty much done here."

Esposito spoke up, "I've seen exactly what I came down here for; I'm done here. Thank you, Todd. Nice work. What about you, Steve?"

"No, I'm done here as well. I just can't figure out how he got cleaned up so fast. In Arizona, they need five guys to do a tasting and they totally trash the kitchen doing it. What did you do, order this food from room service?"

I answered, "They don't serve food like this anywhere in this hotel. This is my friend, Chuco. He learned how to make these recipes from his mother."

Steve was satisfied with my answer. "You're all done here, Todd. We fly out in two days, so relax and enjoy the rest of your time here."

I gave Chuco my knife kit right then and there, top-full of Henkel's. Steve saw me do it. "Why did you do that? Those look like expensive knives!"

"Oh, you should see what they have to work with down here. Besides, I can buy more and this guy can't." Also, Chuco had just saved my ass.

I could not get over how easy it had been. I spent the next couple of days saying goodbye to all my new friends and surfing as much as I could. I swore I would never drink again, and I didn't. In Mexico, anyway.

Chapter 22

WHEN WE GOT TO THE AIRPORT to fly home, we all bellied up to the check-in counter. Steve looked at Raphael and me and said, "This isn't a four-man job. Go stand over there." As we were walking away, I had to ask Raphael, "Man, we are working for Dr. Jekyll and Mr. Dickhead. How can you tell who this guy is?" Raphael just groaned, "I've been with him every day for the past two months. You haven't seen anything yet."

We got up to customs and Steve told me to go ahead of him. I was sweating it. I had about twenty cans of chipotle chilies, at least a dozen cans of *huitlacoche*, and a whole stuffed Armadillo I had bought on the beach. The lady asked me if I had any food, plants, or vegetables in my luggage. I looked back at Steve and asked, "Hey Steve, are cocaine and heroin plants or vegetables?" The customs lady laughed and told me to go through without even opening my bags.

As we were walking to the terminal, Steve was glaring at me. "Look, I don't appreciate your smart ass comments all of the time, and customs is no place to be a fucking comedian. I don't want to hear you say one more fucking word until the wheels are up on that aircraft and we're out of this country."

When we got on the plane, Steve told his wife to sit with Raphael, and me to sit with him. All of a sudden, he was acting like my best friend again. On the flight, he asked all kinds of questions about food and told me what a great job I had done in Acapulco. He said everybody really liked me there, even Señor Chopski.

I spent that whole flight wondering, *How can this guy make you feel so good about yourself and have you walking on air one minute, and then make you feel bad about yourself the next? And not only how, but why?*

Eventually, I would learn that Steve Ast was one of those guys who was so smart and so driven that no one knew what made him tick. It only took him less than ten years to make himself the vice president of Princess Hotel Corporation.

We landed late at night and I was so happy to see Stacey. Steve asked us to give him and his wife a ride home and told me to take the next two days off with my family. We went to McDonald's and then I asked Stacey to take me to the resort. It was a full moon and the restaurant was still under construction. I just couldn't wait until we got home. I was so happy, my life was so great; I wiped off a stainless steel counter and made love to Stacey right there in my new kitchen.

✳ ✳ ✳

Steve had already told the other chefs that Esposito had said I had the best tasting yet, and they had to learn how to step it up. I had technically worked in a Princess kitchen longer than any of these chefs, just at another resort. Nevertheless, they all treated me like I was new.

The executive chef Reed Groban introduced himself to me. He congratulated me on a great menu, and on the success I had had in Acapulco. Reed, to this day, is someone I would call a friend. He has been the executive chef of the Scottsdale Princess for more than twenty years. Before that, he worked at the Washington DC Sheraton where he was executive chef for nine years. Reed had a lot in common with Steve: he was Jewish, he had a lot of experience, and he was a genius. I don't mean that word lightly, I mean it literally. Reed Groban is way too damn smart for anyone's good. This cat knows his twenty-one times tables. He's like an idiot savant, or rain man, if you will.

And just like Steve, nothing gave him greater pleasure than fuckin' with people's heads. If he was discussing the amount of sauce to be produced for a large banquet, he would rattle off rocket-fast, "Well, we're feeding five hundred and thirty-two people, and we need an ounce and a half of sauce per portion. That's seven hundred and ninety-eight ounces divided by one hundred and twenty-eight in a gallon, so according to my calculations, you will need six point twenty-three gallons. Go ahead and make seven."

Then a person would walk up to him, ask a question, and within ten minutes Reed would ask him a series of questions that would leave the poor guy wondering if he was good enough to even be pursuing a career as a chef. Just like Scientology. It was Reedology, and a lot of people couldn't handle it. I liked him because he would always get my passive aggressive comments faster than anyone else.

The banquet chef they had hired was Tom Tompkins. He had done his externship from the CIA with me, in the banquet kitchen at the Anatole. The whole time I was in Mexico, Tom was telling Reed and any chef who would listen that I was good. Nice work, Tom.

Steve had hired a lot of talent and all of the chefs he'd hired were jockeying for position. I didn't go out with any of them at night, not even Tom. I would just go home to my family. We did have Tom over for dinner one night, however. He spent the whole night providing me with a safety manual on how to handle Steve Ast. Just like he was hazardous waste or something. Tom had been working with Steve for the past couple of years at the same resort where I had locked myself out of my hotel room in my underwear, the Four Seasons in Austin. What a small world.

La Hacienda was the last restaurant to open, so, besides a couple of tastings, I spent all of my time in other outlets helping them open. I may not have been the best chef there, but I certainly knew I could outwork the rest of them. Roget had always told me, "No matter how bad you are, if you are the first one there and the last one out, you will always be better than everyone in between." There were only two people that were always there before me and still there when I left: Reed and Steve. All they did was talk for a living, though. I had to load and unload, lift, carry, chop, and plate. So, they didn't count.

Banquets was the first to open. The first party we did was such a clusterfuck, Steve snapped and grabbed a speed rack full of salads and hurled it at the cooks. Speed racks are big and I was surprised at how strong he was. I just stepped back and laughed my ass off. It wasn't my department.

The next to open was Las Ventanas, the three-meal restaurant. Carey Neff was the token black guy that the Princess had hired. I liked Carey. I was watching TV the other night and saw him. He's now the corporate chef for Jenny Craig; go Carey.

I don't know if there's anything harder than opening restaurants at a three-hundred-million-dollar, five-star resort. We would have nights from hell called "trial feedings". The hotel would invite two hundred and fifty people to come eat for free and fill out a guest comment card before they left. At the first trial feeding, I worked the line with Carey. Talk about a mess. This guy's cooks were not even trained. Steve was sitting down, eating, and Reed was holding a bunch of photos taken during the tasting. The executive sous-chef Charles Decranis was trying to expedite.

Every time a plate would come up wrong (and this was every single time), Reed would kick it back and say, "Do it again." Nobody knew how to do it again: not me, not Carey, and certainly none of the cooks. Finally, I said to Reed, "Give me the pictures."

He glared at me. "No."

"Look, it's not my restaurant, but if you don't give me the fuckin' pictures, no one is going to get anything to eat."

"I only have one copy, and I can't check your work if I don't have the pictures."

"I will put the picture up with every plate when we serve it, just give it back after you check."

"Fine." We were finally able to get going.

I was so pissed at Carey. "Carey, what the hell? Why didn't you train your cooks?"

"Man, I thought that's what this was for." The guy was working his ass off and fuckin' miserable, like the rest of us.

"Well, those are all real people out there. They want something for dinner, and Papa Smurf there isn't going to let anything pass through the window unless it's right."

Right then, the fire suppression system went off on the line. I couldn't have been happier. Steve jumped up from his table and over the line and shoved sheet trays into the hoods so it quit spraying on the guests. *How did he know how to do that?* Once again, this guy really impressed me.

Eventually, all of the restaurants were open except for La Hacienda. It was time to start doing tastings again. I was all ready to go. Steve walked in the kitchen with Reed, Raphael, and the executive steward in tow. He greeted me and then just dropped to the ground. He didn't even bend his knees. The guy knocked his own feet out from under him and caught himself with his arms, like he was doing push-ups. He looked under the line I was prepping at, and started screaming at the executive steward because there was still construction litter there.

It had been a few months since I had been back from Mexico and, sad to say, I was getting used to Steve. I had just started to lay out all of my menu items, just like in Mexico, when Steve screamed, "Don't start throwing this shit at me Todd!" *What did he just say? Did he just call my beautiful food shit?*

"My food isn't shit."

We just stood there like a couple of gorillas with our arms braced on the line. We stared each other right in the eye for over a minute without saying a word. Reed was behind Steve trying to signal to me like a mime to *shut the fuck up*.

We continued with the tasting, and what was just dandy in Mexico was not nearly good enough here. Steve kept saying go get this, and go get that. He was adding stuff to plates that had no business being there. They don't even have this stuff in Mexico. After a couple of hours, he had bastardized everything that I had worked six months for. He made Raphael take pictures of it, like this was what we were going to serve.

I could barely stop myself from walking out. "This isn't La Hacienda, you're turning it into Steve Ast's personal Mexican restaurant." He slammed his hand down against the table.

"That's it. Tasting *over*. Todd, we're not going to continue unless you learn how to adjust your attitude. Now, you can adjust it yourself or you can let me adjust it for you. I want to see each and every one of these dishes again at seven a.m. tomorrow morning." He stormed out of there like Darth Vader, his lab coat blowing behind him.

I was there at four a.m. making everything again. I refused to do it the new way, so I stuck to my original menu. When Steve walked in he came right up to me, put his arm around my shoulder and said, "Todd, things got a little out of hand yesterday. I have been going through a lot in the past few weeks, and I was way out of line calling your food shit." He was so sweet.

"Okay, Steve, I understand. No harm done."

Then he continued, "You know, I was thinking all night long about what you said to me; you know, about how I was trying to turn this into Steve Ast's personal Mexican restaurant… I finally came to the conclusion that it *is* Steve Ast's personal Mexican restaurant, and if you have a problem with that then there's the door."

What a fuckin' dick. Reed and Raphael were so embarrassed for me that they wouldn't even look me in the eye. We were back in gorilla mode, but the difference was this time he left my plates alone. He told Raphael to shoot them just the way I had planned them. Steve was such a fuckin' trip. I got my way with the food because he had thought about it and *I* was right, and he got his way with my ego because he had thought about it and *he* was right.

Steve was every bit as condescending to Reed and Raphael as he was to me. He was an equal opportunity humiliator. Whereas Señor Chopski would humiliate people as one would shoot a shotgun—a widespread, superficial, blanket effect on all who crossed his path—Steve was a precision marksman with specific ammunition for who he was going to attack; a well-planned, single shot straight through the heart. It was interesting to witness the effects of Steve long after he had left the room. Just like the eddies in a pond after casting a stone, Steve, too, would have a ripple effect. Well, really, it was more like a tsunami effect with nothing but destruction in its wake.

I could not, for the life of me, figure out why I still wanted this guy's approval so bad. I didn't care if Reed liked me, or if Raphael liked me. I wanted Steve to like me. I wanted him to tell me that I was good chef. Maybe it had something to do with brainwashing, or Stockholm syndrome, or the same reason battered women keep going back to their husbands, or why battered shrimp keep jumping back into the fryer. Who knows.

Chapter 23

BY THE TIME LA HACIENDA was ready for its first trial feeding, my crew was trained on being trained. I had spent so much time with these kids. Every one of them not only knew their stations inside and out, but they knew all of the stations.

We had a young kid from one of the Point resorts on sauté. His name was John Black and he was only nineteen. I had Tracy for my sous-chef, and Debbie in the pantry. I'd brought them with me from the conference resort. When Reed found out they were lovers, he made Debbie go work in the main kitchen. Probably not a bad call. I hired this young girl named Teri Chin for the pantry. She was a sophomore in high school with no experience at all. I don't know exactly what it was about her that I liked so much. She was very quiet and very stoned during her interview. I had interviewed a lot of candidates, but most of them seemed too old and set in their ways. I guess that was it.

Finally, I asked Reed if I could have Jarred Bohanin, a twenty-year-old cook in the cafeteria. He said no at first, but I finally got him to cave in.

Our crew was so tight. They would all come over to my house at night to drink beer, smoke weed, and talk about work and our plans for the future. Reed knew we were different than the other crews at the resort. First, none of us would wear hats. That would really piss him off. Second, none of us would take our required breaks. Sure, we would all take a minute to walk outside around the building to smoke a joint, but we would never punch out and go down to the employee cafeteria. The other outlets started to call us the phantom crew because nobody would ever see us. La Hacienda was a free-standing restaurant, so there was never really a need to go to the main building. We had our food delivered to us and we all just stayed in our own little world.

We would have a family meal every day at four o'clock, and we would take turns fixing dinner for the group. We were a family in every sense of the word. Everybody was so loyal, and I loved them all dearly. On the first night of trial feedings, Steve had two hundred and fifty people all show up at the same time. Just one of his little ways of trying to stick it to me. We were so ready. I thought, *Bring it on.*

Reed, Steve, and Charles Decranis were all right there comparing the plates to photos. I didn't need Reed's photos this time. Every person on my crew had their own set. I always thought it was messed up that only Steve and Reed had the photos—they should have given us all copies. Instead, I made all the plates in advance, took photos, made copies for everyone, and paid for them myself.

I worked the middle with the high-end ticket items. I had roasted five whole pigs and three whole goats that first night, and they all looked beautiful. I mean, as beautiful as a goat can look.

We had swamped the waiters in thirty minutes. That's all you have to do on any night in any restaurant. Once you get ahead of them, you only have to cook as fast as they can serve. The only thing you have to watch out for is if the room clears at once. That means it will then be seated at once, and you have to be prepared for the next push.

Charles had a stupid idea. "Todd, we all know that you're a great line cook, but how about your crew? Leave the line and let's see how it works without you." I looked up at Steve and Reed for direction, but they were so pleased it was going so well that they didn't say a word.

"Charles, this isn't some kind of an experiment, this is a restaurant. I need to stay right here and watch the food."

"Todd, I wasn't asking you, I was telling you-"

"And I'm not *asking* you," I cut him off, "I'm *telling* you to *go to hell! I'm not leaving the line!*" Charles could not believe his ears. It actually took him a minute to digest it. Steve had to turn his back so Charles couldn't see him laughing, and Reed just stood there shaking his head, smiling, looking me right in the eye. I just looked back at him thinking, *I am glad that I can provide entertainment for everybody, now get this prick off my back.*

None of us expected what happened next. Charles screamed, "Ok, that's it, you're fired! *Pack up your things and get off the line!*" I *so* badly wanted to use the same line that Misha used on me when I fired him at Joe Vera's, but, before anyone could do anything, Steve grabbed Charles. He put one hand on the back of his neck and the other on his arm, and escorted him out of my kitchen.

"You don't fire anybody and you never will without talking to me first, especially someone I have this much money invested in." He was plenty loud enough for us to hear him, all the way to the door.

When Steve returned to the line, it was just like nothing had ever happened. He and Reed just continued talking about logistics, and we just kept plating orders. My cooks started to gloat, but I just shook my head. No gloating allowed. Things were not as calm as they seemed: I had fallen for this game before. I was sure Steve was going to tear into me for it, I just didn't know when or how.

The very next morning, Steve's secretary called me in my kitchen at seven a.m. and said, "Mr. Ast wants to see you immediately." *Here we go.* At least I was exhausted. I was probably too tired to fight with him. The walk from the La Hacienda kitchen to Steve's office had to be at least half a mile. I hated that walk more than anything because the only reason he would call me to his office was to scream at me more than normal. He needed the comfort of a shut door. The only thing I hoped for was that Charles wouldn't be in there when I got there.

The second I walked in, he snapped, "Shut the door and sit down." This was the first conversation that I had ever had with Steve where he flip-flopped his attack style. Normally, he would be all sweet in the beginning as he gently walked you down the alley. The whole time he would be pouring gasoline on you without you knowing it, and then, just when you had fallen for it, he would toss a lit match at you.

This time, he spoke in a low, harsh voice. "Todd, I want you to know that what you did last night was gross insubordination. Charles is the executive sous-chef of this resort. You had no right to tell him to go to hell, but at the same time, that's exactly what I would have done. Charles is a fuckin' putz and we all know that. He is the biggest mistake I have ever made at this resort. Now, Reed is going to come get you. You're going to sit down with him and Charles this afternoon and you're going to apologize to Charles for your actions."

"Steve, I am not sorry for anything that happened last night. I had one of the best nights of my life and things went great. Why should I be sorry?"

He snapped his head back and forth, "Todd, you're not listening to me. I didn't say you had to feel sorry, I said you just have to say you're sorry. There's a big difference. And things did go great last night; in fact, it was the smoothest trial feeding that I have ever seen in my career. It should have been, because you had six months to get your deal down."

"Why do you only compliment me when we're alone?"

"Listen, you ungrateful fuck, I told you I was impressed last night and I made sure I said it loud enough for everyone to hear. You're lucky I compliment you at all. You did a great job last night. You do a great job every night, and for that I give you a paycheck. Would you like me to keep the check and just pay you compliments?"

"You're right. I'm sorry. I stand corrected."

"Now, keep your mouth shut about the context of this meeting. Go get ready for tonight because I invited even more people for today." As I was walking out the door, he said, "Todd, just so you know, the day you tell me to go to hell will be the last day you ever speak to me."

"I understand. Thank you, Steve." After that, I spent the whole walk back thinking: *It's a trick. It's a trick. He's really not that cool. It's just a trick. I really don't like him that much. It's a trick. He's going to be a prick again in no time at all.* And, of course, he was.

◇ ◇ ◇

I was in the men's room in the main building when I saw Jarred walk out of the same stall with a cook from another restaurant. I called after them, "Hey, if you guys get caught smoking dope in here, there's nothing I can do to save your jobs. I need you right now, so stop it." Jarred shrugged me off.

"We weren't smoking dope."

"Well, you looked like a couple of fags walking out together, what in the hell were you doing?"

Jarred just answered, "I sell coke." At that, the other cook tore out of the bathroom, thinking that Jarred had just gotten him fired.

Without any hesitation, or even thought for that matter, I blurted out, "I want some." *Why had I just said that?*

I hadn't done coke since the last time it fucked me up in Austin,

Texas. That was over a year ago. Jarred was unfazed, though.

"I didn't say I did coke, I said I sold coke. I never touch the stuff, and if you want some you have to order it a day in advance. I keep it at home."

Before my brain could catch up to my mouth, I told him, "Bring me a quarter gram in the morning."

Jarred brought me a quarter gram that day and every day for the next six months. I never told Stacey. I never bought more than a quarter, and it was always long gone before I was ever off at night. I honestly thought that I had learned how to control the drug, as opposed to the drug controlling me.

Chapter 24

WE WERE ONLY OPEN A WEEK when Elin Jeffords, the food critic for The Arizona Republic, started coming around the resort. She did a four-part series on the restaurants at the new Scottsdale Princess Resort. The first restaurant was Champions, the steak house out in the middle of the TPC Golf course where the Phoenix Open is held every year. She gave them two stars for food, two stars for service, and three for ambience. The highest you could get in any category was four stars. Even though she had given them two stars, she still ripped them for food and service.

Steve and Reed both went berserk. Their bosses had just invested three hundred million dollars and they were starting to worry about their impact on the investment.

The next restaurant on the firing line was Las Ventanas, Carey's restaurant. Elin Jeffords went in for breakfast, ordered Eggs Benedict, and the headlines the following Wednesday read in big, bold print: "Soggy Muffins, Curdled Hollandaise, and a Short Black Hair." *Oh my God.* I was riding to work that morning and I had not seen a paper yet; I was listening to Dave Pratt on the radio. He read it over the air and was making jokes about it. I saw Carey in the hallway when I first walked in, and I felt sorry for him. Carey wasn't that great of a chef, but he was a good man. She had given him one star for food and then wrote that he didn't even deserve that. One star for service. Two stars for ambience. This whole thing had gone from really bad to even worse.

She went on and on for two pages about how bad the food was at the Princess. I couldn't sleep at night because I knew this lady had my future in her pen.

I never worked harder in my life. I made every batch of everything myself. I really expected to see Reed and Steve hanging over my shoulder, but they were never there. They had bigger fish to fry: Marquesa, the fine dining restaurant. Marquesa only fed fifty people a night; how hard could that be? Apparently pretty hard, because those two just about lived at that restaurant.

All for naught. I got up at five that morning and ran to the news stand. The headlines read: "The Princess Adorned Herself with a Silk Purse Called Marquesa." In even bigger print, it read: "In a Sow's Ear". Another one-star review. Steve couldn't even hold his head up in the hallway anymore. I was certain that the owners were going to fire Reed and Steve both.

I had no idea what more I could do to prepare my crew or myself any more than we were. So, before I went to bed one night, I got down on my knees and prayed to God not to let Elin Jeffords trash us. I had watched every single plate of everything before it left the kitchen, over the past three weeks.

Her reviews came out every Wednesday, and everybody knew I was next. People would walk up to me and say, "It's ok if you get slammed in the newspaper next week, Todd, she's doing it to everybody." I would answer, "I am *not* getting slammed."

The Monday morning before my review was scheduled to come out, I answered the phone in the kitchen. The woman on the line was crisp, professional, "Can I speak to the chef?"

"Speaking."

"Hi, this is Elin Jeffords from the Arizona Republic. How are you today?"

"Great. Is there any reason I shouldn't be?" She chuckled. "Chef Todd, I was in for dinner three times last week and had some of the best meals I have had at the Princess."

"Thank you." I could barely get the words out.

"I have some questions in regard to the preparation of your food. There is a predominant flavor in the black bean soup that I have never tasted before."

"That's *epozote*, an herb that is used for medicinal purposes in Mexico. They always put it in beans to avoid flatulence." *Was I really talking to this woman about farts?*

"I see," she laughed a little. "Your roast suckling pig carved tableside was excellent. Can I ask how many whole pigs your restaurant goes through in one night?"

"We are up to eight now."

"And where were you trained?"

"I completed a formal French apprenticeship under the direction of Roget Cortello, but all of this food came from spending a few months doing research and development in Acapulco."

"Impressive," she replied.

I then just straight up asked her, "So, am I going to get the single star like all of my workmates?"

She laughed, "Well, if you can keep this whole conversation a secret until after Wednesday, then I'll tell you."

"I can do that." *Come on, lady, don't tease me.*

"You got a perfect score on food and a superlative review. One of the best I've ever written."

I thanked her and promised again not to say a word. I hung up the phone and called Stacey and told her, but I didn't tell another soul about the fact that I knew that I was about to rock the Princess.

It was so tempting to start acting even cockier than I already acted. I probably did anyway, but at least I remember trying to be cool about it. One time, Steve asked me if I was worried about it. I just said, "What's there to worry about? My crew and I have worked hard and our food rocks. If she gives us a perfect score and a stellar review, then she knows good food when she sees it. If she slams me, then she doesn't."

He took on his dangerous voice, "Oh, so you think she was right about the other restaurants?" I knew better than to answer that question.

"I have never even been to one of them after a trial feeding, so I have no idea what they're doing over there now." He looked at me like he wanted to slug me.

That Wednesday morning, I drove down to the Republic building at three a.m. to get a copy off of a distribution truck. I was not disappointed. I couldn't have written a better article, myself. Everybody at La Hacienda was walking on air for weeks.

Some corporate bigwigs flew in from New York and had a secret meeting with Raphael and me. They told us how pleased they were about the success of the restaurant. In the next few days, they said, there was going to be a great big shake-up. No matter what happened, they wanted to make sure we were both planning on staying on board. We told them we were and they said great.

We both left that meeting thinking that Steve was going to be fired. Raphael was thrilled, but I couldn't help feeling sorry for Steve. He had worked so damn hard to do what he thought was best, even if he was acting like a jerk.

Two days later they fired the general manager, not Steve. Raphael couldn't believe it.

Chapter 25

LA HACIENDA WAS ROCKIN'. Every chef in town was eating there. In fact, all kinds of other hotel people were eating there. Leona Helmsley checked in and ate there three times a week. Christopher Gross would come in, and one time I was too busy to go out in the dining room after being requested so a strange guy just walked in the back to tell me how much he enjoyed his meal. It was Jacques Pepin, the chef for the president of France.

I was getting a lot of job offers. These millionaires who owned a restaurant up the street called The 8700 were sending their GM in every Sunday brunch to keep sweetening the pot. I finally told them I would do it when they offered me double what I was earning at the Princess. But, only under the condition that I could bring my crew with me. They agreed.

I gave notice. Steve had made a counter offer, but when I told him what I was going to get paid he told me to forget it. So I left. I made sure that the crew came over slowly within the coming weeks so we wouldn't put La Hacienda in a jam.

It felt really great to be out from under Steve's thumb, although my new boss wasn't nearly as smart as Steve. In fact, he was kind of a goofball. I'll take a kind and considerate goofball any day of the week over condescension, though.

I once heard that the building for The 8700 cost eleven million dollars. Whatever it cost, it was beautiful. They had these famous forgery oil paintings: Van Gough, Modigliani, and Picasso. They were very good forgeries, but none the less forgeries. The owners were Robert and Anita Keyes; they owned banks all over the country. I dealt with their daughter Karlyne most of the time. She was my age, twenty-five or so. Vincent was the one who laid out the kitchen, but he started having a love affair with Karlyne. Dad put the brakes on that fast.

One day, Karlyne and I were chatting and she tried to tell me how humble her beginnings were. She told me a story about a time when she and her two little sisters didn't have money for the ice cream truck when it passed by, playing its music.

"Todd, it was the saddest thing that you have ever seen. All three of us just sitting there crying because we didn't have any money and we couldn't have any ice cream."

I thought to myself, *Well, looks like it worked out all right because now you can take one of two private jets your dad owns and fly to France just to go shopping.* And she did.

It only took a couple of months to get my crew in line and the restaurant in order. We were serving very high-end Southwestern Cuisine with one hell of a Mexican influence.

I would run *cabrito* for a nightly special. One night, I had a baby goat sitting outside the back door thawing on a table. When I went out to get it, there was a great horned owl perched on top of it, trying tonight's special. I scared him but, trust me, he scared me more. Instead of just flying away, he tried to take the goat with him. He could only make it about a foot off the table, though, and then he would have to set the goat back down. It was too heavy to fly with. But no matter what, he wasn't going to let go.

I went in and told John, Teri, and Jarred to come check it out. When we all came back out, he was still there with the goat in his clutches. I told

John to go get me a tenderloin. He did, and I carefully eased up on the owl and tossed the tenderloin on the goat. The owl took one peck at, grabbed it with his talons, and flew away with it. Beef tenderloin was a lot easier to get in America than baby goat. Definitely a fair trade.

✧ ✧ ✧

Around that time, I went to a winemaker dinner at the Loews Paradise Valley Resort. While I was being served one of the courses, I noticed a man at the dinner. He looked so familiar, but I couldn't remember where I knew him from. Then, a couple of courses later, it came to me.

It was Robert Lawrence Balzer, the food editor from Travel Holiday Magazine. I got right up and walked over to his table.

"Do you remember me?'

He smiled, "You know, I had seen you earlier tonight at the reception. I knew we had met, but I just couldn't remember where."

"I was Roget's apprentice." Roget, still making my introductions eleven years later.

"Ah yes," he cried, "Of course, Todd!"

"You should come into The 8700." *How cool to see this guy here!*

"Perhaps I could. I'm quite busy, this is a working trip for me. What I would really like is *huitlecoche*, but I know that you can't get it in America."

I grinned, "I brought some back with me from Mexico, and I've been waiting for just the right time to serve it the traditional way, Crepes *Huitlecoche*."

"Excellent! You will be my first stop on my dine-around tomorrow!"

Robert Lawrence Balzer came in for dinner the next night. A few months later, The 8700 received the Travel Holiday Award for the first year with a great write-up in Travel Holiday. Then, I started to get lots of great write ups. Elin Jeffords gave me another perfect score and stellar write up. Nikki Buchanan from the Phoenix New Times was in one night, as well. I used to make nightly rounds to all of the tables, and I met her as she was writing right there at the table. I remember thinking that she was very cute. I would fly to Napa Valley, do a winemaker dinner, and two days later in the local paper there would be a photograph of me, right there, carving a pig on a spit with the headlines reading: "Chef Wings Way on Culinary Mission". I would have no idea how they even got the photo, let alone found out what I served.

But my controlled cocaine use was getting more and more out of control. The bigger my head got, the more blow I would do.

Chapter 26

I WAS ASKED TO FLY TO Georgia O'Keefe's estate in Santa Fe, New Mexico to do a dinner for the Minnesota Institute of Fine Arts. I had been reading everything I could get my hands on about Southwestern Cuisine, and one of my favorite books was the *Pink Adobe Cookbook* by Rosalea Murphy. I went to her restaurant, The Pink Adobe, for dinner my first night in Santa Fe and there she was, sitting with another woman at a booth with her dog Rex. I walked up to her and introduced myself. That was how I found out she and her friend Nedra Matteucci, the lady next to her, would be at my dinner the following night. I had dinner and drinks with both of them until it was pretty late.

Nedra took me back to the guest house I was staying at on the estate. I couldn't sleep, so I went swimming in a black swimming pool that just kind of sitting there, in the desert. There was this great, big sculpture that Georgia had done that stood about twelve feet high and twelve feet wide, sitting right at the edge of the pool. The sculpture looked like a giant snail shell with a four-foot hole bored out of the center of it. I was just floating in the water and the strangest sensation came over me. I knew that I was floating in water, but the black bottom coupled with the dark sky made me feel like I was just floating in space.

Just then, the moon started to rise on the horizon. In just a couple of seconds, it had risen until it fit perfectly in the center of the hole in the sculpture. She had to have placed it there on purpose because it was just too fuckin' cool. It was one of the most beautiful things I had seen in my life. Right then and there, I knew I would be an artist someday. I just wasn't sure when. And I'm still not now.

When I was flying back with the GM of The 8700, I told him, "I'm going to be an artist."

He replied, "Todd, you can no more say that you're just going to be an artist than someone can just say that they're going to be a chef."

"I don't care. I'm going to be an artist."

We never discussed it again, but when Stacey picked me up from the airport we went straight to Arizona Bronze. I bought a bunch of microcrystalline and started to teach myself how to sculpt.

When I told Stacey I was going to be an artist she said, "That's nice honey, I'm pregnant." I was ecstatic.

I thought of all the things I had spent hours teaching Chelse, that she then spent hours teaching Parker: how to place the colored doughnuts on the yellow pole, how to operate the Jack in the Box, how to play peek-a-boo. Chelse would sit and read to her little brother Parker for hours. He had no idea she was making every single word up. All he knew was that he sure did get to read a lot of cool books with his big sister. Nothing gave me greater joy than my children.

Stacey was an awesome mother and wife. She would get up early, make coffee, and iron my chef's jackets while I got in the shower. She fixed breakfast for the kids, loaded them up in the car, and took me to work every morning. Stacey spent every day as a full-time mom, and that's hard work. I couldn't even do it for a couple of hours without screwing things up.

I was still excited about the thought of a new child, when she continued, "I have something to tell you, though, and you're not going to like it. When you were gone, I had to ask your mom to go to the doctor's with me so she could watch the kids while I was having my examination."

Stacey paused for a second and looked me right in the eyes like she was trying to collect everything she had to say. "Todd, when I came out and told her I was pregnant, she shushed me. She told me, 'Listen, don't even tell Todd, honey. I'll take you to have an abortion before he ever flies home. And no one will ever have to know. You already have two beautiful children. A boy and a girl. That's perfect. And enough. Kids are so expensive and take such a big part of your life away. Just let me take care of this, honey, and you'll thank me later. I promise you.'"

Stacey took a deep breath and continued, "I told her, 'Are you kidding me? If Todd found out, he would never speak to me again. He loves kids.' She told me, 'I know, sweetheart, that's why we just have to keep it between us.'"

Right there in the car, my mind went from the beautiful thoughts of a new child to how my own mother could even suggest something like that. I cannot explain the protective instincts of a father. But all of you fathers know exactly what I am talking about.

I was so pissed off. "Stacey, pull over and stop at a pay phone, I'm fuckin' calling her right now."

She wouldn't, though. When we finally got home, I was so upset I couldn't even dial right. I had never discussed my mom trying to kill me, but right now seemed like the perfect time. I had always felt really bad that my mom tried to abort me, but that was nothing compared to her trying to kill one of my children.

As soon as she answered, I tore into her. "You thought just because I had to ride in your womb for nine months, that that gave you the right to kill me? Well, you're wrong. I am a survivor and I not only dodged all of the hangers and sharp objects you tried to stab me with when I was inside of you, but I dodged hot coffee, hairbrushes, telephones, abusive and perverted husbands, and anything else you tried to hurt me with, the whole time I was growing up. That's fucked up, you know that? I should be able to look at my children's grandmother as a fellow protector, not a killer. Stay the fuck away from me and my children."

She tried to say, "Oh, baby, I am so sorry. You don't understand. We were on drugs when you were conceived, and they had TV commercials with babies with club feet and blue faces, I was certain that you would be deformed. I was just trying to protect you from a hard life."

"You... what? You wanted to protect me from a hard life?" I hung up. She called back. Stacey answered it and I took the phone away from her and hung it up. I unplugged it.

I had waited a long time to say that. I hadn't done any coke for a week because I had had that dinner in Santa Fe to do, but I sure as hell wanted some now. I came out and watched "MTV and Me". The kids warmed up the microcrystalline and started to sculpt. All the while, the same four words just kept rolling in my head: *What a fuckin' bitch*.

I went back to work. I had already gotten some great press for my last meal, but do you know what? I couldn't feel good about anything; not the press, not my crew, *nothing*. Once again, I had allowed my mom to steal every ounce of pleasure in my soul.

Chapter 27

MY CREW WAS DOING A great job. I had signed John Black up for the apprenticeship program two years before, back when we had first opened La Hacienda. Now he wanted me to hire his best friend, Chris Mattocks. In fact, for months on end Chris would come in every other day and ask me if he could be my apprentice. He was the ultimate surfer dude: spiked blonde hair, never wore a shirt, and drove some really cool, English, convertible sports car. Chris was an only child and his parents were loaded. The day I finally conceded, mostly because I was getting sick of him asking, he was so happy.

Only a few days later, we were having a meeting in the general manager's office on the top floor. The general manager kept looking out the window. Finally, he sighed. "Todd, you have to come check this out." I looked down in the parking lot. Right below us, Chris and John were sitting in Chris's convertible, lining up a few giant rails of coke on a CD case.

"What do you think they're doing?" The GM asked me.

"You know what they're doing," I answered. Just then, John put a rolled-up bill to his nose and sucked the coke down. The GM looked at me.

"Who is that guy with John?" *Great.*

"That's my new apprentice I just hired. Remember, I was telling you about him."

"Well, now they're both fired. Not for doing coke, but for being so stupid to do it right under my office."

I scrambled to go to bat for them, "Bruce, listen, they're both good boys. Please, just let me handle this. I promise it will never happen again." I was getting so much press that our numbers had gone from one hundred and fifty thousand dollars a month to well over two hundred thousand dollars a month. Bruce was getting a percentage, so he never wanted to say or do anything to piss me off. It was almost like he was working for me.

"Okay, fine," was all he could manage.

I ran downstairs and smacked both of those boys so hard in the back of the head it knocked the coke right out of their nostrils. Chris started out on my shit list, and pretty much stayed there for the next six years. He was just such a cool cat you couldn't stay mad at him for very long. He was a natural; a great cook from the moment he stepped foot on the line.

John had been right by my side ten to twelve hours a day for over two years, at two different four-star restaurants. He was getting pretty damn good himself. We were at Taliesin West, Frank Lloyd Wright School of Architecture, doing a real big dinner when I told John I had decided to make him my sous-chef.

"You still have a year left on your apprenticeship," I told him, "but I was a sous-chef the last year of my apprenticeship."

"This is so amazing, Chef! Could you do the produce order so I can go out with my girlfriend tonight and celebrate?" He was practically dancing.

"Oh, so this is how you're going to start? By shrugging off your responsibility on me?" I pretended to be mad. "Go fill out the logbook and I'll do the order."

Before I left that night, I looked at what he had written in the logbook. He had written: *This is the greatest day in my life. I'm not going to let Chef Todd down. I'm ready for this! The whole crew is behind me and The 8700 is going to be the greatest restaurant in the world!* I was so pleased with John and how seriously he was taking his career. It made me feel great that I was able to develop these kids into hardworking, talented men.

The following morning, I was walking out to my car at seven a.m. when the director of catering pulled up in my driveway.

"What are you doing here?" I was too surprised to be polite.

"Todd, John was killed a few hours ago." It almost didn't even register.

"How?" *I was just with him ten hours ago, what could have happened?*

"He was out drinking at Shepard's real late last night. His girlfriend was driving down Cactus Drive and she drove right into McDonald's at Tatum Boulevard." I felt like my legs were going out from underneath me. She continued, "They were going over eighty miles an hour when they hit the building. John died two hours later."

All I could say was, "I just made him my sous-chef last night."

I was too upset to drive, so she took me to the restaurant. I called all of the crew and woke them up. I told them to come into work right now. Some of them tried to blow me off, but I used a tone of voice that they knew not to fuck with.

Jarred, Teri, Tracy, Debbie, Chris, Arturo… all of those kids had been with John every day for the last two years. I called them all into my office. When Teri asked, "Where's John? How come he didn't have to get his ass out of bed?" I just did it, then. I told them, "John's dead."

Debbie instantly started screaming and bawling. Chris tried to pretend like it was a joke. He kept saying, "No way man, no way man." Teri was the one who asked, "How?" After I had explained what happened, Jarred slammed his fist right through the door of my office, all of the way. Then he ran off. I told him to come back, but he didn't.

It was a Saturday, and I told them they didn't have to work if they didn't want to. But I was going to. Tracey just murmured, "What the fuck else are we going to do?" I handed them the logbook and told them to all read what John had written in the last hours of his life. Each and every one of them wrote something about John, next to what he had written. I did lots of coke and drank gin all night. I didn't know what else to do. The food was sad and a little bit slow that night, but it was still really good. I think that's what John would have done if it had been me.

We kept rolling along at The 8700 for the next six months. I was doing coke all of the time now and everyone knew it. It's amazing what people will let you get away with as long as you fill their till with money every night. I would go into the food storeroom to snort lines on top of some can. I wasn't even hiding it that much. I locked myself in there one night without my key, and they had to call Bruce to come let me out. He knew what I was doing in there. He was beside himself.

"This has got to stop."

I yelled back, "Settle down, hotshot!" And that was it, he fired me right in front of everyone.

The whole crew came to my house that night and asked me what I was going to do. I told them I didn't know. They told me that I had to stop doing so much blow, that I was going to die, and Stacey agreed with them. I did my last line right in front of all of them. For a little while, anyway.

Chapter 28

THE THING IS, I DIDN'T EVEN WANT to do coke if I wasn't working. I had the next couple of months off because I was looking for a job. Steve was super cool. He didn't hire me back, but he hired me as a consultant for the month just before Christmas. So, my family had a nice holiday.

I landed at the Hyatt Regency Scottsdale at Gainey Ranch. I was hired as executive sous-chef, a prestigious position in the valley. It paid thirty-five thousand dollars a year, less than half of what I was making at The 8700.

I had to call in sick on my very first day at the Hyatt because Stacey went into labor. When she had Parker, she was in labor for twelve hours. When she had Chelse, she was in labor for sixteen. So, I knew I had some time to kill. I went outside the hospital to smoke a joint, and couldn't believe what was going on when I came back.

Stacey was screaming at me, "Todd, what the fuck? Where were you?" and some nurse was yelling, "Stop pushing, stop pushing!" This lady was trying to shove the head of my baby back in Stacey.

"*What are you doing?*" I wanted to grab her hands and pull her away.

"There's no doctor here, and I don't know how to do this!" *What the hell?*

"You don't have to do anything but catch the baby, and it's coming out." I told Stacey to push and my second son just slid right out into this nurse's hands. The nurse was happier than I was that it was over.

She turned to me, "Do you want to hold him while I go get scissors to cut the cord?" I held my beautiful son in my arms and whispered to him, "Welcome to earth."

The nurse came back and started to cut the cord.

Holding my son, I said, "*Stop.*"

"Why, do you think it's too long?"

"No, you have to clamp it in two places and cut between the clamps."

"Oh, that's right." *Wow.*

We named our new, ten-pound baby boy John Hyatt Hall because he was born on my first day at the Hyatt. Good thing he wasn't born on my first day at the Princess…

John was all cleaned up, weighed, foot printed, and photographed before Stacey's obstetrician walked in.

"Well I guess we just saved a lot of money," I told her.

"It doesn't work like that," he replied. *Bummer!*

John was the fifth baby ever born at the new John C. Lincoln hospital. They had only opened a short time before. I thought that it was kind of weird that my friend John died at the old John C. Lincoln hospital, and my son John was one of the first to be born at the new John C. Lincoln hospital. That's just way too many Johns to keep track of.

✧ ✧ ✧

When I went to work on my first day at the Hyatt, the executive chef Anton Brunbauer told me that I was going to be in charge of an event being held at The Scottsdale Princess that night. Nice, my first night at the Hyatt would be spent back at the Princess. Life is so weird.

Anton Brunbauer was and still is the meanest man I have ever met. He is Austrian, and just fuckin' mean. Not just to me, but to every person that crosses his path. He was a far better chef than almost anyone in the valley, including myself, but he was just so mean-spirited that no one ever said anything nice about him and he got zero press.

At the Hyatt, Anton worked fifteen hours a day, six days a week. He didn't sit in the office and go to meetings like Reed. He cooked food every day. He cut all of the meat rocket-fast for the whole hotel. He had his hand in everything.

At about ten o'clock in the morning, he would start drinking beer. Right in his office in front of everybody. He smoked cigarettes in his office right in the kitchen. At three o'clock, he would tell some cook to go get him his first mug of iced coffee. The cook would go to the service bar and say, "One iced coffee, please." The bartender would grab a bottle of Johnny Walker Black, which had a great big label on it that said "KITCHEN". The bartender would fill Anton's mug with scotch.

Here's the kicker: I worked side by side with Anton for a year and he was never drunk once. He never even smelled like alcohol. He never slurred a word. He drank at least four beers and a lot of scotch every day, but never got drunk. I finally decided that Anton was an alien.

I never sought Anton's approval the way I did Steve's. I hated his fuckin' guts. I tried as hard as I could for that guy, and nothing was ever good enough. I got so sick of being his whipping boy.

There were some great restaurants and some great people at the Hyatt. There was some great food, too, but Anton made me hate every minute of the time I spent there. I was in charge of everything as long as he was not in the building. He was in the building from eight a.m. to ten p.m., six days a week. I had to be there before he arrived, and I wasn't allowed to leave until he left. When he was on vacation, I talked to the general manager.

"Is Anton trying to make me quit?" Serious question.

He didn't seem surprised when he answered, "No, Anton always speaks very highly of you in the executive committee meeting."

"Why am I always in trouble? No matter what happens wrong, it's always my fault. And he totally treats me like crap."

He just shrugged, "That's Anton. No one really knows why he's that way with his assistants. He's been the chef here for three years and he has never had an executive sous-chef last longer than a year. Just think, you're almost done." And he walked away. *Was that supposed to encourage me?*

◎ ◎ ◎

I had been watching this cafeteria cook selling blow. Technically he was in my area, so I could have fired him, but instead I just told him to start bringing me a quarter gram every day. I was convinced that smart coke dealers always got jobs at large resorts, and actually requested to work in the cafeteria so they could sell coke to all of the employees. It was just too coincidental to have a dealer both here and at the Princess cafeteria. It was the perfect cover because no employee would ever be in trouble for getting caught in the cafeteria passing things back and forth.

I guess I wasn't the only one who noticed, because a couple of months later he was caught in the act. Human resources said they wouldn't have him arrested if he made a list of everyone he sold to. Guess whose name he thought of first.

Chapter 29

I ALWAYS WONDER WHAT my life would be like if the only place people could get any drugs was at a hospital. Maybe I would not have been born. Maybe my biological father would not have been running from the law and bumped into my mom.

Would my mom have been pleasant in the mornings if she wasn't jonesing for her speed to kick in? Would she still have tried to abort me? She wouldn't have worried about me being deformed. Would I have been an engineer like my daughter if I hadn't spent my entire high school education stoned?

I think it's a waste of time to play the "What If?" game. What I do know for sure, is that in some sick and twisted way each of these drug-induced traumas and tragedies have always left me a special little gift. Every job I have lost, every ounce of respect I have lost, and all of the time I have lost have all been compensated for with something even more valuable.

I don't know if there's a word to describe it with, but I can recognize a quality in other people who have led similar lives without ever even speaking to them. I'll give you a clue for how to detect us: we will never be seen in the checkout aisle, giving a new cashier a hard time for taking too long. In fact, we will make her feel better about herself and tell her to take her time.

A couple of weeks before I got fired from the Hyatt, my sister Cindy was visiting us from Texas. She asked me to take her to Sedona. I had no idea how beautiful it was up there, and the serene beauty made me feel peaceful. I really did feel at home. I hated my job at the time, so I stopped at a little place on Oak Creek called L'Auberge De Sedona and applied for a chef's position. The food and beverage director told me that he had a great chef from France, but he would keep my number just in case.

He called me at ten-thirty at night two days after I was fired from the Hyatt. His chef had just given notice, was I still interested? Call it fate, fortune, nature, or God, but something was telling me to move to Sedona. I accepted the executive chef position at L'Auberge De Sedona. I didn't have any money to rent a new house, so Stacey and the kids stayed at our house in Scottsdale until I got my first check.

The first day I walked in the kitchen to meet my new crew, it made me cry. Right on the line cooking were Tracy and Debbie, the badass lesbians who had always been the driving force of my crew at The 8700. This job was certainly meant to be. I camped out on the creek in a tent for my first two weeks. Tracy and Debbie offered me a couch to crash on at their apartment, but I declined. Sleeping by the creek at night next to the restaurant reminded me of my childhood in Logan Canyon. I did front a quarter ounce of weed from them, though.

I got us a house on 70 Rock Top Road, right in front of Bell Rock, in the village of Oak Creek. I bought a mountain bike and I rode the eight-mile trek from the village to L'Auberge every day. After topping the hill at Bell Rock, I would always say a prayer while coasting down the other side. I'd thank God for my beautiful family, for getting to live and work in this beautiful place. Then, I'd ask Him to please bless me with the inspiration to create totally badass food that day.

The first order of business was to get all of my crew back. I asked Tracy if she wanted to be my sous-chef. Her words were, "I didn't move to Sedona so I could spend all day and all night trapped like a rat in some kitchen." I took that as a no. Chris was still living at home and working at The 8700. Teri had gone back to La Hacienda.

Neither one of them hesitated when I called and told them they had to move to Sedona. I let them be surprised as I was when they walked in for their first day of work and saw Tracy and Debbi. When Tracy saw Chris she said, "You're going to let this surfer douchebag back on our line?" Then they hugged. Now I needed a sous-chef. Misha popped into my head. I found him in Missouri and he flew right out, sight-unseen. We had Misha, Chris, and Teri all living with Stacey, the kids and me until they could find places of their own.

I hired another guy from Johnson and Wales Culinary School, Will Le Roux. Will fit in perfectly. I cannot tell you the value of a crew that you have spent training for over two years. Everybody already knew exactly what I wanted and how I wanted it. We rocked L'Auberge. We had only been there a couple of months when Elin Jeffords gave us a perfect score. Four stars for food, four stars for service, and four stars for ambience. The headlines read: "L'Auberge De Sedona is as solid as the Red Rocks". And it was.

L'Auberge had a prix fixe menu that changed nightly and we could cook whatever we wanted. I was ordering as much food from France as I was from America. Turbot, brill, loup de mer, John Dory, chanterelles, and, of course, we preserved our truffles every January.

Robert Mondavi, Mikel Grgich, and Kathleen Heitz would come in, and too many movie stars to even begin mentioning. I will tell you that we had to kick Freddy Krueger out of the restaurant for screaming at his girlfriend in the dining room. And, one time after Barry Goldwater had just finished the long bus ride to the resort from Scottsdale, he walked up to the bar and said, "I just want the tallest glass you have full of ice."

When the bartender handed him the glass he said, "Now, fill it with vodka."

We were not only getting a lot of local, Phoenix, and Scottsdale press, but we were starting to get a lot of national press. I was doing winemaker dinners once a month with the top labels in the industry. My crew and I had doubled L'Auberge's food revenue. The food and beverage director Marc Bolloco, who you would think would be ecstatic over our success, was starting to get jealous of all the attention I was getting. He was a chef in France, but I never even saw him cook so much as a strip of bacon.

Whenever someone famous would come in, Marc would go put on a chef's jacket, sneak through the front door, and take credit for my food. I caught him red-handed one night when I stepped into the dining room. I got into a tiff with him about it. So, to teach me a lesson he started putting his name on all of the winemaker dinner menus as "executive chef" instead of "director of food and beverage". He would demote me to "chef de cuisine". I was hired as executive chef, my business card said so, but things were just going too well and I didn't want to be punished anymore. So, I just kept my mouth shut.

I would read anything that I could get my hands on about food. There was a magazine called Food Arts; every month they would have full-page ads for Pelugrá butter. They had this cat named David Burke with the coolest food I had ever seen. I would rip the pages out of the magazine and paste them all over the kitchen to remind myself and my crew that we still had a long way to go.

❂ ❂ ❂

I entered the Bocuse d'Or, Paul Bocuse's international culinary competition. There were over four hundred entries just from America, alone. They would pick twelve finalists to compete with one of their apprentices in the national competition in Chicago. I won; I was a finalist, and I was going to Chicago to compete against the top twelve chefs in America.

I couldn't believe the list of competitors. They were the movers and shakers of the national food scene. Then I saw a name that jumped right out at me: David Burke, my culinary idol.

Having an Arizona chef up for the gold in an international competition like this was a very big deal to the press. I was in Food Arts, as well as USA Today. The more attention I got, the bigger dick Marc became. I had just about had a gutful of his bullshit.

We would go into the weekly food and beverage meeting with our bottom line bigger than it had ever been in the history of L'Auberge. Our dining room sold out for a week in advance, the guest comment cards showed a higher score than ever before, and this little prick would just bitch and bitch and bitch about everything we did in the kitchen. A lot of it had to do with the fact that not one member of my crew would even give him the time of day. None of them had any respect for him, and I couldn't be held responsible for that. They were all very sharp kids and they saw right through his bullshit.

Instead of just getting some blow, like I would in the past, I promised myself that I wasn't going to blow *this*. No pun intended. Marc was certain that I would not make a move until after the Bocuse d'Or, so he acted like a prick on steroids as often as he could.

Our competitor, Los Abrigados, had a food and beverage director named Edd Zielinski who was starting to pal around with me at local events. His wife Nancy worked at L'Auberge in catering. I had breakfast with Edd and he told me that my crew and I could come over to Los Abrigados if we wanted to, but we had to wait for the right time.

About a month before the Bocuse d'Or, Greg Lamond, the six-time winner of the Tour de France, stayed with us for about a week. I didn't get a chance to make it to the dining room the first couple of nights he dined with us, but I kept track of his table and sent out some duck liver and French fish, complements of the chef.

When I finally did meet him and introduce myself as the chef, he was surprised, "I thought Marc was the chef! You've prepared the best duck liver we have ever eaten in our lives!"

"Ah," I said, "Marc suffers from *complexe de Napoléon*." Greg, who spoke fluent French, started busting up laughing. He felt bad that I had to put up with someone stealing my talent, so we planned a menu for the next night to try to catch Marc in a lie, right at Greg's table. Marc must have heard reports of me palling around with Greg, because he wasn't seen in the dining room again for the remainder of Greg's stay. I did get to go on a bike ride with Greg. He signed a jersey and gave it to me, which was pretty cool.

We had two seatings at L'Auberge, and the crew and I would go smoke a joint after the first seating had their entrées. I had just hired this awesome pastry chef Kevin, so after we smoked we all went in the pantry and started munching on the new pastries. I was throwing chocolate truffles up in the air and catching them in my mouth when Marc walked in. Every one of us had either a pastry in our hands or mouths. Marc just threw a fit. He was stomping his feet and shaking his fist and yelling in half-French and half-English. He looked just like a little kid throwing a tantrum. The fact that he was only four feet tall with a pinhead just sealed the moment.

Tracey just looked at me and then looked back at Marc, and laughed so hard that she accidentally spit chocolate all over his suit… and that was it. That was all we needed. All of us just started laughing hysterically. Marc's face got so red I thought his head was going to pop. He just ran out of there, totally embarrassed.

Misha called it to our attention that we all were going to pay for that one. I thought to myself, *Life is just too short to spend it worrying about how much trouble you're going to be in tomorrow.* I had spent my whole childhood worrying about that. It was time to stand up for myself and put a stop to this nonsense.

That night, I went out to the bar and wrote my letter of resignation. My crew asked me what I was doing, and I told them that we were all going to work across the street. I had finally had enough of Marc. None of them even questioned me. They all just sat down and wrote their letters of resignation also. We all slid them under the door of human resources. Nancy told Edd what happened and he said we could come over but not for a few weeks; I said fine.

The owners of the resort came up to Sedona and asked what was up. I said we were all sick of Bolloco and ready for a change. It was a nice feeling knowing that I was finally leaving somewhere and cocaine had nothing to do with it. Edd hired us just a week before the Bocuse d'Or.

Edd, my brother Nick and my mom flew out to Chicago to support me in the competition. I was receiving another award in Chicago from Chefs in America; they had selected me as one of America's best chefs.

Chris and Nick were out painting the town red while Edd and I went to the restaurant show and swam some laps at the hotel pool. Those two showed up at the award ceremony totally trashed. I thought they were funny until they were announcing the award for the Chef of the Year and Chris screamed out, "TODD HALL!" just before they could say the name of the real winner: André Soltner from Lutèce. I have never been more embarrassed in my life.

The night before the competition, all of the chefs had dinner at the Omni Hotel. I looked for David Burke, but didn't see him. I asked another competitor where the competition was being held and he said, "Right there, across the street." I thought, *Nice, we're staying at the Omni, and we can just walk across the street at five-thirty AM.* The competition started at six. We hit the sack early, and in the morning we went across the street. There, fifteen minutes before the competition was set to start, someone told us that it was actually at Kendall College ten miles away. I about died; those assholes lied to us.

There we were, standing in a parking lot holding our knives and silver platters, with no car and no way to get to Kendall College. Just then, a white car cranking AC/DC squealed in the parking lot and skidded to a stop right next to us. The driver and passenger were wearing chef's coats. The passenger leaned out the window and said, "Did those fuckheads tell you it was over here too?"

"Yeah! They did." What a fuckin' mess!

"Get in the back."

The chef in the passenger side was reading a road map, so I didn't get a look at his face. He kept yelling at his apprentice, "NO, turn here!"

Then, he finally put the map down and reached over the seat and said, "Hi I'm David." I couldn't believe it; it was David Burke.

We got to the competition twenty minutes late and they almost disqualified us. Our assigned kitchens were right next to each other. We both went to the pot and pan room, and it was completely empty. There was not so much as a spoon left there to cook with. We were both fucked.

David didn't hesitate. "Come on, follow me." And we walked out the back door. I had no idea what we were doing but I knew he was a hell of a lot better chef than I was so I just followed him. As we walked he muttered, "I smelled bacon cooking when we walked in here, so there has to be a kitchen somewhere." We followed our noses until David pulled open a door and, just like that, we hit the motherlode.

It was the cafeteria for all of the college students. David yelled, "Grab that cart!" and we both just started loading up as much as the cart would hold. We walked out the back door with all of it, never speaking to a soul that worked there. When we got back to our kitchen, we had more shit than all of the other chefs put together. Then we got crankin', making the required duck dish and Dover sole dish. In the end, all the entries looked so awesome I had no idea where anybody stood.

The awards ceremony was held at some hotel over a seven-course meal. My mom, Edd, Nick, Chris and I all had to sit at the same table as Marc Bolloco. The executive chef of The Four Seasons Chicago ended up winning, but I wanted to see how I scored.

I asked one of the judges if I could see my score. He told me that they didn't do that. I knew we would be better competitors if we could see what mistakes we made, so I pressed him.

After discussing it for a minute, the judge took me up to Jean Banchet and gestured at him, "Tell him what you told me." I repeated my request.

Jean just replied, "If we cared about your opinion, then we would have asked you for it."

I got pissed and pointed back at the other judge. "He just asked me for my opinion. In fact, he told me to give it to you." Banchet just gave me a dirty look and turned and walked away. I was totally beat and ready to go back to Sedona.

Chapter 30

A COUPLE OF WEEKS LATER, I had a winemaker dinner with Heitz Cellars. It was well-known that Joe Heitz made the best red wine in America, Martha's Vineyard. I had reached the pinnacle in the wine industry. The first time I met Joe, he wanted me to make one of each course so he could sample and pair them with the wines he was featuring. Once I was done, I waited for at least ten minutes until he finally said something.

"A hell of a lot better than I expected to find in Arizona." That was it, I had passed his test. He just turned away and walked back to his suite. Before he left, he and his wife Alice left me a couple magnums of Martha's that he'd signed.

A week later, he wrote me a handwritten letter telling me how much he enjoyed my food and asked if I would like to come cook at his home for a special dinner for his friends. When Stacey and I drove down the Silverado Trail and turned onto Joe's road in St. Helena, I couldn't believe it. Most wineries have big signs and tasting rooms with lots of people trying to sell you shit. We got to the end of Joe's road, though, and there was this great, big chain link gate with a giant yellow sign that said, "END". I thought for sure I had turned on the wrong street. Then, I noticed the same rock building that was on the card he had sent me, so I opened the gate and we drove in.

As we approached, Joe walked out to greet us. I had to ask.

"How can people find your winery if you don't have any signs?" I pointed back at his don't-fuck-with-me fence.

"Why in the hell would I want anybody to find my winery?" he grunted. I didn't even try to answer that question.

Later that night, Joe took Stacey and me to dinner at Auberge du Soleil. I watched him pay over a hundred dollars for a bottle of his own wine. I asked him why he did that and he said, "Two reasons. One, there's not a better bottle of wine on their list, and I thought we deserved to treat ourselves to the best. Is there something wrong with that?"

"No, not at all. Thank you." I replied.

"Two," he went on, "the more of my wine they sell, the more they're going to buy, so I am just creating more business." It all made perfect sense to me.

The other winemakers would sarcastically call Joe Heitz "Smiling Joe", because they thought he was a little grumpy. I always thought he was a no-bullshit kind of guy and he either liked you or he didn't. I felt honored that he liked me.

When we got back to the winery, he gave us a tour and showed us to the guesthouse. He had a couple of good bottles of wine in there, he said, and invited us to help ourselves. He also showed us a guestbook and asked us both to sign it. Then he left.

I opened a bottle of wine and spent the next hour seeing who else had slept there. I found Robert Lawrence Balzer's name, along with James Beard's and Julia Child's. Everyone that was anyone had signed that book, not just in America but in the world. I thought to myself, *This man could have any chef in the world come to prepare this meal, but he chose me.* It was truly the greatest honor I have received in my entire career.

I woke up before dawn the next morning and it was raining. I had brought my mountain bike with me, so I got dressed and went for a ride. It was a habit now and I would never dream of cooking without riding first.

I went flying down to Beringer Vineyards and placed my hands on the foggy windows to see inside. I felt like a starving man looking in the restaurant window. I had applied to the School for American Chefs at Beringer years before and didn't get accepted. But, there were Madeline Kamman and about ten student chefs. You had to already be a well-established chef to even think about making it into this school. One of her students opened the door and asked if I needed anything, but I said no and peddled away.

For the dinner, I had prepared a lamb consommé and some salmon that I had cured and smoked myself. I had also brought a saddle of a black buck antelope that had been shot just for the dinner and a bottle of my truffles. Joe decanted some phenomenal wines before dinner. I listened to a story about Joe Heitz and Joe Phelps sitting on a roof, drinking a bottle of Madeira from George Washington's wine cellar. It was a very special night for both Stacey and me.

The next day, Stacey and I were invited to attend two luncheons. The first was with Margaret Beaver, Robert Mondavi's wife, and the second was with Dennis Cakebread of Cakebread Cellars. Margaret gave me a very nice Mondavi golf shirt, so I put it on. When I got back to Joe's, he glared at me.

"Come with me." We walked to one of his buildings and handed me a Heitz Cellars shirt. "Now, since you had the audacity to wear a shirt like that on my property, before you leave for Arizona you're going to be polite and stop by to thank the Mondavis for such a fine lunch. Wearing this shirt."

I just laughed, "You know what Joe? I give you my word that I will do just that." And I did.

Chapter 31

MY CREW WAS DOING BETTER than ever and I was selected that year as one of The Best Hotel Chefs in America by The James Beard Foundation. I had gone down to Tuscan for a hot food competition. When I was queued up to compete, I could not believe who the chef was in the kitchen right next to mine. It was Takashi. I was so happy to see him. He had already been cooking for thirty minutes, but he still stopped to shake my hand.

The mystery basket they gave us had a whole Mahi, mussels, chocolate, fresh berries, a few potatoes, shrimp, sea scallops, cream, butter and flour. I saw the mussels and wanted to make *billi bi en croute* the way Takashi had taught me, in honor of him. But there was no saffron. Shamrock was holding a food show downstairs and I asked Edd to go find some saffron. The rules say you can bring an ingredient as long as you bring enough for all of the other chefs. Kind of like bubblegum in grade school.

Edd came back with the saffron, and I offered some to Takashi first. He said, "You're going to make my soup, aren't you?"

"I am."

They gave every competitor an apprentice, but I didn't want mine to screw anything up. I handed her a bag of small water balloons and told her to blow them all up to the size of a baseball and tie them off.

When she was done, I had her dip the balloons in chocolate and place them on a sheet tray, but only halfway. When the chocolate had set, I popped the balloons. I had perfect little chocolate cups to put some marinated fresh berries in for dessert.

Then, I took the Mahi and filled the belly with julienned celery, carrots, and onions. I wrapped the whole fish in parchment paper, and then I covered it in some Sedona red rock clay I had brought with me. I sculpted a killer looking fish out of the clay with gills and scales and placed it in the oven.

I then started my mussel and saffron soup and let it reduce in cream, just like Takashi had shown me. I had taken a class by Jacques Pepin, where he'd taught us how to make puff pastry in a food processor, so I had the dome ready when my soup was done. I then made shrimp and scallop mousse. I rolled a tube of it in cellophane and tied it off tight. Then, I put a potato in a Japanese food slicer until it became one long, continuous strand, just like a shoe string. I wrapped the potato around the outside of the cellophane of the mousse. Another chef was watching me and went to go get the master chefs. He was calling over to them, "Come quick! This guy is about to deep-fry cellophane!"

When the potatoes completely surrounded the tube of mousse, I dropped it in the fryer until the whole thing was crispy. Most chefs don't know that cellophane won't melt in a fryer. I had dropped so many things that were still wrapped in there by accident, I'd figured it out. Anyway, when the potatoes were crispy I pulled out the tube. I cut one end of the cellophane, held the mousse in place with one hand, and I yanked the plastic out of the center of the mousse, just like it was a used rubber. In fact, that's exactly what it looked like.

I sliced my mousse and laid it out on a plate. Now, I had a wonderful shrimp and scallop mousse wrapped in crispy shoestring potatoes. A totally bitchin' first course. Then, I presented Takashi's *billi bi en croute*. When they broke into the dome, it made the whole room smell good.

Finally, I took my big fish sculpture out of the oven and carried it over to the judge's table. I smacked it hard with a meat mallet and broke my sculpture into a million shards. I cut open the parchment paper and the best smell filled the room. Pulling the vegetables out from the belly, I placed some on each of the judge's plates with a portion of fish. I topped it with some brown butter, lemon and fresh chopped parsley. Dessert was already done, so I whipped some cream and piped it on the marinated berries in their cute little chocolate cups.

I not only kicked Takashi's ass, I kicked everybody's ass. Takashi kept saying to the judges, "That's my recipe! That's my recipe!" He didn't care about winning, but he sure wanted the judges to know when they tasted the soup that it was his recipe. I even told them it was definitely his recipe. Takashi took second place and got the silver medal. I was only one point away from a perfect score, and that has only happened twelve times in the history of ACF culinary competitions. I was the captain of the Arizona Culinary Team and on my way to another national competition.

I had also entered in the cold food competition and a sculpture I had made of a covey of quail in flight had taken the silver medal. That night, Edd took me out to a meal at Takashi's restaurant.

Chapter 32

HALLOWEEN CAME AROUND and Stacey was the same thing she always was at Halloween: a fat chef. She was pregnant every year so it was an easy costume. All she had to do was put on one of my jackets. Chelse always wanted to be a princess and Parker always wanted to be an Indian. John wanted to be an Indian too, like Parker. We got him a Teenage Mutant Ninja Turtle costume and he really liked that.

It had been raining for a few days and the creek was overflowing. The creek flooded every year, but this was the worst I had seen. I had recently taken classes and passed the test to be an EMT, and it was nine a.m. when I got my first call as a member of the local volunteer fire department. A truck had been swept off a bridge and into the creek. I left a note for Tracey to do the produce order. I'd recently promoted her to executive sous-chef. She was supposed to have already been there, I figured she gotten held up because of the rain.

I was walking up the creek with a search party and it was raining like hell when a call came over the radio. We were instructed to look for a man in a chef's uniform, who had just been seen gasping for air in the rushing water. I thought about it for a second and realized that Tracey lived at the Rainbow Trout Farm, and she would have had to cross the bridge on her way to work. She also drove a tan Toyota truck, which had been witnessed sliding off the bridge. I knew it was Tracey. I started running up the creek as fast as I could and ran into the search party ahead of me. I was soaking wet and in uniform when I heard over the radio, "Call off the search, we found him and he is running towards us."

"It's not me, it's Tracey! It's Tracey! Keep searching!" I was completely frantic. I was so upset that they pulled me off the search team. Bill Bouller, my instructor from the classes, told me I had to wait at the command center. They weren't going to start looking for two chefs because I couldn't think straight. I sat out in the rain for over five hours because I couldn't stand the thought of telling my crew that we had lost another sous-chef. *Oh God, Tracey.*

It started to get dark and they still hadn't found her. She had been seen bobbing and screaming at different points along the creek, and they pulled her truck out a half mile down from where it had gone in. I went back to the kitchen and told the exact same people who I had told John died, that Tracy had died. I remember Catherine the spa manager said, "You don't know she's dead yet."

"Yes, I do," was all I could reply. "We may not have found her body but I know she's dead." I could feel it.

Three days later, they found Tracey's body under a stack of logs. We had her funeral creekside at the resort. I was getting sick of loved ones dying, and I started doing coke again. Everybody knew it. Everybody knew why and no one said a word about it. I had thirty people all in denial, just like I was.

◊ ◊ ◊

I cannot tell you guys how hard it is for me to write this book. I have always been able to run to drugs to avoid the pain, trauma, and tragedy in my life. Guess what? You have to experience those feelings eventually or it will kill you. The past and reality have a way of catching up with you. So, as I relive my life through this book for the first time, I am really feeling the pain. It's just like it all happened yesterday, and it's no fun. I am clean as a whistle now and I am going to stay that way, but it's like a lifetime of hard work that I have put off until now.

It's been years since I have even thought about the death of my brother Tracey. I may have not cried then, but I sure as hell did when I wrote about it. I loved John and I loved both Traceys. I wish I had mourned for them when I was supposed to.

※ ※ ※

The more coke I did, the bigger a dumbass I became. David Burke was coming to Sedona to stay with us for a while. He had just left the River Café. He was going to open his own place, The Park Avenue Café, and he had some down time in between. David was headed to Napa to do a dinner, and he planned to stay with us en route. When Stacey and I went to pick him up at the airport, we had to stop at The Phoenician so he could stash some of his cured salmon in the walk-in of some mutual friends, Alex Stratta and James Boyce.

After we dropped off David's salmon, I was jonesing for some coke, so I went to Van Brune Street and stopped at a Circle K to buy some beer. I asked a hooker if she knew where to score some coke. This chick just hopped in the van next to Stacey. Stacey jumped out, screaming at me, and started running down Van Bruen.

David told the hooker to get out of the van, and ran into Circle K and bought one of those cheap bouquets of flowers they have at the checkout stand. I pulled up to Stacey and David jumped out and gave her the flowers. He finally got her to get back into the van.

You get all strung out on that shit and you can't even see the way that it changes you. We went back up to Sedona. Elin Jeffords had invited us to dinner. Christopher Gross was there along with Barbara and Terry

Fenzl. The last time we were at Joe Heitz's house, he had asked Stacey what year she was born. She'd told him 1965 and he had come back with a bottle of his 1965 cabernet. We drank it that night with Chris, Elin, David and Barbara. The wine was fantastic, as well as the company. Why wasn't this good enough for me? Why in the hell did I always have to fuck up my life, just when it would be going great?

    I had a beautiful wife who I was madly in love with, and three of the best kids on the face of the earth, with another one on the way. I was one of the top chefs in the nation, I had a great job that flew me all over the country just so I could play with food, and I wasn't even thirty years old yet. Why was this not enough? Why did I have to abuse myself with blow? Unfortunately, it would take a hell of a lot more blow and a hell of a lot more pain, trauma, and tragedy to answer that question.

Chapter 33

I KEPT DOING BLOW AND fucking up. I had gotten so wasted one night at the bar of my own restaurant, I couldn't even sign my own name on the guest check. A couple of days later, Edd found the check and asked me if it was my signature. I honestly couldn't remember. We started looking for a forger when the bartender reminded me of the night they'd had to drive me home.

I had imported wild pigeons from Scotland that had been shot with a shotgun. I spent three days cleaning buckshot out of those birds for a winemaker dinner/comedy show. The pigeon was the first course. I had thought about whether I should call it "pigeon" or "squab". They're the same thing, but most Americans don't know that. I chose to call it "pigeon". Big mistake. There was already a buzz in the room about eating pigeon before I had served anything. I took the birds up to one hundred and fifty degrees Fahrenheit to kill any bacteria, but the meat was like venison: blood red.

I went to the dish machine like I always do after they cleared one of my courses to see how much the guests had eaten. No one—not even one person—had even so much as touched their bird. This had never happened to me before. I had just fucked up big time. I went into the bathroom, laid out a couple of huge rails of coke, and went back into the kitchen and slammed a couple of Styrofoam cups of some expensive champagne. Blow and alcohol kind of even each other out, so believe it or not I wasn't even that drunk. But I certainly was scared to death that I was becoming a failure. I had five more courses to go, and I focused. They were all well received: the plates at the dish machine were empty.

After the meal, they called me and my crew on stage and we received a standing ovation. This was what I was used to. When I got up to the microphone I said, "You can take a guest to the park but you can't make him eat pigeon." Everybody laughed and we went back to the kitchen. Edd got me to come out and listen to the comedy show, so I went and sat down at his table.

The comedian came out and his first joke was about my food, and everybody was yuckin' it up. His second joke was again about my first course and everybody was still laughing. I heard Nancy, Edd's wife, say, "Edd, get Todd out of here." He just ignored her, but she knew that I was about to snap. Then, when his third joke was still about my food, that was it. I had had enough. I stood up and marched over to the stage and got right in this asshole's face. It scared him because he could see how pissed I was and I'm a big guy.

Everyone was still laughing, so I was loud enough to make sure that every one of them heard what I was about to say. "I have been working on those fucking birds for three days, and I failed. Is that what's so funny? Because I failed? You earn more money in one night than I do in a month and that's all you can do? Make fun of my food? You're a fuckin' hack." I turned around and I was mortified. *What had I just done?* The whole ballroom was dead silent except for one-person way in the back: Joe Martori, the owner of the resort. He thought that me screaming at this comedian was far funnier than the actual show.

I just walked through the crowd, and when I opened the door to leave I heard, *click*. The exact same sound that you'd hear when opening the door to an empty ballroom. I had never heard that sound before when it was full.

Nobody could believe what they had just heard and seen. The next morning when I got to work, they took me off property to the fire department and a physiologist said that I needed some help. My choices were: check into an outpatient substance and alcohol abuse program in Flagstaff, or resign. I had a kid on the way, so I chose the program.

❂ ❂ ❂

Flagstaff is almost an hour drive up one of the most beautiful canyons in the world, Oak Creek Canyon. I was entered into a daily outpatient program which started at five-thirty p.m. and ended at nine-thirty p.m. every weeknight. It was group therapy and there was a wide variety of people, most of whom were like me and sent there by their employers.

There was one guy who was seventeen. When I asked why he was there, he told me that his mom had found a little bit of weed in his pants pocket while doing laundry. His mom was the director of the rehab center. Being someone that had smoked weed every day for over twenty years with just about everyone I knew, I thought that outpatient rehab was a ridiculous place for an impressionable teenager to be.

Everyone else was much older and pretty rough. I had been going to class for a little more than a week when some guy got up and confessed to the group that he had slipped back into his evil ways and let the group down. He almost started to cry, and he was being so melodramatic that I thought he had started banging up heroin again or something like that. So I finally said, "Get on with it. What did you do?" He said that he had found half a joint in his garage while moving and he'd lit it up and taken a few puffs.

I started to laugh. "Oh yeah? Well, I found a whole joint in my ashtray. I smoked all of it on the drive up here, just like I do every day, and I am going to find one for the ride down as soon as I walk out this door tonight."

The whole group looked at me like I was the devil. I said, "Look, I am here because I have a problem with cocaine and I agreed to not doing any coke again. I promised not to drink for the six weeks while these classes were going on and I haven't. Nobody said anything about smoking weed." Some fifty-year-old, chronic alcoholic who was an executive at AT&T said, "This is rehab and nobody gets to smoke any weed during rehab." And then I said, "Well, that's a shame, because a lot of you guys could certainly use it to mellow out. Everybody seems way too uptight around here to me." Eventually, I agreed to stop smoking weed too. I honestly thought I was there for blow. In fact, whenever I was jonesing for blow I would just tell myself, *Well at least you have some good weed.* Now what was I going to tell myself? I couldn't drink, I couldn't smoke weed, and I certainly couldn't do blow anymore. I needed a new vice to trade for the other three I had just lost.

The fifty-year-old guy from AT&T would always go out and chew tobacco on break, so one day I told him, "Let me try some of that." It certainly wasn't weed, but it made me feel dizzy. I figured that was better than nothing. I hated cigarettes back then and I had never smoked them in my life.

The counselor that ran this group had no education, no degree in anything; in fact, he was a high school dropout. He was a recovering alcoholic. He would just sit and tell us stories about how he would get drunk and call the White House and bitch at the operator because she wouldn't let him talk to Dwight D. Eisenhower. After repeated calls, he claimed that the Secret Service knocked on his door. I don't know if I believed anything this guy said, and I knew he certainly wasn't qualified to help me with the very complex problem of why I abused myself. It only took me a couple of days to learn to say exactly what he wanted us to say in order to get though the class with as few debates as possible about the real reason people abuse substances.

If someone asked me today why I abused myself all of those years, I would say that I did it to survive the same way that the water snakes ate poisonous newts to survive in Logan Canyon. The newts are so toxic that if a person were to ingest just one drop of their saliva, they would be dead in less than an hour. But, since they're the only thing the snakes have to eat, they do it anyway. The venom paralyzes the snakes for an hour, but at least they survive. So, the snakes have two options: eat the newts or die of starvation. Over the years, there has been an arms race going on: the newts get more and more toxic, and the snakes become more and more resistant to their poison.

I had to teach myself not to feel at a very young age, even in utero, in order to survive. If I hadn't, I surely would have died. So, when drugs came into my life, they were nothing more than an instrument that helped me develop my fine art of avoiding pain. As life would become more toxic, just like the newt, I would build resistance by doing more drugs. I had my own little arms race going on with life's pain and drug use. The ironic thing is that drug use is one of the major contributors to pain. What a predicament.

If someone asked me, "How did you finally institute the peace treaty and the disarmament of pain and drugs to stop the race?" I would say that you don't have to have a painful life any more than the snake has to eat newts. All the snake has to do is change his environment. Find somewhere else that's less painful, somewhere that doesn't paralyze you every time you try to satisfy yourself.

You can find pain in just about everything if that's what you're used to looking for, just as you can find peace in everything, if that's what you're looking for. We get so used to keeping our eye out for pain so we can avoid it, that we walk right by the peace without enjoying it.

At this point in my life, I am a professional peace collector. I explore anything and everything to try to find it, just like Exxon searches for oil. And I tell you, I have one hell of a collection that I am very proud of. The motherlode of peace is the calm, still spirit inside you, but the trick is that you can't have any interference or pollution or you won't feel it. No different than if you put a telescope in the middle of the city; you can't see anything because of the interference of the light pollution. You have to set up in a dark place. You could never hear the nuances of a fine orchestra if they were playing in a subway terminal. You would miss most of it every time the train went by.

The same goes for the peaceful spirit within. Once you master the ability to really feel it, then the pain in life is placed in another position. The pain, then, is what becomes polluted and difficult to receive. It can even be blocked out from the interference of your own spirit of peace and wellbeing.

Now, I am not pretending to think that I am done with the pain in life. If something happened to one of my children, I know it would hurt so bad I wouldn't be able to stand it. What I am saying is that all of the pain from the past isn't getting very much attention from my internal dialogue anymore.

I have slowed down and thought closely about my life and what used to cause me to run to drugs. If I do drugs, then I won't be able to enjoy anything, especially my loved ones, myself, and the natural pleasures in life. By enjoying these simple pleasures, I inadvertently tune out the pain.

I went to all of my sessions and learned that there were about as many different reasons to use substances as there were people in the group. The only thing I regret from the whole deal is the final night. Everyone had to go around the circle and discuss what they had learned from the class. After that, they gave you a medal with the serenity prayer embossed on it. The kid whose mom ran the place asked me for a ride home. When he got in my car, I had a six-pack waiting for me on ice and a joint of Thai weed in the ash tray. I immediately lit up while I was still in the parking lot.

The kid was mortified. "What about everything you just learned?"

"Dude, they are doing nothing but using guilt manipulation to try to stop you from enjoying the few things you can in life. Your mom's the head manipulator. You're not a bad person because you smoke weed and don't ever let anyone tell you that you are."

He wanted nothing to do with the joint and I never offered him a beer, but I did feel guilty for calling his mom a manipulator in front of him.

✦ ✦ ✦

Stacey's due date was two days after my last class, and we lived so far from the nearest hospital that we checked in and the doctor induced labor. Todd Cody Hall was a perfectly healthy, beautiful baby boy. The following nine months in Sedona were very pleasant. I quit senselessly driving myself to get more medals and accolades. I was enjoying my family, riding my bike, and having barbeques with friends at beautiful places. I stayed away from blow for the entire nine months. Maybe the class did help me and I just didn't know it.

Chapter 34

I WAS SCHEDULED TO TEACH a cooking class down in the valley at The Sheraton San Marcos, and a fellow chef named Eddie was teaching a class after mine. The night before our classes, Eddie called another chef named Joe and we all met at a bar. Eddie bought an eight ball of coke and we drank until one in the morning. We went back to Eddie's room and did lines and talked about food until it was time for me to teach my class. So much for my nine-month dry spell, and it's not like anyone had to twist my arm.

I went right back into blow mode as soon as I hit Sedona. I was snorting more than ever before. I was always a happy user, but now I was turning into a miserable prick. My crew told me; my wife tried to tell me. It went on until one night I came home at three in the morning and fell down in the driveway and broke a beer bottle. I had to be at work a few hours later and I had stopped riding my bike.

On her way to drop me off at work, Stacey's expression was strangely blank. "Todd, this has to stop."

"If you don't like it, then you can move."

She didn't say another word.

I got off of work about nine hours later and had one of my cooks give me a ride home. Everything was gone. It had taken us three days to move into that house and somehow she was able to move everything out in nine hours. We had a lot of shit. I was amazed that the house looked just like it did before we moved in: empty.

She had rented a U-Haul and her dad and two brothers had packed everything up and taken her back down to Phoenix. I deserved it. I kept partying for another couple of weeks and it was one of the most miserable times of my life. I missed my kids so much, and I missed Stacey too.

Then the owners of The 8700 called me at my office at the resort and offered me eighty grand a year plus twenty-five percent ownership in the restaurant. I called up Stacey and said if I promised to stop doing blow and staying out after work, and got us a nice house in Scottsdale, would she come back? She agreed.

I told The 8700 that I would do it based on a couple of conditions. Joe Martori had just bought me a new van and it would be rude to leave after receiving such a gracious gift, so I needed them to write a check out to Joe for twenty-five grand so I could keep the van. They agreed, and then I told them I needed ten of the eighty grand up front. They agreed. I leased us a big four-bedroom house with a pool in Scottsdale. I bought a new racing street bicycle and prepared to get cleaned up again.

On my last day at Los Abrigados, I received a telegram from The James Beard Foundation, telling me that I had been nominated as The Rising Star Chef of The Year. I was one of four finalists and I had to go to the awards ceremony held at the Lincoln Center in New York City in a couple of months. I really did need to get cleaned up… and quick.

As soon as we moved in, I rode my new bike to The 8700 every morning to open the doors at six AM. It was seventeen miles from my house. I had to leave my house at five. After I unlocked the door, I would ride another fifteen miles to The Boulders and get some breakfast. I'd make it back to The 8700 by nine or ten. I would work until two, ride home and take a nap, and drive back to work at five. I'd do dinner and come home at nine or ten at night.

This routine cleaned me up. When I flew to New York for the

awards ceremony, I took my bike with me and rode it around central park every morning. The finalists were me, Bobby Flay, his then-wife Debra Ponzek, and Todd English. Debra Ponzek won. I asked Bobby if we were losers. He said, "No, Todd, we're not losers. We're big fuckin' losers." At least I didn't have to sleep with the winner that night, like he did.

I was introduced to Martha Stewart at the Lincoln center in 1992. I had never heard of her before, but the person next to me assured me she was big, very big. One of my regular guests who I had been feeding for years, Mrs. Osafski, flew her private jet to New York just to support me at the awards ceremony. She had bought me this beautiful silk tie with James Beard's face on it. After the ceremony, Jack Daniels threw a private party for all of the chefs at James Beard's home, and I got a chance to finally meet Charlie Trotter. A lot of the time, famous chefs can be arrogant, but Charlie was a very friendly, down-to-earth guy. He had some beautiful food.

The following evening, we went to David Burke's new restaurant, The Park Avenue Cafe. His food was tighter than ever, and the new restaurant was packed. David's creativity goes beyond the food at this place. You can see his tracks all over the restaurant, especially in all of the unique containers he thinks to serve his beautiful and tasty morsels in.

We had a great summer with the kids. I remember Chelse came home one afternoon and asked me, "Daddy, Jennifer has a diving board and a slide at her pool. How come we just have a slide?" I instantly thought to myself, *My God, my children are going to grow up to be Scottsdale Snobs.* I couldn't help using the same line all parents do: "When I was your age..." We all know the rest.

For some reason, I would always equate riding my bike, constantly working, and senselessly driving myself to being clean as doing well, or, at least, semi-normal. In my mind, it had to be true: just look at how well I was doing. I had plenty of money, and I was getting a ton of press since I'd moved back into the valley. The food critic for The Republic had changed, and the new one said of me, "If there's better food out there it's not cheaper, and if it's cheaper it's not better." Perceived value has always been the ultimate compliment for me.

Even though I had not started to do coke again, I was far from clean. Now that I am clean, I have come to the conclusion—and this might sound crazy—that you can abstain from drugs and alcohol and still not be clean. If you can't just relax and enjoy life and your loved ones without having to do anything else, then you are probably not really clean. Restlessness is definitely a symptom of something. I would keep myself so busy, set high goals, and even achieve them, but I never learned to enjoy any of it. I would go from project to project; benefit dinner to benefit dinner; bike ride to bike ride; all nonstop, high-speed and, yes, drug free. As long as you don't consider pot a drug, anyhow.

I was so manic, I couldn't even have a conversation with someone without trying to finish their sentences for them. Even though I hadn't done any blow, I was far from being cleaned up. I had to be so tired when my head hit my pillow that I would instantly fall asleep. I had to leave no chance that I might think of all of the bad things that I had done and had been done to me. I thought this was normal. My entire life, I had never learned to relax. I had gone from a childhood with my defenses always up, for fear of what could happen at any second, to an adulthood where I senselessly drove myself to assure that my children had a better life than I did.

It's just like Don Imus. Even though he quit smoking, he is still addicted to nicotine and has to chew that gum every hour. Even though I was not abusing substances, I was abusing circumstances and opportunities. The real crime here, is that society rewards you for circumstance and opportunity abuse. They have a word for it: success. Sometimes being successful is every bit as self-destructive as being a drug addict. It doesn't matter if you blow off your family because you're on a cocaine binge or because you're on a work binge, you still made a wrong choice. Your children need you a lot longer than a few hours a week.

Cody was eighteen months old now. If you added up all of the consecutive time I had spent with him since he was alive, it wouldn't have amounted to more than a few weeks. I thought this was what I was supposed to do. Although I couldn't see it then, a pattern was starting to develop. I would work like a maniac until I was ready to drop, then I would use coke to pick up the pace until I got fired. If there is anyone to blame here, and you all know how I feel about blaming, it is the person that decided to start the twelve-hour-a-day, six-day-a-week work week for all chefs. Why can't we work eight hours a day, five days a week, like the rest of the world?

I'll tell you why, because selfish restaurant and hotel owners look at their chefs like property. They want them constantly around to show off as often as they can. They want them at every meeting in the morning and at every table at night. They figured out years ago that the more often the chef is in the kitchen, the more money they put in their pockets. Greedy bastards like that have caused many a great chef to sacrifice his or her family, health and personal wellbeing for a job. All this, just so the chef can make more money for his or her "owner". Do you really think the owners of The 8700 *liked* me so much that they were willing to pay me double my original salary? They could have hired another chef for half of that.

I don't think they even liked me at all, but they sure as hell did like the money I made for them and the notoriety I brought to their restaurant. They would constantly say and do anything in their power to make sure I lived at that restaurant, and they were no different than any other restaurant or hotel that I have worked for. I have never once had a general manager, or food and beverage director say, "Hey, Todd, why don't you try to spend more time out of the kitchen and with your family? You have been working seventy hours a week and that's a little too much." They know it's not healthy, and they sure as hell don't do it themselves, yet they ask their chefs to do it. Shame on all of them.

All of you food and beverage directors, general managers, and owners know *exactly* who you are, and you need to stop it. Your chefs are real people, and, even more importantly, they have real families who, thanks to you, they never get to see. I always love the food and beverage director that walks up to you in the morning and says, "Where were you last night at ten? I understand that they had a problem with a table. Oh, I almost forgot to tell you, there's a pop-up pre-con meeting in the executive board room at eight tomorrow morning. Make sure you attend." Do you know how bad I have always wanted to say, "Where are you on any night? Home with your family. Like I should get to be every once in a while."

Chapter 35

IT WAS EIGHT O'CLOCK ON Saturday morning, September fifth of Labor Day weekend. The 8700 had sold out for that night a couple of days ago. I was lying on the couch holding Cody in my arms and feeding him a bottle while watching cartoons with John. Chelse and Parker had already had breakfast and were out riding their bikes in the neighborhood.

Cody may have only been eighteen months old, but he was heavy. His head was twice as big as any other part of his body. He would suck on his bottle for a minute, and then put it in my mouth. I would pretend to suck on it and say, "Yum, this is a great bottle!" And he would yank it out and put it back in his mouth.

It was time to get ready for work, and Stacey had already set up the ironing board and turned on the iron so she could get my chef's jacket ironed before I was out of the shower. I was in the shower thinking of all of the cool food I was going to cook that night and hoping that they didn't send me any shitty produce, when I heard the most God-awful, blood-curdling scream coming from the backyard. It was Stacey, and I knew it. Without even thinking, I ran out of the shower, naked, to the back patio sliding glass door. I never broke my stride and when I saw her in the pool with all of her clothes on, I knew what had happened. I made a flying leap from the shallow end and landed in a perfect dive at about the halfway point. I could see Cody lying on the bottom of the pool under ten feet of water.

I grabbed him in my arms, sprang my feet off the bottom of the pool, laid him on the side, and hopped out. I was trained how to do this, but I had an overwhelming sense of doom. I had to tell myself, "Todd, if you don't settle down and carefully do what you have been trained to do, your son is going to die." Cody was cold and blue. I had resuscitated people before, but never an infant. You can hurt a child worse than they already are if you do it wrong. *Clear the airway, clear the airway, clear the airway.* I gently covered his little nose and mouth with my mouth and slowly blew in until I felt the right amount of pressure, I then placed my hand on his belly and carefully compressed it. He threw up water and choked. I quickly repeated what I had done, and he threw up the formula that I had fed him earlier.

I'm going to do this, I'm going to do this, I'm going to do this. He threw up, coughed, and choked, but he wasn't breathing on his own. I couldn't feel a pulse. *Oh God, Cody, come on son. Just cry, please God, please just cry.* I started full lung resuscitation, coupled with chest compressions, constantly telling myself in perfect rhythm just like a metronome, *Don't blow his lungs out, don't break his ribs, don't blow his lungs out, don't break his ribs, don't blow his lungs out, don't break his ribs.* I was still naked working my son when a paramedic said, "Step aside."

I screamed, "*I'm not stopping until you hand me an infant Ambu bag!*" The paramedic ran back to his truck to get the resuscitating device.

I stepped away when I saw the bag, and the paramedic started bagging Cody. I watched to make sure that he was doing it right. A helicopter was landing, and we put Cody on a gurney. John had been sitting on the other side of the pool watching everything. He was four years old. Stacey was hysterical and tried to climb in the helicopter, I had to pull her back. I already knew that neither one of us would be riding with Cody.

I yelled at the pilot, "Where are you transporting to?" He yelled back,

"Phoenix Children's." Phoenix Children's Hospital in downtown Phoenix. Scottsdale Memorial North was right down the street, but Phoenix Children's Hospital had a trauma center just for near-drowning infants.

Chelse and Parker had run home to see why there was a helicopter at our house. Stacey tried to get the van keys and drive straight to the hospital. I grabbed ahold of her and John, and told Chelse and Parker to get in my room. I had just gotten us all alone when a lady from the fire department walked in and tried to get more information. I screamed, "Get the fuck out of my room." She hurried out. I told everybody to get on their knees against the bed, and led all of us in prayer, begging God to please not take our son and brother. I have never prayed harder or wanted anything more in my life.

My secretary, Mindy, came right over. When we walked out of the room, I told Mindy to stay with the kids. Stacey and I were driving to the hospital.

The lady from the fire department was walking with us, holding her clipboard, and trying to tell us that we couldn't leave yet because she needed to get more information so they could help Cody. I snapped at her, "That's bullshit, they have all of the information they need to save his life, now get the fuck away from my van."

The whole ride to the hospital Stacey kept asking why they didn't take him to the hospital by our house. Why did we have to drive so far? I kept telling her that he was at the best hospital in the world for child drowning.

Most people would be asking themselves, "Oh God, how could we let this happen?" The only thing I could think of was, *Oh God, please let him have low blood gas levels, please God, please let him have a normal pH, low blood gas levels, low blood gas levels, I got there in time, I got there in time, oh God, please let him have low blood gas levels.*

By the time we had parked and gotten to the ninth floor of the hospital, it had been forty-five minutes; an hour and ten minutes since I had pulled Cody out of the water. I ran to the nurse's station and told them who we were. The head nurse stepped up and started her normal child-near-drowning talk that she had to give way too often to hysterical parents.

I didn't give a shit that he was on a resuscitator, or that they had done this, or that they had done that; the one and only thing I wanted to know was what in the fuck the pH level of his blood was.

"What were his blood gas levels?"

She looked me right in the eye and lied, "I am not certain what his blood gas levels are."

"Bullshit, where's his chart? The first thing you did when he hit your floor was draw blood and send it to the lab. That takes ten minutes. What are his blood gas levels? Where is the toxicity report from the lab?" Stacey had gone into the room where they were working on him.

Finally, the nurse walked me over to the stand without saying a word and handed me the lab report. His gasses were off the chart. Cody was dead. He was still lying in bed breathing from artificial resuscitation and his heart was beating, but I knew beyond the shadow of any doubt that Cody had died. It is impossible for anyone to survive that long without oxygen to their brain. We had all worked our asses off to keep him alive and he still didn't have any oxygen in his brain.

I told Stacey that Cody had died, and she slugged me in the chest. She screamed, "He did not! He's right there! He'll be fine! How could you say something like that?" I remembered watching technical training videos while I was studying to be an EMT, of fourteen-year-old kids who had been vegetables on life support for twelve years because they fell into a pool when they were two. I told myself right there in that classroom that that was the cruelest thing you could do to a person. Let the dead rest in peace, regardless of what kind of machines we invent to keep someone's heart beating and lungs breathing.

Cody's heart had stopped beating at the bottom of that pool and I was the one who decided to make it beat again, not God. Cody's soul left his body right after he took his last breath, before he fell in the water. A perfectly innocent soul, I might add.

You can make a heart start beating again, you can keep blowing air into someone's lungs, and after a while you can even get their blood to start flowing again. But once their brain has gone over thirty minutes without any oxygen, they have died. Period, end of story. *Their brain has died.* That's not life; that's a hollow, soulless shell being driven by machines. It has absolutely nothing to do with being alive.

I knew this. It wasn't something I heard on the street, it was something I had been trained in by professional instructors, and they tested me to make sure I had a clear understanding of it. Now I just needed to figure out how in the hell I was going to come to grips with it and make Stacey understand that that wasn't our son in there.

The chief physician of the intensive care trauma unit had been standing next to us, listening to us fight, without ever saying a word. Finally, he took a deep breath and said, "I need to speak to both of you alone."

As we were walking towards a little chapel in the intensive care unit, he asked me what I did for a living.

All I could say was, "Does anything even matter anymore?"

We sat down and he started, "This might sound cold and insensitive to you right now, but it's my job to make sure you both have a very clear understanding of the situation here. Mrs. Hall, I am so sorry to say that your husband is right. Cody has died. It may appear to you that he has a chance, and, please believe me when I tell you that if for even a moment I thought that he did, we would not be having this conversation." Stacey was now screaming hysterically. After she was able to settle down, he continued, "In the state of Arizona, by law we are only able to discontinue life support within the first twelve hours upon receiving the patient. After twelve hours, you need a court order signed by a judge to discontinue life support. Unfortunately, I have seen many parents so consumed by grief that they were unable to make that decision in the timeframe. The worst thing that can ever happen to you is to have your situation be compounded and dragged out for weeks, months, or even years at a time. Cody has irreversible brain damage. He will never speak, move, laugh, eat or breathe on his own again. We need both of you to make the right decision and consent to discontinuing life support."

I stood up, "Do it now, unplug it right now." Stacey started slugging me and screaming, "No, no, oh God, no…"

The doctor tried to console her, "Please don't misunderstand me, you don't have to make this decision now. It's noon. You have nine more hours until there's nothing that any of are able to do. I am going to leave you alone to discuss this in private."

Stacey just started to beg me, "Please, Todd, don't do this, don't kill my son."

"Stacey I love you so much, please understand that Cody has already died, please…"

This was the longest nine hours of my life. Stacey said one word at eight fifty-eight p.m., "Ok." I told the doctor to take him off. Todd Cody Hall died in Stacey's arms ninety minutes later at ten-thirty p.m. on Saturday, September fifth of Labor Day weekend.

Quietly, Stacey told me then that earlier that morning when she'd taken my chef's jacket out to lay it on the bed while I was in the shower, she had noticed John hiding in the closet. He was peeking through the door, looking like he had done something very wrong.

She opened the door and asked him what was wrong and he wouldn't answer, so she started looking for Cody. When she noticed the pool gate had been opened, she ran out and saw him at the bottom of the pool. She jumped in, but couldn't reach him with all her clothes on, so she surfaced and screamed as loud as she could.

The latch on the pool gate was four feet high and there was a toy inside that John had wanted, so he'd gotten a milk crate from the back patio and stood on it to unlatch the gate. He'd gone to get his toy without realizing that Cody had followed him out there. There was a plastic ball floating at the deep end of the pool and Cody had tried to walk out and get it.

When John heard Cody fall in, he was afraid of getting in trouble because he knew he wasn't allowed to be at the pool without one of us. So, he hid in the closet.

We drove from the hospital and picked up the kids. I drove to the Hyatt Regency Scottsdale. I walked in the hotel kitchen while Stacey and the kids waited in the car, and of course Anton was still there. He had already heard what happened. I told him we needed a room. He nodded and told me to go get my family and meet him at the front desk. He gave us a four-bedroom casita. We finally got the kids to sleep, but Stacey and I didn't sleep that night or the next few nights.

We stayed at the Hyatt for the next day and night while we made the funeral arrangements. I kept thinking of what I had failed to do right, and for the first time I realized why I had gone to so much trouble to become a certified emergency medical technician. The only thing that could have possibly been worse than what had happened would have been to have just stood at the side of the pool, not knowing what to do. I did know what to do and I had done it all correctly.

Cody was born in Sedona, and we could not think of a more beautiful place to bury him. I always go up to Sedona to visit the grave, and every time it still kind of creeps me out to see the name Todd Hall on a headstone. L'Auberge De Sedona made accommodations for all of Stacey's family and Los Abrigados made accommodations for all of my family.

We held Cody's funeral creekside at the exact same place we had held Tracy's funeral the year before, with most of the same people present. My grandpa was in a wheelchair and couldn't breathe without an oxygen machine, but he still made it to the funeral. That was the last time I ever saw him.

All of my brothers and sisters showed up and it was the first time we had been together in many years. Both resorts comped all of the rooms. Stacey's family behaved and left respectably. My family cleaned out the mini bars, made phone calls and room charges, and some of them split without even checking out or paying for anything.

Chris had graduated his apprenticeship a few weeks before all of this happened. I had offered to make him my sous-chef, but he declined. It was very bad luck to be my sous-chef, I guess. Nevertheless, he was still in charge of The 8700 while I was gone. My first day back to work, Chris told me that Robert Keyes, the owner, had been telling people that my son had drowned because my wife and I were on drugs.

I went ballistic. I ran over to the bank where his office was, blew right past his secretary, and flung open his closed door. He was sitting in there with his bank manager.

I just screamed, "So I hear you've been telling people that my son died because my wife and I were on drugs."

"I didn't say it like that."

I didn't lower my voice one decibel, "*Then how did you say it, Bob?*"

"Look, Todd, we can clear all of this up. I will recant what I said if you just go right now and take a drug test. If the results are negative, then we will all know that drugs had nothing to do with your son dying."

"I have nothing to do with my son dying. Who in the fuck do you think you are? Only God knows why my son had to die, and you are not in charge of what happened at my house. You are the coldest, most insensitive person on the face of this earth, and you can take your drug test and go fuck yourself with it."

I never stepped foot in The 8700 again. We had just gotten done with feeding the kids breakfast on a Saturday morning and we were watching cartoons. No one had done any drugs. No one had smoked any pot. No one was even hung over. We were both getting ready to start our day with our children, just like we did every Saturday morning.

None of us knew how to act anymore; I just kept telling myself that I had to be the man of the family and take care of everybody. Stacey would not talk, smile, or laugh. She could do nothing but cry for what seemed like forever.

A wealthy friend of mine offered to open a restaurant for us right next to the Hyatt. He was an importer, but he could get a tax credit up to one hundred and fifty thousand dollars for creating a new small business.

So, we opened Todd's New American Cooking on Halloween night, only seven weeks after Cody had died.

Chapter 36

I WOULDN'T LET STACEY or the kids out of my sight, so I converted the dry storage room into a playroom, and the kids stayed right there at the restaurant with us every night. I had never been big on canned food anyway. It hurt so fucking bad for so very long; I could not believe that this excruciating pain would not pass. On January first, my backer pulled out. He had invested all that he could get credit for. He wished us luck and said goodbye.

I hadn't done any coke yet, but I was drinking a whole bottle of Tanqueray a night and constantly smoking pot. When our partner bailed, I just lost it. I started shooting up coke after everyone had gone home. Stacey would take the kids home, and I started coming home later and later every night. She went back to the restaurant and caught me with a needle in my arm.

She didn't really even freak out, she just took me home. I just stayed at home for the next four or five days and shot about a half ounce of coke into myself. Stacey would pick the kids up from school and go straight to the restaurant. She came home and said that I had to stop or I was going to die. I think that was actually my plan. She told me that I was the only one that knew how to do the batch report on the credit card machine, and there was over forty thousand dollars in it. If the power went off, then we would lose it all.

I dumped what coke I had left in the toilet and told her I would take care of it in the morning. That night, Stacey rolled over next to me in bed and I was burning up. She took my temperature and it was over a hundred and four. I had two bright red stripes running down the center of both of my arms. She took me to the hospital, told them what I had been doing, and I was rushed to emergency surgery. I had pumped coke not only into my veins, but into my muscle tissue. It had gone septic.

"Septic" means you have puss flowing in your blood and it can stop your heart instantly. They gave me two one-hundred-percent blood transfusions and made ten three-inch lacerations on the inside of my arms, five on each arm. They spent the next five hours sucking all of the puss and bacteria-infested blood clots out of the muscle tissue and fat. My doctor later told me that it was so rotten in there, it made the operating room stink until they couldn't stand it. I have the most horrific scars on both of my arms to always remind me of how close I came that night.

My doctor said that my bloodwork was so bad that they honestly thought that I wasn't going to make it. I found out later that my grandfather was in an emergency room and died at the exact same time that they thought I was going to die. I was in the hospital for over a week and I missed his funeral.

I had a friend from a hotel go to my restaurant and do my batch report; we hadn't lost the money. When I was finally able to make it back to the restaurant, I did a winemaker dinner with Joe Heitz. Minnie Lane, a guest and friend of mine, attended the dinner and told me she wanted me to meet her at her hotel for breakfast in the morning.

The next morning, she handed me ten thousand dollars and told me that it was none of her business, but she thought I should close the restaurant and take a little better care of my family. I took her advice and we just locked the door and never went back. We moved back to Utah. The Hotel Utah had been closed for over ten years, and the Mormon Church had just done a fifty-two-million-dollar renovation on it. They had asked me to re-open it for them. They had converted all of the rooms to office space, but they still had the two restaurants: The Roof and The Garden. I opened them up with great success, and after about nine months I started doing coke again.

Right when I started to do coke, I was diagnosed with Planter Carcinoma. I had a tumor growing on the bottom of my foot. The cells were multiplying at such a slow rate, they were certain that it was isolated to my foot. I had surgery and I couldn't walk for about a month.

When I returned to work at The Hotel Utah, they sat me down and very gently discussed my addiction. They handed me a large severance and wished me well. I knew I had to get the hell out of Utah; it was just too easy to get drugs. I wanted to stop so badly, but I just couldn't stand the pain. I knew I just couldn't keep running, but I did anyway.

I called Bradley Ogden in San Francisco and asked him if he knew of any work. He told me that he had heard of a lady named Erna who owned a Relais & Châteaux in Yosemite. She was having a winemaker dinner that weekend with Far Niente, and her chef had just walked out on her.

I called Erna and she flew me out the next morning to do the dinner. I had already known Dirk the winemaker for years, as well as Gill, the owner of Far Niente. I had done dinners with them before in Sedona, and I was also one of the chefs featured in their *Dolce* cookbook.

After the dinner, Erna offered me a job. She gave me five grand upfront and rented us a beautiful home on Bass Lake. Our new home had a mile-long private dirt road that only lead to us. It was right, smack-dab in the middle of Sierra National Forest. I went back to Bountiful to get Stacey and the kids. We had four and a half acres, and all of the land surrounding us was national forest. We had a creek running right next to our house, and we had to drive across a bridge to get to our front door. There was no television. My children were about to learn what it was like to live in the middle of the mountains, just like I did when I was a kid.

Erna's resort was just like L'Auberge, only smaller. It had been open for ten years and we would have all kinds of famous people staying there. Wolfgang Puck would even come up and stay with us. I felt great, and I hadn't even thought about doing coke. Everybody smoked a lot of pot, and they all grew it themselves. Although nobody did any coke at Bass Lake, everybody was doing this new drug called meth. When an inversion would come in, you could smell it cooking, in the air. There were hundreds of meth labs all over the forest. The whole fuckin' town was totally spun.

The first time I tried meth, Stacey and I were at this little bar called the Snowline. A guy in the bathroom was snorting a white powder.

"Hey, man. Want a line?"

"Sure." I thought he meant coke. I snorted it and it just about ripped my face off. It scared me. I didn't know what I had just snorted, but I sure as hell knew it wasn't coke.

He thought I was going to slug him, "I'm sorry, man, I thought you knew it was meth."

"You should cut that shit with some rat poison to mellow it out," was all I could manage to say.

The second time I did meth was at work. One of the waiters thought it would be funny to put a quarter gram in my diet Snapple on a very busy night without telling me. I called everybody outside, and said, "I don't know how it happened, but I am fuckin' flying. I want to know which one of you did this to me." Pat confessed, and I told him not to ever do that again. I couldn't sleep for two days.

Chapter 37

I HAVE LEARNED MANY THINGS in my drug-induced career. I think most people think of a drug addict as someone who has constantly and consistently used drugs. This very well may be the case for some addicts. But I had definitely developed a legible pattern, and if you designed a model of my drug abuse, the graph would have very consistent valleys and peaks. I would go six months without using at all, and then I would have three months of light use, similar to a recreational drug user. Then, three months of hardcore abuse.

Now, if we designed a model of my work habits, it wouldn't look very different from the drug abuse model. I would work ten to twelve hours a day, five or six days a week for the six months I was clean; then I would work twelve to fifteen hours a day, six or seven days a week when I was a recreational user. I'd burn out a few months later, unable to work at all; then I'd get cleaned up and do it all over again.

In the first chapters of this book I was adamant in expressing that it doesn't matter why people choose to abuse themselves. I didn't just wake up one day and say it doesn't matter why; for years on end, I spent three months of every year abusing drugs in the most self-destructive way, asking myself, *Why am I doing this?* I came to the conclusion that I had so many reasons that I couldn't tell which the culprit was. It's kind of like going to a police lineup with eight identical clones and trying to identify the one who mugged you. Maybe it was all of them, and the information does nothing to help stop the abuse.

I had just started the recreational part of my cycle with Erna. The only difference was that I had a new medium to create my artistic self-destruction with: methamphetamine. There has been a spiritual arms race going on since the beginning of time, and the creation of meth has placed the darker side way in the lead. Meth is as American as Harley Davidson and apple pie, created by Americans, for Americans. In the beginning, you wouldn't find it in the dark alleys of the city streets; you found it in your local trailer park or construction site.

It kills me to see CNN all worried about things like the bird flu pandemic. You will hear them say, "Twelve died here", or, "Ten died there." Meth kills thousands every single day, all over the world. That's the pandemic that I am worried about. I truly believe that methamphetamine will be the decline of Western civilization as we know it. If you get hooked on meth, you will wish you had the bird flu.

I think the reason it never makes the news is because it has its roots in white trash America and that's something no one likes to talk about. It doesn't matter where its roots are; it has grown into a blossoming vineyard with its vines reaching out and grasping every part of society, all over the world.

Some people can do meth for a long time without screwing up their lives (if you call a couple of years a long time). The first year you can buy a half gram for forty bucks and it will last you a week. You can go to work; you can function in society. The only thing you can't do is stop doing meth. Even if it's just one small line every morning, you still need to have one small line every morning.

Here's the breakdown of the meth food chain. Every day in Arizona, there are twenty-five people who either die or are permanently incapacitated because of meth. There are many more who would have died if they hadn't been arrested—not for possession, sales, or use, but domestic violence, sex offenses, burglary and sophisticated, fraudulent schemes. Tweakers stay up all night long for days on end, thinking of sneaky ways to steal from everyone else. Just ask anyone who works at a credit card company about the escalation in fraud associated with the use of methamphetamine.

For every thousand users in jail, there are five thousand bringing their schemes to fruition in society, who won't even be arrested for the next six months. For every five thousand of these tweakers, there are ten thousand who are still able to hold down jobs. They look spun and they're starting to lose their teeth, but they have been hardcore users for over five years. You see them working at auto parts stores and convenience stores, in landscaping and mechanics, and at junk yards and construction sites. They will lose their jobs and advance to the next level of professional schemes, in no time.

For every ten thousand tweakers who have used for over five years, there are twenty-five thousand who have used for less than two years that you wouldn't be able to identify if they were living in the same house as you. A lot of them are high school and college students. This drug sneaks up on you and you honestly think that you're going to be fine. Only one in four meth users is able to kick it for a year or more.

Chapter 38

BY THE TIME I WAS BURNT out and ready for my hardcore cycle, meth wasn't giving me the rush I needed. I had only been using it for a few months, and in the beginning it doesn't make you feel really high when you do it. It makes you feel a little bit high for a really long time. I needed some coke.

I drove a hundred miles down to Fresno on a Super Bowl Sunday morning and tried to pimp rocks of crack off the street. I asked this lady on the street corner if she knew where to score, and she told me that for twenty bucks she would send someone over to my van. I agreed. In a couple of minutes, a fourteen-year-old kid hopped in the passenger side of my van and pointed a gun at me.

My first thought was to try and grab the gun, but I didn't want to give him any reason to shoot me.

The kid shoved the gun in my face. It was almost touching me. "Give me all of your money and I will get out of the van." I just stared at him and thought about it for a second.

"Fuck you. Go ahead and kill me, I am not giving you my money."

I put the van in gear and started to pull out. I then heard the loudest noise that I have ever heard, and it scared the shit out of me. My ears were ringing so bad, I thought I was deaf.

Then he shot again. I was going about twenty miles an hour and he had opened his door. I slammed on the brakes and he smacked the windshield. Turning around and with both feet, I kicked him out of the van and he fell on the ground on his back. He shot a third time; this shot hit me right in my chin and knocked my head back so hard, I thought I'd broken my neck. I hit the gas and started looking for a pay phone. It was Sunday morning and the downtown streets were empty.

I started to get gas pains and I felt something warm all over my belly; my tongue was starting to swell, and I was having a hard time breathing. I pulled up my jacket and I was soaked in blood. My God, I'd thought he'd missed the first two times. How in the hell is it possible to get shot twice in the abdomen and not feel it? I'd just taken two thirty-eights in the gut and I didn't know I was even shot, until I took one in the head.

I went from feeling gas pains to feeling like someone had shoved a branding iron all the way through me. It started to burn so fuckin' bad, I couldn't stand it. I started to get really scared and driving fast as hell. The first car in front of me was a cop car so I started honking my horn and flashing my lights, but he wouldn't pull over.

We went through three intersections before he finally stopped his car in the middle of the road, jumped out, and drew his gun on me. In the middle of the road, he yelled, "Get out of the car!" He was wearing a camouflage jumpsuit that said Gang Task Force.

I screamed, *"I've been shot!"*

"How do you know?" One of the all-time stupidest questions I have ever been asked.

I just pulled my jacket up and I was soaked in blood. He hurried and grabbed his radio and called for an ambulance.

After that, he came over to me. "Sir, I need you to lie down."

"I don't want to lay down," I snarled at him. It was burning so bad; I couldn't stand it anymore, so I started to pace around my van.

"Fine, do what the fuck you want."

When the ambulance arrived, there were a ton of cops all around me, asking the same two questions: "Who shot you? Where did you get shot, before you drove here?" A news camera was filming me and a reporter was sticking a microphone in my face. I just yelled, "Everybody get the fuck away from me!"

I was so happy to finally get to lay down on the gurney, and they slid me into the ambulance. I had been on lots of ambulance rides, but never as a patient. I was totally exhausted. The more tired I got, the less pain I was in. I was so fucking tired, I couldn't keep my eyes open anymore and all of the voices were becoming very hard to hear.

I was just about ready to fall asleep when that scripture came into my mind and I thought, *Father, forgive them, for they know not what they do.* Fuck that, I was going to kill that little bastard if I ever saw him again. Jesus may have been able to think that, but not me. I was going to kill that prick just as soon as I could stand up again.

My ears finally quit ringing and I felt great. I was just going to catch a nap for a minute on the ride to the hospital. I couldn't remember ever feeling that tired before. I was about to fall asleep when my internal dialogue said, *Wait a minute, you stupid fuck. If you take a nap right now, you're going to wake up dead. You're not sleepy; you're fucking dying.*

I said to myself, *I have a point here. I had better try to stay awake.* My next thought was very weird. I wasn't that worried about dying, but suddenly very glad that I never actually finished paying the IRS. I started to picture Stacey getting remarried and being happy. Then I pictured the guy she remarried trying to rape Chelse, and I went crazy. I was not only wide awake, then—I was fuckin' pissed.

Then I was able to hear things again, and the first thing I heard was some lady paramedic screaming, "He's fifty over sixty, he's dumping! He's dumping! We're losing him!"

I screamed back, "I'm not fucking dumping, and you are not ever supposed to say that! What in the fuck is wrong with you? You're never supposed to tell the victim that he's dying!"

Then the guy sitting next to me said dryly, "It doesn't sound like you're losing him to me."

The ambulance doors ripped open and they wheeled me into the emergency room. Twenty different people were talking at once as each and every one of them was shoving something up a different orifice of my body. All of them were asking me, "What are you on? What are you on? What drugs have you taken?"

I told them, "Nothing."

They wouldn't quit asking me, "You have to tell us. You won't be in trouble. Just tell us what you're on."

I finally said, "Look, I love drugs and I take them all of the time, every chance I get. I was trying to get drugs when I was shot and that didn't really work out so well, so just fuckin' believe me when I tell you that I am not high right now." No one asked me that question again.

The next thing I remember is the scissor lady. She had a pair of scissors that could cut through steel. She started at my jacket and in one slick swoop, she was at my boots. I had just spent three hundred dollars on those ostrich boots and I sure as hell wasn't going to let her cut them up. I sat right up, pulled them both off, and threw them across the room. One boot knocked over a little wheeled cart with all kinds of utensils on it.

Sitting up ripped out every single tube that they had just spent the last five minutes shoving into me. The head dude got pissed and yelled, "Alright that's it, strap him down and knock him out!" In less than one second, some big ass black dude pinned me to the bed while someone else strapped me down so tight I thought it would kill me, if the bullets didn't. Another person held a mask to my face and I fell asleep.

It seemed like I was only asleep for a second when I woke up. I was in the recovery room, but I had no idea why. I was so thirsty, I thought I was in the middle of the Sahara dessert. A nurse walked by and I asked her, "Why am I here?"

"You're in the recovery room."

"I know I'm in a recovery room. I didn't ask where, I asked why."

Matter-of-factly, she stated, "You were shot."

Oh my God, it wasn't a dream. I'd had a dream that I had been shot just before I woke up.

I asked, "Am I all right?"

"You seem to be," she replied. "You were in surgery for over six hours."

"Hurry, pull the blanket off of my feet," I told her. She looked at me funny, but she put the end of the blanket on my knees so I could see my feet. I hurried and wiggled my toes. *Nice, I wasn't paralyzed.*

"Did they take anything out of me?"

She nodded. "You lost half of your intestine, half of your spleen, and at least half of your blood."

"They all grow back, right?" She said she thought so.

"I am so thirsty and my tongue is swollen. I have to have some water."

"You can't have any water, and your tongue is swollen because somebody shot it." *Oh fuck, that was worse than being paralyzed. What if I couldn't taste?* I hurried and licked some dried blood that was on my hand next to the IV. I couldn't taste any blood, but I sure as hell could taste the betadine they had wiped on my hand before they shoved the IV in. It was nasty; I could taste just fine.

The nurse gave me a funny look. "Why are you licking yourself?"

"I had to make sure I could still taste."

She started laughing, "Are you going to lay there and check out all of your body parts to make sure they're working?"

"As many as I possibly can." She then tried to explain to me how the morphine pump worked. I had already hit it a couple of times, but it only worked every half hour.

The next thing that happened was one of the all-time strangest coincidences that has ever occurred in my life. A guy was rolling me from the recovery room to my room and we stopped to wait for an elevator. There was a TV mounted on the ceiling and the news was on. Right when I looked up, I saw myself being rolled into the ambulance. When I saw my boots on TV, it made me wonder where they were. I remembered taking them off in the emergency room.

Later, in the recovery room, Stacey just stood over me and cried, "Don't you dare leave me alone with these kids, Todd." We were in a disgusting, dark room. There were about eight other beds and there was a Sheriff's Deputy standing guard.

Lying there, I motioned to him, "Did I get arrested while I was sleeping?"

"No," he replied, "but all of these guys have been arrested."

"Why am I in the infirmary, then?"

"This is where they put all of the people involved in drug-related crimes."

I was in that room for forty-eight hours. Finally, I told Stacey that I was going home, and that I was in a bad hospital. My doctor told me I couldn't. I said I knew that he couldn't hold me there against my will.

I was fed-up and miserable. "Stacey, go park out front and get me a wheelchair."

"No, Todd."

I wasn't taking that for an answer, though. "Don't make me get up and get my own chair, Stacey." She went and got one.

We left the hospital after midnight, and we were back at Bass Lake by two thirty. The doctor on the graveyard shift handed me a prescription for morphine when he saw me wheeling down the hall towards the door. We filled it at a twenty-four-hour pharmacy before we left Fresno.

I was waiting at the door at the Bass Lake medical clinic when they opened the following morning. There was a semi-retired doctor there, who used to work trauma at Cook County General Hospital. He x-rayed me and told me they had only taken one of the bullets out; there were still two in me. He would wait a few weeks until I had a chance to recover, and then remove them as an outpatient surgery. He told me I needed to come down to his office every day for the next week so he could make sure I wasn't starting to have complications. He gave me a prescription for some very strong morphine and a shot.

I was trapped like a rat in bed for over two months. For the first time in my life, I couldn't run away from myself by going to work or staying busy. The only thing I could do was lie there and think.

My mom called me while I was still in the hospital. At the time, she acted all pissed off because I was going to inconvenience her with a trip to Bass Lake. She demanded, "What do you want me to do, Todd?" I just told her to do what she wanted. She never came out, nor did she even call more than once a month. Ever since I left my house at seventeen, my mom has called me once a quarter, just the same as your tax accountant does. She keeps the conversation superficial. She may ask how you're doing, but if you say anything besides "great" she hurries and says, "I love you honey. I got to run."

I lay in bed thinking that if one of my children had been shot three times, not hell or high water could keep me from them. Stacey's parents got in their truck immediately and drove twelve hundred miles to make sure I was all right. Stacey's mother had just had a facelift and wasn't even supposed to travel yet.

I often looked out my bedroom window at this seven-hundred-year old oak tree we called Big Bob, and asked myself why I was even born. Pretty soon, the kids would come hop in bed with me and tell stories about their latest adventure in the woods. Then, I knew exactly why I was born.

I thought I was supposed to die when I poisoned myself back in Scottsdale, and I thought for sure I was supposed to die when I was shot. Then I realized, it was just like when I tried to fire Misha: God wasn't going to let me off the hook that easy. He was going to sit and watch me while I buried myself with drugs. I came to the conclusion that I was never going to get to die. If I got on an airplane and it crashed, I would be the only one still alive, crawling through the carnage.

Physically, I was a lot more messed up than I realized. My doctor told me that he was not going to release me for work for another six to nine months. If I lifted over ten pounds, I would rip up what little guts I had left and I would be back in the hospital. Of course, everybody was constantly telling me how lucky I was. Funny, I didn't feel very lucky.

Chapter 39

THE VICTIMS OF VIOLENT CRIME ACT allowed me all the free counseling I wanted. I had had a gutful of myself and I wanted as much as I could get my hands on. I selected Dr. Jill Shearson. She was a professor at UC Davis, but she also had a home at Bass Lake and she would spend half of the week at each place.

At this point my life was so fucked up, I was her dream patient. I had never been to a shrink before so I had nothing to gauge it with, but there was one thing I knew for sure: this lady was smart. She would not only get the finest subtleties of my passive aggressive humor, she saw right through it as a tool I had developed at a very young age to help intimidate and control those I was trying to communicate with.

I went to Dr. Jill twice a week for almost a year, and I honestly think we both kept each other on our toes. At that time in my life, she had certain theories that I called bullshit on. Now, years later, I'm thinking, *Wow, there might have been something to that*. Kind of like when Roget would teach me something about food that was too complex for me to understand yet. By no means did I agree with everything she tried to feed me, but a lot of it made sense. Some things were borderline questionable, but she always had text after text to back her theories up with. Dr. Jill was just like an attorney who used case ruling after case ruling to try to win the verdict.

The first order of business was my family, so she had all of them come in multiple times. In the beginning, she wanted to see just John, Stacey and me. She was deeply concerned with John feeling responsible for Cody's death. Stacey hated talking about it at all, but she went to the sessions.

Four or five sessions all boiled down to John coming to the conclusion on his own terms that Cody's death wasn't his fault, rather than us telling him that it wasn't his fault. He would sit there and play with his toys. One day, Dr. Jill asked him, "Hey, John, when you grow up are you going to have any kids?"

John shrugged. "Sure."

She continued, "When your kids are four years old, are you going to let them open the gate to the pool?"

John wouldn't even look up. "I am not going to have a pool."

"John, just pretend that you have a little four-year-old boy and you also have a pool. Do you think that you would let him open the gate?"

John got pissed and said, "No, four year olds are too young to open the gate. They might die."

Dr. Jill nodded. "John you're a very smart young man, you are absolutely right."

All of this was just tearing Stacey and me up. Dr. Jill wasn't done, though. "John, please remember that this is just pretend, but I have one more question to ask you: if your little four-year-old boy learned how to open the gate and something bad happened to him, whose fault would it be?"

John quickly responded, "My fault. Four-year-olds don't know. I am his Dad."

"That's right John, four-year-olds are too young to know, aren't they?" John nodded his head in agreement.

Dr. Jill then commented on what a talented artist he was, and they talked a moment about the picture he was drawing. Then she softly asked,

"John, whose fault was it that Cody died?" John just pointed his crayon at Stacey and me. She pushed, even more quietly. "Why?"

John answered, "Because four-year-olds are too young to know."

"That's right, John, four-year-olds are just way too young to know how to open the gate, aren't they?" John nodded.

Stacey and I were both bawling. Dr. Jill handed us some tissues. "I'm sorry that I put you guys through that, but please keep in mind that it's just not about you." Stacey never went back to Dr. Jill.

I looked forward to our appointments for no other reason than they got me out of bed. I was having reoccurring nightmares about the shooting. I had to get shot again at least a dozen times until they stopped. I also started to get very bad panic attacks. One time I was sitting in the car, waiting for Stacey while she was in the store, and a teenager started to approach the van to ask me a question. I freaked out. I honestly thought he was going to try and kill me. I screamed, "Stay the fuck away!" and rolled the window up and locked the door. I think I scared him more than he scared me. I thought to myself, *What has happened to me? I'm a pussy. I'm scared of my own shadow.* I would become so filled with anxiety, it would take ten hours to settle down. A car backfired once and I thought for sure I had been shot again.

I also started to become very paranoid about the safety of the children if they weren't home from school at exactly three thirty. The bus would drop them off right at the end of our road, but I was just certain that a bear or cougar had gotten them.

I was sick of being scared every time our dog sneaked up on me. I stumbled onto something that made me settle right down on my own. I had just experienced a panic attack and someone I was with was smoking a cigarette. I blurted out, "Give me one of those!" I don't know if it was the nicotine, the arsenic, the strychnine, the rat poison, or any one of the other four hundred and ninety-six chemicals they put in these shit sticks, but it worked. I immediately settled right down. I have always hated cigarettes, and I hate them even more now that I'm addicted to them. I am still the only person I have ever met who started smoking at age of thirty-five. My only consolation is that I'm thinking that something else will probably kill me before they do.

Dr. Jill was a true professional. She would prescribe one antidepressant, check my blood to make sure that the levels were right, and then ask how it made me feel. If it didn't work, she would try another. None of them seemed to give me any relief. In that year of my life, I was on Prozac, Paxil, Depakote, Effexor and Lithium, but none of them stopped the panic attacks. I was committed to this program and for the first time in my life I wasn't self-medicating; Dr. Jill was medicating enough for both of us. I wasn't even smoking pot.

Dr. Jill's number one theory that she was always trying to sell to me was about the powers of *in utero*. Please understand I am a chef, and probably the only thing that I am worse at than writing, is explaining something while writing. I am quite certain that I am about to butcher the shit out of Dr. Jill's explanation of *in utero*. In fact, I don't even know how to spell the words right. *Utero* is not in spell-check, so now I will proceed to butcher it some more until my editor fixes it.

Dr. Jill claimed that giraffes evolved from a type of deer. When the mother giraffe was pregnant, she would be afraid that her baby would not be able to reach the leaves on trees. Over centuries of worrying about it, Dr. Jill asserted that giraffes actually changed genetically and grew longer necks and legs. I didn't think it had anything to do with *in utero*, but everything to do with the fact that the ones who were able to reach the leaves got to eat. The giraffes who ate well lived long enough to mate.

"You were born with a genetic, burning desire to feel attached, wanted, and good enough," Dr. Jill would begin. "We are all naturally born with these same desires, and we need these things to survive. The difference with you is that someone tried to take the most crucial, emotional aspects of life away from you while you were developing in the womb. In fact, your mother tried to take life itself away from you. She continued with her plan by not respecting your needs growing up, but that had far less to do with your behavior than what happened in utero.

"Throwing hot coffee on you was nothing more than the icing on the cake. Your childhood experiences may seem important to you because they are all that you can remember, but they didn't cause your problem. Your problem started long before. Your mother's attempt to discard you in utero caused you to be born with a developmental sense of separation, of not being wanted. Separation anxiety, if you will. Don't be hard on yourself for the way you have lived your life. I think you have done a tremendous job of surviving, and most people with your circumstances are dead or spending the rest of their life in prison.

"You have been dodging bullets since the time of conception, and you have managed to have an incredibly successful career and create a beautiful family in the process. Some people take drugs because they are selfish and want to have fun and feel good all of the time. You took drugs to try to stop feeling bad. You tried to self-medicate, rather than coming to a professional like me, to be medicated."

"So you're going to try more medication on me?" I had been through the gamut of medication by this point.

"No, Todd, I'm not. I don't think you have any actual chemical imbalances. I think you suffer from separation anxiety and a lack of self-confidence."

"Lack of self-confidence," I laughed. "You have that way wrong. I have been scolded for being overconfident, my whole life."

"Todd, you know damn well that that's just what you've been selling people your whole life. The only problem is that you're too smart to buy into it, yourself. You have been able to convince everybody but Todd. It's just like John: you can tell him it wasn't his fault until you're blue in the face, and it won't make a bit of difference until the day that he tells himself."

"Todd, humility is the purest form of conceit. Until the day comes that you can experience the joys of humility and not have to have every answer first, or care who sees you using food stamps, or worry that your food is better than all of the other chefs', then you will have truly proven that you are self-confident. The only way to really prove your self-confidence is to not have to prove anything at all."

"All right, Jill, I agree with you. Now, how do we fix it?"

"Let me ask you a question, Todd. How do you become a nationally acclaimed chef, who is recognized by the James Beard Foundation?"

"Well, that takes years. First, you have to serve an apprenticeship under a real chef. Then, you have to read everything about food that you can get your hands on, and spend every day of your life cooking it for about ten years."

"That's how we're going to fix it. No one can teach you to behave any more than someone can teach you to cook. All anyone can do is show you how they behave; you have to teach yourself. Todd, this is going to take years. Just because you now know why you act the way you do, doesn't mean you're going to be able to change the way you act.

"Sure, you're clean now because you just about got shot to death.

What's it going to take for you not to do drugs? And I mean for at least a few years. You have the ability to kick the nastiest habits because you do it every year. Firing you doesn't work, almost dying by pumping poison into your veins doesn't work, Stacey packing up everything and leaving doesn't work, and having your son die in your arms doesn't work. What makes you think that just because someone shot you a few times, you'll stop?

"Todd, you now know why you are so self-destructive. It has proven to be an important part of your survival. But, you need to understand that knowing *why* is not going to make anything any easier to handle. You know why Cody died; he drowned. Does that make you feel any better about it? No, not at all. You're going to feel that pain for the rest of your life, just like you're going to feel the pain of what happened to you in utero for the rest of your life. The only way that you're going to fix this is by dealing with it on a daily basis for the next several years. And self-medicating is not dealing with it. That only postpones it or compounds it.

"Don't be discouraged if you slip back into drug use; statistics say that you have a better chance relapsing than not. Just never forget that nobody is better at kicking than Todd Hall. They should give you a medal for that. As long as you always try to stand up and fight this, as opposed to running away from it, you will eventually win. We're going to find you some sort of spiritual connection to combat the separation anxiety, but only you can give yourself confidence.

"Time's up. Listen, we're going to have a funeral for your mother next week and I want you to write the eulogy. I can't wait to hear it. I know how creative you can be when you want to be. Have a great weekend."

"Jill, my mom's not dead."

"Well, she would be if I had anything to say about it. We are still going to have a funeral for her next week, so come prepared."

All of this was a lot to digest, and it's been eleven years since she first told me. I made the huge mistake of not listening. Sure, I had heard what she said, but I didn't listen closely enough. She gave me everything I needed that day to really turn my life around, but I did exactly what she told me not to do.

For starters, I worried about *why*, as opposed to *why not* and *how not*. This whole concept of *in utero* was so intriguing that I focused more on it than I did the task at hand: stay clean and quit senselessly driving myself. In the past eleven years, I don't know one more thing about *in utero* than the day she told me about it. I can't even tell you if I fully agree or disagree with it, and do you know what? It doesn't matter. It's the *why* part of the problem, not the *how not to* part of the problem.

I find it ironic that she focused on my understanding of why for hours, and then told me it doesn't matter why. Right in that office, that day, she gave me the only two ingredients necessary for me to make a full recovery, and she spent all of one second on them: a spiritual connection and self-confidence.

I missed the importance of the spiritual connection. Like I said, I just wasn't listening closely enough. I am in the middle of my third drug-free year, and I owe every second of that time to my spiritual connection. This should be the first thing on every addict's list. It can help you with all of the other things you're going to have to start dealing with.

If I had paid closer attention to this, I would have been clean for eleven years now instead of just three. Oh well. What's eight years of a life like mine, anyway? Besides, it gives you more to read.

I'm not sure, but I think Dr. Jill was some sort of Zen Buddhist monk or something. I think she even taught monk-type classes. To help me find a spiritual connection, she gave me a book, *Syd Arthur*. The only thing I got out of the book is I now wash my rice really well before I cook it.

I wanted to get better, so, looking for a spiritual connection, I decided to start going to the local Mormon Church. This felt every bit as weird to me in California as it did in Utah. I just didn't fit in. Besides, I had started smoking, and that's a huge no-no. If you're trying to build your self-confidence, then I don't suggest you try the Mormon Church. It always made me feel guilty as hell. Probably because I was.

One thing that did make me feel good was asking all of the businesses at Bass Lake for donations at Thanksgiving. I used the proceeds to buy a shitload of turkeys and the accoutrements. I borrowed a pizza parlor for the day, and cooked until we'd fed all of the families that were having a tough time. It was a great Thanksgiving dinner. That was cool.

Chapter 40

THE DAY MY DOCTOR RELEASED me to return to work, I made two phone calls. The first was to Reed Groban, the executive chef at The Scottsdale Princess Resort, and the second was to Minnie Lane, the founder of Lane furniture. I didn't ask Reed, I *told* him I wanted La Hacienda back.

"Todd, you don't just call me up and order a four-star restaurant for a job like it's a hamburger from room service."

There is one thing that Reed gets a tremendous amount of satisfaction out of, and that's telling people no. Reed really loves to say no whenever people ask him for anything. Reed would have gotten great pleasure out of saying "No, Todd, you can't have La Hacienda back". But he didn't. He never said yes, but that didn't matter. I knew I had it.

"Thank you so much, Reed."

"What are you thanking me for? I never said you could have it."

"I know, but thank you so much, Reed." I hung up.

I then called up Minnie and told her I was going back to the Princess. I had enough money to get a truck to move with, but I didn't have any money to rent a house with. She graciously agreed to help us with a house.

I couldn't believe it when I saw the house she had arranged for us to live in. It was not only a luxury home with a pool and a guest house, it was on a third of an acre in Paradise Valley. It was right across the street from the Camelback Inn, in one of the most expensive neighborhoods in the United States of America. This woman was a saint. I have never had anybody help my family as much as Minnie Lane has.

I had a few weeks to kill until I started back at the Princess, so I wanted to check up on where I stood in the culinary community. I had locked the doors of my restaurant and bailed after almost killing myself from shooting up. Word of this had not only gotten out, but become very distorted. At this point, after all, I'd been gone a few years. There were rumors circulating that I had been killed in a shooting in Fresno. Some people screamed, "I thought you were dead!" when I walked into their restaurants.

I needed to build a press campaign and clear the air. I started inviting food critics over to my beautiful home, preparing meals for them, and telling them my bullshit version of what I had been doing for the past three years. I tried to minimize and rationalize what was now starting to become a big fucking train wreck. I pretended that I had been trying to catch a flight to Phoenix that Sunday morning, and a beggar had approached my van asking for money. I think I even threw a baby in there somewhere, for good measure. It always helps to throw a baby in if you're going to make up lies, because people love babies.

Anyway, I told people that this baby-carrying beggar had asked me for some money, and I pulled out a big wad of cash. When she saw me pull a twenty off the top, she went and told a gangbanger that I had a lot of money on me and he jumped in my van and shot me.

Of course, you know the truth was that I *did* give a lady twenty bucks, but I asked her to please *send over* the gangbanger. Then I *welcomed* him into my van to get shot. The lady wasn't a beggar with a baby; she was probably a hooker, but that was close enough for my purposes anyhow.

At that time, I didn't think that the truth would clear any air. Now I realize that if I had just given it a chance, I probably would have been able to put the past behind me right then and there. I was the only one who didn't know that everybody was already aware that I was a drug addict and still liked me anyway. I wasn't just a drug addict, after all. I was a kind person, a good father and husband who loved his family more than life itself, and one hell of a chef. Most of my friends looked at my problem with addiction like an astigmatism, a harelip, or some other handicap that I was trying to recover from. They did all of this while I insulted their intelligence by trying to pretend that I had my addiction licked.

◊ ◊ ◊

John came home with a new friend named Roark, who lived a couple doors down. They wanted to go swimming in our pool. I told them they couldn't until I had spoken with Roark's parents. I asked Roark what his father did for a living and he said he was a writer. I thought, *Nice, I could try to fit this into my press campaign. He must be one hell of a writer to live in this neighborhood.* I asked Roark who his father wrote for. He said, The New Times. I thought, *Wait a minute, I have had at least a dozen write-ups in the New Times.*

I asked Roark his last name. Lacey. Right then, I called up Elin Jeffords who used to work there and asked if she knew a writer named Lacey at the New Times. She laughed at me and said, "Todd, Lacey isn't a *writer* at the New Times, he *owns* The New Times. And a dozen other newspapers across the country."

Well, that explained how he could afford to live in that neighborhood. Roark called his mom. Instead of giving him permission to swim over the phone, she came over and stood in our living room to make sure the new neighbors weren't child molesters. I would have done the same thing if the circumstances had been reversed.

Her name was Kathleen Ferris. She was very friendly and polite and gave Stacey and me a warm welcome to the neighborhood. Kathleen was an attorney who had worked with my old boss, Joe Martori. I told Kathleen that I had never met her husband, but I was certain that he knew who I was. I later learned that Kathleen was one of Arizona's leading authorities on water rights. I imagine that could come in pretty handy, living in the middle of a dessert. In any case, she told Roark he could swim with John, and I told her I would walk him home when they were done.

The whole time that they were swimming, the wheels were turning inside my head. I was thinking of how I could land this big fish in my press campaign. When I walked Roark home, his father Michael was swimming in their pool. I went over and introduced myself. Michael was also very friendly and asked me where I was working. I told him an abbreviated, bullshit story of what I had been doing the past few years. I pretended that all of the stories about me being killed and what I had or hadn't been doing were creating a real problem for me.

Then, I straight up asked him, "Michael, can you publish an article about me in the newspaper so I can clear the air?"

He was cautious. "Todd, I have been approached by many people in the past twenty years with similar situations, and it hasn't always worked out the way they intended."

"I really have nothing to hide. All I want to do is set the story straight."

He agreed and took my number, "Well, Todd, one of my writers will be contacting you in the morning, then."

I walked home with John thinking, *That was just way too easy.* I was right. Be careful what you ask for: you just might get it.

Before I make one more comment in regard to the New Times article, I have to clear something up. The article was flattering compared to what I have shared with you in this book. They focused far more on my successes than on my addiction. They not only left the door open for me to regain my place at the top of the food world, they *held* it open for me and gave me every chance to move forward with my life.

Here's the problem: I wasn't in the same place then that I am now. I had no spiritual connection and I had no self-confidence. Sure, I could say I was ready to come clean, but it was that same old, bullshit story that Dr. Jill told me I had been selling to people my whole life. In fact, I was getting so good at selling this crap, I had just sold it to a man who owned twelve newspapers—one of which had at least two million readers living within a fifty-mile radius of me. I had hit the motherlode of self-degradation and destruction, because I had begun to sell it to myself.

It is so funny that this article came out ten years ago. A lot can change a life in ten years. I only have one thing to say about this whole fucking thing: if you ever decide to come clean to more than a million people at once, make *damn sure* that you are secure with who you are and that you are ashamed of nothing. If you're not, the shame and guilt will consume you.

I have never imposed my views on my children; I just throw them out there and wait to see if I get any nibbles. However, I read a book that made such an impression on me as a teenager, I actually required all of my kids to read it when they were teenagers.

The book is *Illusions* by Richard Bach. The same author of *Jonathon Livingston Seagull*. *Illusions* was required reading in the Hall family. There is a parable in the book that says:

Learn to live your life being ashamed of nothing,
Even if your life is published in the newspaper,
Even if what is published is not true.

The only two things that the New Times published that weren't true were two lies that I had told them. The first was the way that I had got shot. The writer never said I lied about it, but he said that the detective who had investigated it said I was lying. The second was that I was raised by a good Mormon mom. It's funny how we fantasize about the things we're not prepared to deal with.

Other than that, everything they published was true. Be that as it may, I was far from ready to admit my life to myself, let alone share it with millions of people. I have never felt more ashamed of anything in my life than I did when that article came out.

I had just started back at the Princess on the first of July. The article came out on the fourth. Steve Ast's secretary called me at home at seven in the morning, and told me to come to his office immediately. I had always prided myself on being able to piss off Steve Ast more than anyone else, but he really blew a fuse over this. He booked a flight for me to Acapulco the next day, and told me I was going down there for a couple of weeks until things settled down. The Princess was getting a lot of phone calls to see if I worked there. He said that if he found out that I had spoken to anyone from any type of media, I wouldn't have to worry about being fired in my first week. Because I would be dead. He was just screaming at me like he had never screamed before.

I left his office that day feeling so bad about myself that I stopped for a six pack at ten in the morning. As soon as I stepped foot in the Circle K, the guy working the register said, "Hey, you're that crazy chef." When I walked out, I saw my face on the cover of the paper at the newsstand. I asked myself, *What in the fuck have you done?* I had Michael and Kathleen over for dinner and Michael asked me, "Todd, what do you want from this article?"

"I wanted glory and fame," I told him. "I wanted to be on the cover of the newspaper holding a fiery sauté pan, and I wanted the headlines to read, 'The Bad Boy of Good Food Is Back.'"

Lacey gave me everything I had asked for. I just wish that he'd known that the last person you should ask, "What's good for Todd?" was Todd. I had gotten it wrong my whole life.

Everybody had something to say about the article. Reading it forced me to take a good, hard look at the way I was seen through other people's eyes. Then, no matter where I turned, people would tell me how I looked through their eyes. It was just way too much to handle.

This was the first time in my drug use cycle that I ever went from clean to hardcore overnight. I started shooting coke in the tops of my hands on the night the article came out. The doctor who performed surgery on my arms had tied all of the veins to the bone, hoping that would keep me from myself—so I had to shoot it in the veins in the tops of my hands, the same place they put an IV in you at the hospital.

As soon as I landed in Acapulco, I had the cab driver stop at a drug store so I could get some clean syringes. Then we went to a street corner to score some coke. I stayed in one of the towers for over a week without ever going outside, pumping drugs into my veins in a dark hotel room—just like Howard Hughes had done, at the same place.

I continued to shoot up every night when I got home from work. The Princess knew it. My hands were getting so scarred up, everybody knew it. I was fired after about four months. The James Beard Foundation had invited me to come do a dinner as one of the Best Hotel

Chefs in America, but I was too fucked up to pull it off and Reed ended up doing it. Michael Lacey called me one Saturday and asked if I wanted to take the boys to a movie with him. I had just shot up and I couldn't even talk straight, but I told him to go ahead and take John.

We lost the house and we ended up moving in with Stacey's parents. Eventually, I moved back up to Sedona and finally got cleaned up for a little while.

I invite all of you to read the article. Go to www.phoenixnewtimes.com and type the word "Epicured" into the search box.

Chapter 41

IF YOU GOOGLE THE TERM "unemployable", the first page is all about me. They say that your resume should never go back more than ten years and you need to keep it down to no more than two pages. This is impossible for me, even if it is single-spaced and a font size of eight. It was actually easier for me to lease restaurant space without a penny to my name than it was to find a resort that would hire me. I hadn't just burned bridges; I had burned the whole damn town.

I ended up doing just that. The owners of the Super 8 motel in Sedona had a little freestanding restaurant right next to the motel building. The structure was one of the first buildings ever built in Sedona, and it used to house nuns doing missionary work. I never felt like I was welcome in that building. I don't think it ever should have been a restaurant. The previous people had just walked out and the owners needed it as an amenity to their motel guests.

They let Stacey and me have it, rent-free. I borrowed five grand from a friend to buy the opening inventory. I named it Café Carneros after the wine region in Sonoma. I don't think we ever fed more than twenty people in one night. I would cook, Stacey would waitress, Chelse would hostess, and Parker and John would bus and wash dishes.

I still had not paid Los Abrigados for the mini bar bill my family had run up from Cody's funeral. Edd would mention it every time I spoke to him. Finally, I offered him trade. He had all of his employees come right over for a free meal. That was the most business that we ever did. It was really a stupid idea, but at least they didn't have the New Times in

Sedona, so I didn't have to worry about someone I bumped into on the street reminding me what a fuck-up I was.

Ron Costello came in for dinner and loved it, so he told his friend Tomaso Maggorie that I was a very talented chef and he should hire me for his new restaurant, Tomaso's 2000. Tomaso was good friends with Joe Martori and used to come up to Los Abrigados years ago. Tomaso was the best restaurateur I had ever met. He had five or six restaurants in Arizona and San Diego. He hired me about six months before Tomaso's 2000 was due to open, and I worked a short time at all of his restaurants.

We opened Tomaso's 2000 with great success. The place was packed and my food was very cool. But just like a pregnancy, it had been nine months and my old habits were due any day now. Tomaso is Sicilian and he has an incredible work ethic. You can find him every single morning at his restaurant on Camelback at seven a.m. sharp. He answers the phone himself, and he knows exactly what's going on at all of his restaurants all of the time.

Sicilians don't like drugs, and Tomaso had zero tolerance for them. The first time he saw me high he gave me a look that crippled me. Tomaso is so powerful that he never has to raise his voice. He is so involved with everything that he never even gets mad or upset. If he even thinks something is going to upset him, he just simply gets rid of it before it ever has a chance. So, I was just at the beginning of my recreational stage when he gave me the boot. Just for the record, the Princess was the last time I ever shot up. I think I was smoking crack when Tomaso fired me the first time.

My foot was starting to hurt when I was working, so I went to a podiatrist. When they removed the tumor in Utah, they must have missed some and it had grown back twice the size. So, this time, they removed the whole tendon. Luckily, I quit smoking crack before I really even started. I didn't have any money. I had to figure out how to stop this deadly cycle.

I joined the Mormon Church one more time. This time I had Stacey take temple classes with me, thinking that if I could just make it to the temple I would get an understanding of what it was all about. On the night of the very last class, Stacey said that she didn't believe it and she didn't want to go any more. So, we went to the Cajun House, watched a band, and got drunk. I was not released to return to work yet, even if I did have a job (which I didn't). But I was starting to get addicted to OxyContin. My doctor would prescribe ten-milligram pills and I would change the one to a four and get forty-milligram pills. I kicked the pain pills and was released for work. I begged Tomaso to take me back.

He did, and, nine months later, meth hit Arizona. It was easy to get and very cheap. I had just barely started to do meth when Tomaso fired me again. Tomaso's son Joey was opening his first restaurant on Coronado Island in a few months, and he kept asking his dad if I could please be his chef. Tomaso thought that Joey was crazy, but he gave me my third chance to get my act together. I got us a house a block away from the ocean and started a new cycle.

We opened Joey's California Bistro on the fourth of July and fed three hundred people for lunch and four hundred for dinner, every single day for the next six months. I started to do meth again, and Tomaso flew right out and fired my ass for the third time. He made sure to tell me that I was the greatest waste of talent he had ever seen in his life.

Stacey had had enough, so we packed up a U-Haul and drove back to Arizona. The only difference this time was I was not welcome in Stacey's parents' home anymore. I couldn't blame them a bit. I had been smoking meth hard and fast for a few months already.

I got a motel room and tried to find something to blame my life on besides myself. I had gone to the new Four Seasons resort that had just opened earlier that day and tried to apply for a job. The girl in personnel had already heard about me and wouldn't even let me fill out an application. She was so snotty I couldn't believe it. I was thirty-eight years old and I came to the conclusion that it was the hotel industry that had wronged me my whole life. It had started with Hodgi handing me speed at the age of seventeen so I could make more money for the hotel.

I was no longer Chef Todd Hall. I was a demon-infested, hollow carcass, and I sat in that motel room thinking of a way to get even with the whole fucking hotel industry. I thought that no one was ever going to hire me again, so I had nothing to lose. If anybody ever owed me anything on the face of this earth, it was the hotel industry. I had made so much more money for hotels than they ever paid me, it wasn't even funny. I had sacrificed my life, family, and wellbeing for hotels. I had spent far more time working my ass off in hotels than I had spent with Stacey, my children, or even asleep in bed. I had given my life, heart, and soul to hotels, and now they wouldn't even give me the time of day.

I went to load another bowl of meth and looked on the nightstand. I noticed that they had given me the wrong receipt when I had checked in. They handed me the receipt for the guy who was checking in next to me. The name on the receipt was Geoffrey West and it had his address in Dallas, his phone number, and his credit card number. This was my chance to get even.

◎ ◎ ◎

Please understand that for the next seventy-two days of this book, I did things I know were very wrong. I had never done things like this before, nor will I ever do them again. I am not proud of what I did. In fact, I am very sorry. And every penny in services that I scammed was paid back in restitution several years later.

In order to pull off all of the stupid shit that I did, you first have to have a real understanding of how hotels work. If you try to scam your way into a Motel 6, you will never do it because scammers try to do it all the time. They're ready for you. If you try to scam yourself into a five-star resort, you will never do it because people that scam things stick out like a sore thumb in a five-star resort. They won't even let you through the front door, let alone fraudulently check in.

◎ ◎ ◎

The first hotel on my hit list was the Four Seasons because they had treated me like shit on that very day. I knew that just a name and credit card number would not even get me past the front desk, but I'd thought of a way around that. I called the Four Seasons from the motel room that night. I said that I wanted to make reservations starting tomorrow and throughout next week. The reservationist told me it was six hundred and fifty dollars a night. I said that would be fine.

She took Mr. West's name, address, phone number, and credit card number, and told me she was looking forward to having me stay at the Four Seasons. I waited until I had to check out of the motel the next day and drove around until about four. Then, I called the Four Seasons again and asked to speak to Mr. West. They told me that they were expecting him, but he had not checked in yet.

I asked to leave a message. I said that I was Miguel Garcia from Southwest Airlines and we had just found Mr. West's carry-on luggage in the overhead compartment of a plane that was now in Boston. Southwest would go ahead and deliver it to the Four Seasons the day after tomorrow. They thanked me and said that they would give Mr. West the message as soon as he checked in.

I put on some nice clothes, and when I got to the front door at The Four Seasons, I acted like I had to go to the bathroom really bad. The door man escorted me. When I came out of the restroom, I walked down the hall, the opposite direction of the front desk, until I found the meeting rooms. I looked for a group that was having meetings in the resort. I found one, 10%.com. The name was posted right outside the door that they were holding meetings in.

I walked up to the front desk and smiled, "Hello, I would like to check in, I'm Geoffrey West with 10%.com. I have a real challenge. I left my carry-on luggage on my flight and I have absolutely no identification, or even credit card or cash for that matter."

The front desk clerk chuckled and said, "Mr. West, I have some great news for you. Southwest Airlines called and they found your baggage in Boston. It will be here the day after tomorrow. We saw that you would be staying with us all week, so we said that that would be fine. We have a complementary emergency amenity kit here for you. It has a tooth brush, a comb, some dental floss, and deodorant. Don't worry about a thing. We have your credit card number on file and we will get an imprint when you check out. Please sign here. You can use these cards to make any room charges that you care to, and Joe is here to escort you to your suite. Thank you for choosing The Four Seasons."

I not only stayed at The Four Seasons all week, I ordered rack of lamb through room service every night and smoked meth every day. I wasn't hungry, I would just order it and then bitch about it later. I actually faxed the headquarters of Four Seasons in Toronto a four-page letter telling them how fucked up their new resort was, while I was still staying there. Instead of one room service waiter, I was now getting four room service waiters, gift baskets and bottles of champagne. Compliments of the general manager.

I stayed there a week and I even had the balls to check out. They never asked to see my credit card or ID. The bill was eight thousand dollars. Then, I went to see someone who I thought was a friend of mine, Gary Sheer. He was the executive chef of The Camelback Inn. When I got there, he was not only distant and aloof, he was downright rude and would not allow me to apply, either. So, The Camelback Inn was the next five-star resort on my hit list.

I didn't have any more credit card numbers, and that just felt too much like stealing to me, so I devised another plan to check in. I found out a group that was staying there, GMC. I walked up to the concierge and said that I was with GMC and I needed to know the name of the meeting planner. She told me it was Jim Davies. Then, I went to the house phone outside the GMC meeting and said, "Hi, this is Jim Davies with GMC. I need to add another executive suite to the master account. His name is Todd Hall. Make sure all incidental room charges get placed on the master account as well. He'll be checking in within the next hour or so." I would always make sure that I checked out with the groups, and I always made sure that I bitched about everything.

I did this for three or four weeks in Arizona, two or three weeks in Palm Springs, and three or four weeks in San Diego, smoking meth the whole time. If you're curious, The Merv Griffin resort in Palm Springs was the best. It was really tough finding something to bitch about there. I used my real name most of the time and always left a three or four-page critique that I would type up in the business center before I left. I guess it was my way of justifying ripping them off.

When I would run out of cash, I would cash a check from Todd's New American Cooking at the front desk for a hundred dollars so I could buy some more meth. I had about a one-hundred-dollar-a-week habit, which is huge for meth. I had to liquid paper the 19__ out and put in 20__, make a copy of the check, and use that. They wouldn't take it if it had a 19__. Did you know that just altering your own check like that can get you charged with counterfeiting and the FBI on your ass? I do.

They knew who I was and they were after me. I would always request a ground floor room with a patio door, and this saved my ass a few times. I locked that swinging thing on the front door and if someone tried to just open my door without knocking I would bail out the back.

Chapter 42

IT WAS THE DAY BEFORE MY birthday, and I was at the Radisson resort in San Diego. I was so sick of everything; I didn't know what to do. I had been living like a king for the last couple of months and I have never been more miserable in my life. I got on my knees and prayed to God to please make it stop, and fell asleep praying.

I woke up on my birthday in handcuffs in the same place I was praying when I passed out. It was finally over, and I couldn't have been happier. I had just bought an eight ball of meth and it was inside the tennis shoe on my foot. When they made me change into the orange jumpsuit in jail, I just took it out of my shoe and put it in the jumpsuit pocket right in front of the cop and he never noticed. I was still totally fuckin' spun during my first two or three weeks of jail.

I ended up doing six months, but the way they did it totally sucked. I would be charged for a couple of hotels, get thirty days, and just when I thought I was going home, they would charge me with a couple more hotels and give me another thirty days. I thought I was going home six different times, but instead they would just take me back to court for more charges. They sent me to a jail in the foothills of San Diego. It was more like a summer camp than a jail. There were no cells, just a lot of cabins and a chain link fence that surrounded at least a hundred acres. You could have a great time there coming and going out of your cabin as you pleased, playing volley ball and baseball all day, and watching movies all night.

Newspaper reporters from Arizona started to call the jail to ask if they had a famous chef there named Todd Hall. The deputies got on the internet and ran my name and couldn't believe that someone who was so recognized in the food world was in their jail. One day they came into my cabin and said, "Todd, you have a phone call."

"What do you mean I have a phone call?" I replied. "You can't get phone calls in jail."

I went to the phone and it was a reporter from Arizona. He said, "Every publication is writing stories about you and I thought I would give you a chance to tell your story." I had had a gutful of press, so I declined.

The deputies said that they could make things a hell of a lot more pleasant for me if I would cook for them. I agreed. They went to the store and came in with a list of food I had given them the day before. We would open the kitchen up late at night and have prime rib, filets, and grilled salmon. After that, they would let me go outside the fence and give me cigarettes.

They told me that I should work in the kitchen and fix their lunch every day, but the civil servants who were the cooks there were such dickheads. I couldn't stand those shoemakers giving me orders and I got fired after a couple of weeks. That was a blow: getting fired even when I was in jail. It was ok, though. I was having a hell of a lot more fun playing volleyball every day than I was cooking shitty product.

After I had finally been in San Diego jails for six months, they let me change back into my street clothes. This was the first time that they had ever let me do this and it was late at night, so I was sure that I was getting out.

Right when I was getting ready to walk out the door, I was re-arrested by some cops from Palm Springs and transported there. I actually stayed in the same cell that Robert Downing Jr. did, according to my cellmates. They sentenced me to thirty days. I was all prepared to do it a few times, just like I had in San Diego, so I about died when after thirty days they let me walk out the door. I was sentenced to five years' probation. They told me to go straight to Utah to live with my brother, and to not even *think* about going to Arizona. If I did, they would arrest me, charge me with a shitload more hotels, and I would be in jail for years.

My brother Nick lived in Zion National Park, and he was the chef at a small hotel called Flannigan's. When I first saw Nick, I couldn't believe it: he was a mess. It looked like our childhood was finally starting to take its toll on him as well. He was drinking from the time he woke up until the time he passed out at night. He would shake so bad in the mornings that he had to have a slug of whiskey before he could even hold a cup of coffee.

I talked to his boss, my mom, and his best friend Tom Ellis, and we all showed up at his house one morning at seven and made him check into the hospital. You have some four hundred enzymes in your liver, and Nick only had twenty left. When he quit drinking at the hospital, he almost died. They had him in intensive care. I took over for him at the restaurant until he got better.

Flannigan's was a gold mine and they didn't even know it. We would feed two hundred and fifty people a night: hamburgers, fajitas, and entrée salads for ten or fifteen dollars a plate. I would walk out into the dining room and see the same European tourists who would frequent Sedona.

These guys were loaded and they not only knew good food, they were willing to pay for it. I told the owner that I could make him a fortune if he let me change his menu. I said, "If you don't double your money, then change it back." I prepped for the next two days and we changed it three days after my offer. I had duck, veal, lamb, great filets, New York's, and lots of fresh fish. My cheapest item was twenty dollars, and most of it was around twenty-five to twenty-eight. The specials were thirty-two.

They had owned this place for twenty years and the first night of my new menu were the highest food sales they had ever had, almost ten grand; the deposit for the night before was two thousand five hundred dollars. Needless to say, they loved me. The waiters *really* loved me. The owner gave me his apartment above the restaurant, bought me a brand new mountain bike, and gave me his Mercedes to use, as well as an American Express Gold Card. He flew Stacey and the kids in whenever I wanted. I was his goose that laid the golden egg.

I always thought it was ironic that I was put in jail for staying at hotels and ordering rack of lamb from room service every night, and as soon as I was out of jail the first thing that I did was go stay at a hotel and order rack of lamb from room service every night. The only thing different was that I was clean and being paid a shitload of cash to do it.

I was glad I could help my brother get cleaned up. Nick had always been a morning person, so I told the owner that we were going to put him back into his natural schedule. They had offered a free breakfast buffet to all of the hotel guests since they'd opened twenty years ago. I told them that was nuts. Zion has a shortage of hotel rooms. They were often sold out three months in advance. You don't have to give shit away for free; in fact, you're an idiot if you do.

So, I wrote a breakfast menu and got rid of the free buffet. We charged people ten to twelve bucks for breakfast every day. This brought in another one to two grand a day, plus it gave Nick a shift of his own that he enjoyed. I would send money back to Arizona, but Stacey never used it to pay the bills. She had a new boyfriend now and they were both crackheads. So, I would have to send the money to Chelse.

The kids flew out on my birthday and we all went to Vegas. We stayed in the Chairman of the Board Suite at the MGM Grand. It was a great trip, and it was also my first year anniversary of being drug-free since I was thirteen.

A few months later, I started to get the itch to get high. All of the cooks and waiters were doing meth around me the whole time I was in Zion. I always said, "No thanks, none for me." We had been four-wheeling in the mountains and they had all been doing lines of meth all day. I was drunk and I finally said, "Give me a little one." As soon as I did it, I knew that I had pissed off God. I felt so guilty.

I had to check in with my probation officer. I had never been charged with a drug related crime, so I was never piss tested. But when I got there, he told me that I had been wanted in Arizona for a long time. They had issued a seven-count, felony-fugitive warrant for my arrest, for one hundred and fifty-three thousand-dollar bail. They were extraditing me back to face charges. He put handcuffs on me and I was shipped back to Arizona. I know the only reason that that happened was because I did meth the day before. I was right, I did piss God off.

Chapter 43

THEY DON'T JUST TAKE YOU straight to Phoenix. You go to the county line and a deputy from the next county picks you up and takes you to the next county. It took three days to make a ten-hour trip. I had already spent twice as much time in jail than I had in hotels, and now I was on my way to the toughest jail in the country. I knew that Sheriff Joe didn't have any summer camps with cabins and movies.

I made it to Phoenix and totally lucked out and avoided tent city. I was placed in a jail in Durango that they called "The Warehouse". I had my arraignment after a few days and they had a record of every hotel that I had stayed in.

Just in case someone gets the wrong idea and thinks it might be cute to try to scam their way into a hotel, this is how it works: if you do what I did and try to piggyback onto a group staying there, you're not ripping off the hotel. They get their money when the group checks out. You're not ripping off the group, because their bank protects them against fraud. You're ripping off a bank. If the group pays with a check then you will be charged with check fraud; if the group pays with a credit card then you will be charged with credit card fraud.

Banks don't care how hard your life is and they will always prosecute to the fullest extent. If you enter a building with the intention to defraud it, you will be charged with burglary. If you sign a room service receipt or a check-in slip at the front desk in the name of Geoffrey West and you're not Geoffrey, you will be charged with forgery every time you sign anything.

I was all whacked out on meth and honestly thought I was playing a fun little game with hotels. Hotels are great record keepers. They had every guest check and lots of video footage of me, from the time I stepped foot on their property until the time I left. In my mind, the only thing I stole was the food I ate and the toilet paper I used. Once again, I was so whacked out on tweak that I honestly thought I was entitled because I left such great guest comment reports of my stay.

The demons in my head would tell me that the worst that could happen was that they would find me and feel sorry for me and ask me to pay it back. I might even get a job out of this because of all of these great reports that I was leaving. That is how delusional meth makes you.

The reality was that no one felt sorry for me, and those reports being sent to headquarters really pissed the general managers of these resorts off. Especially when they found out that I wasn't even a real guest. They formed a coalition and compared video tape and reports. They made sure I was going down, and hard. The only reason I was extradited was because those guys wanted to see me lynched.

The prosecuting attorney and my public defender tried to get me to agree to a plea bargain of pledging guilty to all charges. If I did, they would only give me two years in prison.

"What, two years in prison? Are you high?" I was livid.

"Todd, this is your third offense," they explained. "You spent six months in jail in San Diego and a month in Palm Springs for similar crimes."

"This is not my third offense," I argued. "If you notice the dates on the hotel bills, you will see that I stayed at these places before I was ever arrested for the crimes in California. I admit for seventy-two days I was a one-man crime spree, but I did nothing but sleep in hotels and eat food. I cannot go to prison for two years. I am not like the rest of the people in here. I will never make it."

"Well, they will probably let you out after a year or so if your behavior is good."

"I am not signing the plea bargain and I am not going to prison for two years."

They sent me back to the holding cell with eighty other criminals. In all of the time that I had spent in jail, I never met a man who didn't say he was innocent. I also never met a man who shouldn't have been there. I had spent my whole life in a totally different environment, and I had no idea that such evil people even existed.

I was crushed. I was ready to start bawling, and, in fact, I think I did. What a cruel joke God had played, letting me live at a hotel, eat all of that great lamb, help save my brother's life, and be a hero at a hotel again. Guests stood up in the dining room and applauded for my food again. I was able to take my kids on ski trips and stay in great rooms at the MGM Grand. I had filled my pockets with cash and rode a bike in the morning in one of the most beautiful places on earth. God let me have all of that, just to yank it out from under me and put me with a bunch of heathens for two years. *Why, because I did just one little line of meth?* I was just certain that was why I was there.

I went to the far corner of the holding cell, and got down on my knees and prayed. I prayed every bit as hard as I did when Cody died. *Please God, please don't send me to prison. Please just let me wake up in Zion. Please let this be a dream. Just please, God, send me someone to get me out of this mess. Please.* When I looked up, the cell was empty. They were transferring all of the inmates to another cell.

I got up and walked behind the deputy. He had crammed all of the criminals in the other cell real quick and hurried and locked the door while I was still standing behind him. He got all pissed off at me for not being in the cell and boomed, "Fine! You want to play games? I have just the place for you."

He took me downstairs to the maximum-security holding cell where they kept murderers. There were only a couple of other guys in there. I was sitting there, minding my own business, when they brought in one more dude. In the far corner, someone jumped up when he saw the new guy and the two of them started screaming at each other. You could tell that they were both hardcore tweakers by the presence of evil that surrounded them and the fact that they both had lost their teeth at a very young age.

"You motherfucker! They're trying to pin capping that bitch in the back of the head on me!" the first one screeched.

"Settle down," the other yelled back. "They don't even have any witnesses. They don't have shit on us. They're trying to say they have the car we used and we torched it. They're trying to say they have a pair of brass knuckles we used, and I threw the pipe we beat her with out in the desert."

"Listen, I'm not going down for capping that bitch in the head. I may have beat her ass, but you're the one that capped her ass. All I fuckin' did was open the trunk and hand you the gun. Now they have my fingerprints when you're the one that capped that bitch. You're the one that snatched her ass, and they're charging me with all of that shit."

At first, I thought that these guys were trying to play some kind of game to scare the rest of us in the cell. It was working. I was scared shitless. Then, I realized that my prayers had been answered. I have never used my memory more than I did that afternoon.

What had happened was, these evil men had kidnapped one of their wives because she had ratted on them for something. They tied her up, beat her to a bloody pulp with a pipe, threw her out in the desert, and shot her in the back of the head.

The police didn't have any witnesses, but they were certain that these two guys had done it. They had both been in jail for over a month at separate facilities awaiting trial. There was a keep-away order, which meant that the deputies were never supposed to let them ever be together so that couldn't make up a story together. Someone screwed up and accidentally put them in the same holding cell.

They did nothing for the next two hours but argue about who did what to whom. I committed every single act, place, time, name, and date to memory. God had sent me two murderers of an unsolved crime that had no witnesses, and flashed that crime right before my very eyes. It made me think of how I was shot. They had never caught the kid. Instead of me testifying to my own shooting, I was going to testify to this shooting.

No doubt about it, these guys were natural-born, tweaker killers, and this was a very dangerous thing to do. But, I knew in my heart that it was the right thing to do. I had just begged God for some help, and He'd said, "You help me and I'll help you." This was definitely the task that He had decided to test me with. I had two choices: I could be a pussy and spend the next two years of my life in prison, or I could be courageous and help bring justice to someone who had been violated worse than I had.

My biggest worry was that I would testify against these clowns and they would get off the hook and kill me. But, I reasoned, that's kind of hard to do because I don't die that easily.

I was transported back to Durango and I went right up to the deputy and told him that I had information about a murder. They took me to an office and I told them what I had heard. They told me to go back to the warehouse and that they would be contacting me.

An hour later, two homicide detectives picked me up, and we walked right out the front door of the jail—no handcuffs or anything. I got into a car, and they took me to their office. They gave me cigarettes and then took me into a room where they videotaped every word I said. I had so many detailed facts about this crime, they started to think that I was involved in it.

The only thing that saved me from being charged right along with those guys was that I was in jail in San Diego at the time of the crime. That was the first time I had ever thanked God for being in jail. They made it clear that I would not be given a deal for my testimony. My charges would stand the same. I told them that it wasn't about that. These people were evil. They'd shot someone in the head and they needed to get caught for it so they wouldn't shoot anyone else in the head. I also told them that I had been shot in the head and the kid was still out there shooting people with the same gun he'd shot me with.

The next day I went to court. I was still charged with my crimes. The new deal was that if I testified to what I had heard, pled guilty to all of my crimes, and agreed to pay one-hundred-percent restitution, they would release me from jail for safety reasons on my own recognizance. I would be sentenced for my crimes after I had testified in this other trial.

My prayer had been answered just seconds after asking for it. I was out of jail for the rest of my life, three days later. Sometimes I meet people who try to tell me that there's no God. I know different.

I had to go to the county attorney's office and give a second deposition. A short time later, the attorneys for these guys had me give a third deposition. All three depositions were exactly the same. The attorneys for those two guys showed them my deposition and told them that I was going to testify at both of their trials. It was suggested that they both plead guilty and take the plea bargain that was being offered.

They both took the advice. One of them was sentenced to thirty years and the other was sentenced to thirty-five. They were convicted without the county having to go to the expense of a long, dragged-out trial.

I went to stay with my family. Stacey was smoking crack every day and I started to smoke too. But, instead of sticking around to finish myself off, I caught a bus to Bountiful and stayed with my sister Dawn.

⚹ ⚹ ⚹

The Olympics would be in Salt Lake in six months. I not only got one great job, I got two. I was earning over six figures. I had a house and a brand new Jeep Liberty. I went down to Phoenix and picked up my family. Chelse was in college at ASU, so she stayed down there until Christmas break. This little angel had gotten all kinds of scholarships while her mom was cracked out and her dad was in jail. She was putting herself through college as an honor student on the Dean's List. I was so proud of her.

Eventually, I got my shit together and Stacey got clean as well, so we spent Christmas skiing at Deer Valley. I thought that I had finally gotten it together for good. We were a week away from the Olympics when I got a call from the San Diego Adult Probation Department. I was informed that I had forty-eight hours to leave the state of Utah. Because of 9/11, they weren't allowing any interstate convicts in Utah. I could go to San Diego or I could go to Arizona, but I couldn't stay in Utah. The owner of one of the places I was working had his attorneys try to stop it, but they couldn't.

We ended up packing everything into a U-Haul and heading back to Arizona. I was driving the U-Haul with John, and Stacey and Parker were following us in the new Jeep. I looked in the mirror and watched Stacey slide off the road and into a gully. The Jeep was upside-down and totaled. Stacey and Parker were ok, but the Jeep wasn't insured.

I wasn't doing meth, I wasn't smoking crack, and I wasn't shooting coke. Why was I having so much bad luck? Eventually, it turned out that it wasn't so bad after all. I was able to get the executive chef position at the Paradise Valley resort. I had no idea how, after all that I had done. I lied on my application and said that I had never been convicted of a felony, but on my first day I went to the general manager Doug Cole and told him my story. He let me keep my job.

My brother Nick had started drinking again after being clean all of that time. Three days after he started drinking, he started pissing blood. He went to the doctor and they told him that he had to call hospice, that he would be dead in a few days. They didn't even check him into the hospital. There was nothing they could do for him. Nick called me at work and told me he loved me and that he was really sorry he drank his life away. I told him to shut up, he wasn't going to die. He died two days later on the day after his first grandchild was born.

Chapter 44

"HEY, THE KIDS ARE GONE, why don't we get a little?" Stacey suggested one evening. I had just gotten my paycheck as we were driving down a Scottsdale road together. I was floored. It was truly the last thing on my mind, and I was proud of that. "Come on, just once. I promise we won't get more."

"No, Stacey, don't. We're doing really well right now!"

"Fine. I have money, I'll just get my own." The thought of her getting high without me was just that little bit I needed to put me over the edge.

It only took me six weeks to lose my job.

I didn't know it then, but I was getting ready to smoke myself right into two years of hell. Very soon, I wasn't providing enough meth for Stacey, so she went and found herself some tweaker boyfriends. She would stay out for days at a time.

Stacey, my wife of twenty-three years, still smokes meth every day. She has scabs on her arms and face because she is certain that she has bugs under her skin eating away at her. She is right about one thing: she has something eating away at her, but it's not bugs. It's the pain and hardship she has endured in life. The person I was madly in love with for twenty years doesn't live in that body anymore. I only have to see her a couple of times a year now and it's really hard for me.

Parker and John had had enough of both of us by this point and went to live with their grandparents. I was now alone in a three-bedroom house in Scottsdale that proceeded to become haunted. All I wanted to do was smoke meth and oil paint.

I painted for days on end, then weeks on end, and then months on end. I was finally evicted from the house and I found an apartment right around the corner. That's where I met Louise Aniello. She was eighty-four years old, and she had owned an eleven-unit apartment complex since nineteen sixty-one. I didn't have a penny to my name and she let me move in, all spun out. She knew I was a mess and she had a few people just like me already living there. One of which was her own grandson. It was like I had just moved to the island of misfits. Everybody who lived in her complex was either a drug addict, an alcoholic, or both. The cops were over there all of the time.

Louise was one of the smartest people I have ever met. She had a ton of cash and she was eighty-four, so she didn't really care if people paid rent. She just wanted to help lost souls, and I was as lost as I could be. At least every other month she would evict someone. You didn't get evicted for not paying your rent, you got evicted for not answering your door or for fighting with your neighbors. At exactly nine thirty every morning, Louise would come over and pound on your door with the duck handle of her umbrella and make you come out and pull weeds, mow the lawn, pick grapefruit, water the lawn by hand, or clean the apartment of the last addict she'd just evicted.

It would only be for a couple of hours and then she would go home. At that point, you were welcome to go back into your hole and smoke yourself to death. But the day you didn't come out into the sun and work alongside this little old lady was the day that she would give you the boot. She would pretend that she had no idea that you were high as a kite. But she knew. She was running her own little undercover rehab center.

Louise owned a whole city block in Tempe consisting of nothing but apartments, and she would only rent the apartments out to illegal immigrants who had families with them. Every Friday she would go to the bank, get thousands of dollars in cash, and go around to all of the apartments to cash checks for the immigrants so they wouldn't get ripped off at the check cashing places.

I asked her why she wasn't worried about getting robbed, going from apartment to apartment with all of that cash. She said that they all knew she would kill them if they even thought about it. There wasn't a day that went by that Louise wouldn't remind you that God loved you, no matter how spun you were. I would get unemployment checks for two hundred dollars every Tuesday. I would ride the bus to north Scottsdale and spend one hundred on an eight ball of tweak. I'd use the other hundred for cigarettes, Coca-Cola, and a daily hot dog from Circle K. I would spend the rest on tubes of oil paint.

I would stay up smoking from Tuesday clear until late Saturday night, when I would finally run out of meth. Then, I would sleep all day Sunday and wake up Monday morning at nine thirty when Louise would be pounding on my door. After I was done with the yard work, I would eat and crash until Louise woke me up again on Tuesday morning. Then, I would wait at my door for the mailman and start all over again.

I did this for six months straight, never once paying rent. My power got cut off eventually, so I ran an extension cord to the laundry room. All I needed was one light to stay up all night, painting. After a couple of months of this, things started to change in my paintings. This face would always appear, the same face again and again. I thought it was the lack of sleep or the tweak, but this face would always show up somewhere in my paintings and drawings.

The face was always smiling or laughing. It was constantly

complementing me for my great work. Then, the face started appearing on my palette or in things I had spilled on the floor. This same face. I don't know if it was telepathy or what, but the face was communicating with me. It was telling me what a powerful player I was. The face thought it had lost me and it was glad that I had finally found my way home.

I quit trying to paint things. I would just manically brush paint on the canvas and things would appear. It was hell. I was unknowingly painting hell. It looked more real than anything I had painted before. There were caverns with stalactites and stalagmites, and a good friend of mine who had always been an atheist was lying there with worms eating away at him. The face was laughing its ass off because my friend had led a better life than most people in heaven, but he had broken the cardinal rule of denying the Holy Spirit. Now he had to rot miserably in hell.

The face kept telling me to make sure I didn't make the same mistake as the rest of these people, and try to ride the fence. It told me to make sure that I went all of the way or not at all. Hell was a great place to be if you just did it right. The only people who were miserable in hell were the ones who chickened out and didn't have a conviction, one way or the other. It then showed me lines and lines of people who had been waiting for years to finally receive their classification—people who were not bad enough to get a great spot in hell. They spent their time being tortured for not making up their minds.

If I played my cards right, then I could be like the face and spend all of eternity getting high, wandering the earth and fucking with people, trying to tempt them to do things. The face said it was a blast, and a hell of a lot more fun than being bored to death in other places.

The more time that I spent with this face after the sun would go down, the more time Louise would spend with me in the daytime. What used to be just a couple of hours had turned into all day long. One night, when I was with the face at about midnight, Louise got out of bed and drove over to the apartment. She pulled out my extension cord and screamed at me in the pitch black, "You had better start learning to sleep at night or I am going to kick you out onto the street!"

I was being pulled in both directions by some very powerful spirits. It wasn't long before I couldn't get up when I awoke on Monday morning, to the sound of Louise banging on my door. My kidneys were hurting so bad, I couldn't stand or walk. I was dying, just like my brother. I had to get more meth. It was the only thing that made the pain go away.

Soon after, I not only laid waiting for the mailman every Tuesday with tremendous kidney pain, I started to get what I call "electrical shocks". Every fifteen minutes, my whole body would go into convulsions, just like I was being shocked. I would ride the bus looking like a dead fish jumping around every fifteen minutes. I had to smoke as soon as I scored to make it all stop, no matter where I was.

I was certain that I was going to die soon, and, yes, I had been making my reservation in hell for quite some time now. I was really getting scared. I hung a crucifix on the painting I was working on. That Tuesday after I cashed my check, I was too bad off to make the bus ride to north Scottsdale, so I called my connection. He was in my apartment in about an hour. When he saw the crucifix on my painting, he offered to trade a quarter ounce of tweak for it. I knew that a quarter ounce would be just enough to kill me and to trade a crucifix for it would be certain hellbound eternity. I said no. I still have that crucifix today.

Chapter 45

I WASN'T EVEN DONE SMOKING all of my tweak yet when I finished painting for the night. I unplugged the light and plugged in the TV. I was headed for MTV to watch some music videos when I came across a guy, while changing the channels. This is going to sound so corny but it's true.

This guy had an ear-to-ear smile, and the first thing he said was, "Is your life a mess? Do you feel like you just can't go on anymore?"

This cat was certainly talking to me.

He said, "If you just give Christ a chance to help you and let him into your life, then I promise you things will get a whole lot better. Friend, just say this prayer with me and get yourself into a good, Bible-based church. You will be able to put all of this pain and suffering behind you for good. Now pray with me." The man was Joel Osteen.

I said that prayer with him that night, and I have never done another hit of coke or meth since.

The very next day, I put on my suit and walked to Our Lady of Perpetual Help. If anyone on this earth needed perpetual help, it was me. I had never been to Catholic Church before, but the Mormon Church was too far to walk to. I was way overdressed, and when mass started everybody was always standing up and sitting down. I didn't know when to do it, so I was always caught standing up in my suit when everybody was sitting down. The music was incredible. I felt more comfortable in that church than I ever had in the Mormon Church.

Some people asked me why I was there. I told them that I was a Mormon who hadn't gone to church in a real long time. I said I liked what just happened and I was going to start coming to their church. They told me that it took over a year to convert to Catholicism, and I had to go through all kinds of interviews. I would have to be sponsored. If I just wanted to start going back to church, I should probably go back to my own church. It would be a lot easier, they said.

I went to the Mormon Church for the next nine months; I even took temple classes. When I completed my classes, I asked the bishop when I could go to the temple. He told me I couldn't. This really pissed me off. I had taken these classes twice and I still wasn't allowed inside. Coming down off meth takes a real long time. It took me fifteen months until I could wake up feeling good and laugh again. I still lived in Scottsdale, so I would paint houses, drive a cab, make rock walls, or sell restaurant equipment. I had a new job every month. I wasn't allowed to cook anymore. I worked those jobs not because I was bad, but because I was recovering. You cannot let anything give you too much pressure while you're trying to recover or you will start using again.

I had my gas turned off because I had no money, so I called social services for help. I had been clean a year and John came back to live with me. He got me through the hardest parts. Social services didn't help, but the folks at Our Lady of Perpetual Help came to my house to pay my gas bill for me and get it turned back on. I had pictures of Jesus on my wall from the Mormon Church, and they asked me about it. I told them that I was Mormon, but it didn't work out so well for me.

The next day, Sister Patricia Marie called and asked me to meet with her. I spent a couple of hours telling her my story, and then she said, "Todd, you're an important player. We almost lost you, and we are so grateful that you have finally found your way home. So many people try to ride the fence. You have to go all of the way with this or not at all." She was certain that I was going to be someone who would be a great contributor to their cause. "Todd," she told me, "just keep doing what you're doing and you will take your place right where you belong."

Sister Patricia Marie signed me up for catechism classes, and when I looked at the calendar, the baptism was on the Easter Vigil, which was also my birthday.

◎ ◎ ◎

I started writing this book because I tried to give up cigarettes for Lent. That went right out the window ten hours later, so I decided to give up my life for you. Please learn something from it. Today is the last day of Lent. Tomorrow is Easter Sunday. I have finally risen, and I am done with my book.

I thought Dr. Jill was talking about my mom when she said that I suffered from separation anxiety. It was God the whole time and I never knew it. I was baptized exactly a year ago right now. I feel much higher than I ever did on drugs. I have to thank all of my children for always loving me. And I thank you for making time for me to share with you. I love you all.

CHEF TODD HALL

Epilogue

THAT WAS TEN YEARS AGO—almost to the day. I wrote this book as a recovery tool, and it worked. It has sat in a Google drive for the past ten years and reading it again was simultaneously difficult and gratifying. Michael Lacey, the former owner of Village Voice Media, was the writer I quoted in the beginning. He was the one who told me that "people love a happy ending, Todd, and you don't have that yet." So, I'll dedicate this last chapter to you, Michael, and all of my family and friends who have stuck by me during good times and bad.

At the time I wrote my book, I was no longer allowed to cook. I was driving cabs, painting houses, and selling kitchen equipment. I was fine with that—I understood that it was the punishment for my bad behavior. I was wrong. I was giving up too easily. That's what I want anyone else who is going through the recovery process to understand—you will get your life back if you work hard and fight for it.

In the ten years since I wrote the book, my relationship with my children is better than it's ever been. Chelse graduated cum laude from the Fulton School of Engineering at Arizona State University. To hear her name called during that graduation ceremony was one of the proudest moments of my life. She, of all things, wrote on her graduation sachet how proud she was of me. She has worked at Texas Instruments for over eight years now.

John graduated Horizon High School with honors. He married young and provided me with the most adorable granddaughter. John now runs a successful business that his brother Parker started years ago. Parker created a start-up doing SEO optimization. Using geo-tags and meta-tags, he can take a small business off the fifth page of an internet search and place it on the first, which is really valuable to a lot of small business owners.

As for me, I spent a year traveling the country, feeding rock stars with Clear Channel and Evening Star Productions. I met all my favorite artists. I spent a year doing super high-end catering in the homes of the wealthiest people on earth: Rob and Tiffany Walton from Walmart; Jacque and Bennet Dorrance, who own Campbell's Soup; CEOs of banks; hedge-funds; and even the CEO of Dunkin' Doughnuts.

I spent three years doing nothing but traveling around our country renovating, rebranding, and opening beautiful hotels and resorts for the Pyramid Hotel Group. I worked for the vice president of food and beverage, Doug Cole (the same guy who fired me for smoking meth at Paradise Valley Resort). I spent five years in Boston creating brand new concepts—restaurants that have never existed before. Six years later, they still have waiting lines to get in.

I've been invited to do many winemaker dinners with great winemakers, and participated in hundreds of exclusive events that only the best of the best get invited to. I have been a chef at five star resorts, like The Inn at the Little Nell in Aspen. The GM from Los Abrigados, the guy that sent me to rehab after exchanging barbs with a comedian, called me up out of the blue and asked me to come down to Santa Fe to open a four-star Starwood Luxury Collection Resort and create two new restaurant concepts for him.

I have been invited to be the guest chef for this year's American Harvest Workshop at Cakebread Cellars in Napa—that's going to be fun.

And the crown jewel is...

I was allowed to come back and once again cook at James Beard's Home!

Here's the problem with happy endings, Michael: they don't last forever. No one can ever escape the pain, trauma, tragedy, and death of people you love most in this life. It is an equal opportunity, debilitating part of life itself.

While I was in Boston, John was visiting me and we got word that Parker was using heroin. John helped me pack up my things and we headed back to Scottsdale. I camped out in Parker's apartment and forced him to stop. I chased away the dealers, the friends who were using, and erased the contacts in his phone. I went grocery shopping and cooked him breakfast, lunch, and dinner every day for a month. He was pissed. He did not want to clean up. While he was detoxing, he was downright nasty.

Parker had gotten busted with a gram of heroin a couple of months prior and was awaiting sentencing. He hired a great criminal attorney. I knew a lot of people in the Arizona justice system and I reached out to all of them, requesting that Parker receive jail time for his upcoming sentence hearing because I knew he would start using again as soon as I left.

He was sentenced to four months in Sheriff Joe Arpaio's jail. John and I drove him there. We told him we would see him in four months and we would be there to pick him up when he got out.

I didn't even go back to work. The time flew by; I skied in Aspen for a couple of months, and spent a few weeks in a little cabin on the Firehole River in Yellowstone. I rode my bike in the Tetons and Zion until it was time to go pick up Parker.

When he got out, he was my beautiful boy again—full of life and happiness. It was five in the morning and he wanted me to take him hiking, so I did. Parker stayed clean with no probation violations or drug use for a full year. He even received his one-year sobriety chip. His business was better than ever and we were all very proud of him. I had spent so many nights worried to death that one night I would get *the call*, but that was the past and I was sleeping well.

No one ever found out why, but after Parker had been clean for over a year he used again, just once. That first dose after a year without heroin killed him. His girlfriend found him dead on the bathroom floor with the needle still in his arm.

This was the second son I had lost, but it was different than when Cody drowned. Parker, Chelse and John never gave up on me as long as I was doing my part and trying to stop my substance abuse. They all stayed by my side until I was finally able to put it behind me. Going through that makes you so close to your children. Parker's death ripped my heart out and was the ultimate reminder that no one can ever stop someone else from using drugs. Only you can stop yourself.

There's a hidden, dark corner in our society that is filled with people like Parker and me: people who haven't been able to stop yet, or who have stopped and are miserable, or who have stopped and, for unknown reasons, started again.

That's who this book is for: me, Parker, and the rest. You know who you are.

You don't have to feel hopeless. You just have to be patient and never give up.

The End